PERSONAL PROPERTY

IN A NUTSHELL

Third Edition

By

BARLOW BURKE

Professor of Law
Washington College of Law
American University

Mat #40043430

PREFACE

Personal property is a subject that is often grist for a unit of many required, first-year property courses in law school. It introduces students to ideas useful in other areas of law study—contracts, commercial transactions, and civil procedure, for example. It helps a student distinguish between title and possession. It permits students to see the origins of substantive rules of law in procedure. The substance of the common law is "secreted in the interstices of procedure." See Henry Maine, *Early Law and Custom* 389 (1890). It also engages law students in the study of a set of readily understandable situations; in short, it provides a good way of beginning law school.

Its ready understandability belies its importance: once wealth was measured in land, and one horse, or cart, had relatively little value, and was easily replaced. Personalty with permanent value (silverware, gold jewelry, etc.) was rare. That changed with the Industrial Revolution, when railway cars, industrial machines, and inventory, became a feature of our economic landscape. In a later stage of that revolution, consumer goods became common, and today, certificated rights in shares of stock, bonds, negotiable instruments, patents, trademarks, and copyrights, can be added to the common sources of individual and commercial wealth. Thus today most wealth is in the form of personal property of one type or another.

The fact that students begin law school studying personal property has some limitations. Students study the subject while they are also busy adjusting to a new discipline, types of analyses, technical language, etc.—in short, to our legal culture. That necessary, and required, adjustment is no mean task; many attorneys would like to forget all about it. Students do not have that option and many would benefit from experiencing those first weeks of class again.

This book is written in part so that they can do that. It provides not a substitute for the classroom experience, but an extended analysis of leading cases—the ones likely to be covered in the first weeks of the term. Thereafter this book is a summary of rules and principles of law, a discussion presented on the assumption that the student is later better able to see them applied in particular cases.

This book owes a lot to many people: to my students who help me organize my thoughts; to the editors of the many casebooks I've used who, with their scholarship, suggest relationships it would otherwise elude me; to the co-editors of my own casebook—Professors Ann Burkhart and Dick Helmholz; to my research assistants, Brenda Leahy, Patricia Hamnes, and Stephanie Quaranta, all three of whom patiently answered my questions with solid research.

BARLOW BURKE

Washington, D.C.
December, 2002

OUTLINE

	Page
PREFACE	iii
TABLE OF CASES	xiii

Chapter I. Wild Animals and First Possession | 1
  I. The Leading Case | 2
    A. Control | 9
    B. Custom | 13
    C. Wild and Domestic Animals | 17
        1. Estray Statutes | 23
        2. Stray and Lost Pets | 24
    D. Landowners as First Possessors | 26
    E. More Bee–Hive Cases | 31
    F. More On *Ratione Soli* in the United States | 33
 II. Government as First Possessor | 37
    A. State Hunting Regulations | 41

Chapter II. Possession and the Forms of Action for Personalty | 45
  I. Another Leading Case: Eads v. Brazelton | 45
    A. The Controversy | 46
        1. The Decision | 48
    B. Actual Possession | 53
    C. Citations to *Eads* | 54

Page

II. A Recent Shipwreck Case: *The Central America* 58

III. Trash and Possession 67

IV. Other First Possessors and the Forms of Action 70

    A. The Forms of Action 72

V. A Third Leading Case: Goddard v. Winchell 84

VI. Property in One's Body: Moore v. Board of Regents 91

    A. Other Related Disputes 101

VII. The Plaintiff's Election 102

Chapter III. Prior Possession 104

I. Choosing Replevin or Trover 105

    A. The Consequences of Choosing Trover 108

II. The Reach of the *Armory* Rule 113

III. Justifications for Protecting the Prior Possessor 114

IV. The Measure of Damages 115

V. The *Armory* Rule in Replevin Actions 116

    1. Who Is the "True Owner"? 116

    2. The Defense of Jus Tertii 119

    3. Two Leading Cases 122

VI. The Problem of Successive Finders 131

    1. The Measure of Damages in Clark 139

    2. Salvage Rights 141

VII. Conclusion 141

Chapter IV. Finders 143

I. Who Is a Finder? 143

II. Barring the True Owner's Right 145

Page

III. The Finder's Right ----------------------------------- 146
   A. Public/Private Place of the Find -------- 149
   B. Lost/Abandoned/Mislaid Chattel -------- 150
IV. Other Categories ------------------------------------- 154
   A. Chattel Embedded in or on Top of
      the Soil --------------------------------------- 154
   B. Small/Bulky Chattel ----------------------- 156
   C. Limited Entry Cases ----------------------- 156
   D. The Place of Finding, Type of Goods,
      and Limited Entry Cases --------------- 157
   E. Treasure Trove and Buried Treasure   159
      1. Wreck of the Sea, Historic Ship-
         wrecks, and Embeddedness Re-
         dux --- 161
         a. Finders at Sea --------------------- 163
         b. Salvage ------------------------------ 164
         c. Comparing Finders' and Sal-
            vage Law --------------------------- 166
V. Finders' Statutes ------------------------------------- 169
   A. The Effect of Statutes on the Com-
      mon Law of Finders --------------------- 171
   B. Finders' Rewards --------------------------- 174
   C. Escheat --- 176
   D. Unclaimed, Intangible, Personal
      Property Acts ----------------------------- 177

Chapter V. Bailments --------------------------- 182
I. Their Nature and Definition ----------------- 182
   A. Finders as Bailees ----------------------------- 186
      1. The Right to Sue and the Causes
         of Action ----------------------------------- 191
   B. Bailments, Leases, Licenses and Sales   195
      1. Safe Deposit Box Cases -------------- 195

Page

2. Parking Lot Cases 196
3. Photography Cases 200
4. The Bailee's Personal Injuries in the Bailment for Hire.................. 201
5. Negligent Entrustment 202
6. Sales Distinguished From Bailments 203
C. Returning the Chattel 204
1. Fungible Goods 207
D. Standard of Care................................. 208
E. The Burden of Proof............................. 211
1. The Majority Rule 211
2. A Second View 211
3. A Third Rule 213
F. The Measure of Damages 214
G. The Bailee's Liability for Misdelivery 216
H. Bailee's Failure to Return Chattel 217
II. Commercial Bailments 218
A. Standard of Care................................. 219
1. Warehousers................................. 219
2. Common Carriers 220
B. A Bailee's Burden of Proof and Persuasion for Damage to Bailed Goods.. 221
1. Theft From a Warehouse 227
C. Misdelivery 229
D. Limitations on Warehouser Liability.. 230
E. A Final Word on Innkeepers 233

Chapter VI. Sales and Good Faith Purchasers 236
I. The Problem... 238
A. Void and Voidable Title 242

Page

B. The Good Faith Purchaser 247

C. Insurable Interests in Stolen Chattel 248

D. Extinguishing the True Owner's Title
in Favor of a Good Faith Purchaser 251

II. The Uniform Commercial Code (UCC)..... 252

A. Transfer 254

B. Good Faith................................... 255

C. Value 256

D. Transaction of Purchase 257

E. Entrusting Chattel 257

F. Resale by a Vendor in Possession 263

III. The Identity of the Fraudulent Purchaser 264

IV. Liens 267

Chapter VII. Gifts of Personal Property 273

I. Delivery 274

A. A Deed of Gift 277

B. American Cases 280

C. Symbolic and Constructive Delivery... 283

D. Gifts Through Third Parties............... 287

E. Corporate Stock............................. 290

II. Donative Intent............................... 293

A. Conditional Gifts: Engagement Presents 297

B. Presuming Donative Intent 301

C. Some Problems on Delivery and Donative Intent 303

III. Gifts *Causa Mortis* 306

IV. Acceptance 311

V. Conclusion 312

Page

Chapter VIII. Joint Bank Accounts 314

I. Concurrent Interests in Personal Property 315

II. Joint Bank Accounts 317

    A. Statutory Treatment of Joint Accounts 318

    B. Establishing a Joint Account 321

    C. The "Wallet" Function: The *Inter Vivos* Right to Withdraw 323

    D. The "Will" Function: Gifts to Surviving Account Holders 327

        1. The Totten Trust 334

Chapter IX. Adverse Possession of Personal Property 338

I. Adverse Possession and Statutes of Limitation 340

    A. The U.C.C. and *Chapin* 343

II. Adverse Possession as a Gloss on Statutes of Limitations 344

    A. "Open and Continuous" Adverse Possession 348

III. Conclusion 357

Chapter X. Accession and Confusion 359

I. Accession 359

    A. Conversion and Damages 362

    B. Incorporation of Chattel Into Another's Property 363

    C. Accession to Real Property 368

II. Confusion 369

III. Fixtures 370

Page

Chapter XI. Common Law Estates in Personalty ------------------------------------ 374

  I. Present Estates and Remainders ----------- 375

    A. The Rule in Shelley's Case -------------- 376

    B. Fee Tails ------------------------------- 376

    C. The Rule in Wild's Case------------------ 377

    D. The Doctrine of Worthier Title -------- 378

  II. Future Interests------------------------------ 378

    A. The Rule Against Perpetuities --------- 379

 III. Concurrent Estates----------------------------- 379

INDEX --- 381

*

TABLE OF CASES

References are to Pages

Abrams v. Sotheby–Parke–Bernet, *357*

Adams v. UMS Generali Marine S.P.A., 220 F.3d 659 (5th Cir.2000), *66*

Adams v. Unione Mediterranea Di Sicurta, 220 F.3d 659 (5th Cir.2000), *163, 164*

Adams, In re Estate of, 155 Vt. 517, 587 A.2d 958 (Vt.1990), *337*

Agway, Inc., Commonwealth v., 210 Pa.Super. 150, 232 A.2d 69 (Pa.Super.1967), *38, 41*

Allen v. Hyatt Regency–Nashville Hotel, 668 S.W.2d 286 (Tenn. 1984), *196*

Allright, Inc. v. Strawder, 679 S.W.2d 81 (Tex.App.-Hous. (14 Dist.) 1984), *196*

Amundson, In re Estate of, 621 N.W.2d 882 (S.D.2001), *335*

Anderson v. Gouldberg, 51 Minn. 294, 53 N.W. 636 (Minn.1892), *118, 119, 126, 127, 128, 129, 130, 140, 141, 146*

Armory v. Delamirie, 93 Eng.Rep. 664 (K.B.1722), *105, 108, 109, 110, 111, 112, 113, 114, 115, 116, 117, 118, 119, 122, 124, 126, 127, 128, 129, 131, 132, 133, 134, 141, 146, 147, 148, 169, 249*

Aronow v. Silver, 223 N.J.Super. 344, 538 A.2d 851 (N.J.Super.Ch.1987), *299, 301*

Associated Mills, Inc. v. Drake Hotel, Inc., 31 Ill.App.3d 304, 334 N.E.2d 746 (Ill.App. 1 Dist.1975), *234*

Associates Discount Corp. v. Gillineau, 322 Mass. 490, 78 N.E.2d 192 (Mass.1948), *193*

Atlas Ins. Co. v. Gibbs, 121 Conn. 188, 183 A. 690 (Conn.1936), *365*

Attorney General v. Hermes, 127 Mich.App. 777, 339 N.W.2d 545 (Mich.App.1983), *40*

Attorney General of the Duchy of Lancaster v. G E Overton (Farms) Ltd., 3 All E.R. 503 (Ch.D.1980), *160*

Autocephalous Greek–Orthodox Church of Cyprus v. Goldberg & Feldman Fine Arts Inc., 717 F.Supp. 1374 (S.D.Ind.1989), affirmed 917 F.2d 278 (7th Cir.1990), *356*

B.A. Ballou and Co., Inc. v. Citytrust, 218 Conn. 749, 591 A.2d 126 (Conn.1991), *183*

Baehr v. Clark, 83 Iowa 313, 49 N.W. 840 (Iowa 1891), *258*

Ball, State v., 260 Conn. 275, 796 A.2d 542 (Conn.2002), *43*

Bank of America v. J. & S. Auto Repairs, 143 Ariz. 416, 694 P.2d 246 (Ariz.1985), *366*

Bank of Landisburg v. Burruss, 362 Pa.Super. 317, 524 A.2d 896 (Pa.Super.1987), *77*

Bartee, State v., 894 S.W.2d 34 (Tex.App.-San Antonio 1994), *37*

Barwick v. Barwick, 33 N.C. 80 (N.C.1850), *122*

Beach v. Holland, 172 Or. 396, 142 P.2d 990 (Or.1943), *314*

Bemis v. RMS Lusitania, 99 F.3d 1129 (4th Cir.1996), *163*

Benjamin v. Lindner Aviation, Inc., 534 N.W.2d 400 (Iowa 1995), *151, 172*

Bibby's Refrigeration, Heating & Air Conditioning, Inc. v. Salisbury, 603 A.2d 726 (R.I.1992), *218*

Bilida v. McCleod, 41 F.Supp.2d 142 (D.R.I.1999), *42*

Bischof, Estate of, 770 S.W.2d 474 (Mo.App. E.D.1989), *336*

Blackmon v. Estate of Battcock, 579 N.Y.S.2d 642, 587 N.E.2d 280 (N.Y.1991), *335*

Bol, Matter of Estate of, 429 N.W.2d 467 (S.D.1988), *336*

Bowlin, Estate of v. Ables, 766 S.W.2d 193 (Tenn.Ct.App.1988), *334*

Bridges v. Hawkesworth, 21 L.J.Q.B. 75 (1851), *150*

Brotherton v. Cleveland, 923 F.2d 477 (6th Cir.1991), *98*

Burns Harbor Fish Co., Inc. v. Ralston, 800 F.Supp. 722 (S.D.Ind.1992), *42*

Burtt, People v., 100 Mich.App. 122, 298 N.W.2d 684 (Mich.App. 1980), *13*

Buster v. Newkirk, 20 Johns. 75 (N.Y.Sup.1822), *9, 10*

Cabot v. Thomas, 147 Vt. 207, 514 A.2d 1034 (Vt.1986), *36*

Campbell v. Cochran, 416 A.2d 211 (Del.Super.1980), *173*

Carr v. Hoosier Photo Supplies, Inc., 422 N.E.2d 1272 (Ind.App. 2 Dist.1981), vacated 441 N.E.2d 450 (Ind.1982), *201, 215*

Case of Swans, 77 Eng.Rep. 435 (K.B.1592), *27*

Chance v. Certain Artifacts Found and Salvaged from The Nashville, 606 F.Supp. 801 (S.D.Ga.1984), affirmed 775 F.2d 302 (11th Cir.1985), *154, 162*

Chapin v. Freeland, 142 Mass. 383, 8 N.E. 128 (Mass.1886), *341, 342, 343, 344*

Chappell v. United States, 119 F.Supp.2d 1013 (W.D.Mo.2000), *152*

Charrier v. Bell, 496 So.2d 601 (La.App. 1 Cir.1986), *155*

Chiappetta v. LeBlond, 505 A.2d 783 (Me.1986), appeal after remand 544 A.2d 759 (Me.1988), *73*

Choice Hotels Intern., Inc. v. Manor Care of America, Inc., 143 Md.App. 393, 795 A.2d 145 (Md.App.2002), *83*

City Bank and Trust Co. in Dixon v. Morrissey, 118 Ill.App.3d 640, 73 Ill.Dec. 946, 454 N.E.2d 1195 (Ill.App. 2 Dist.1983), *376*

City of (see name of city)

Clark v. Maloney, 3 Del. 68 (Del.Super.1840), *131, 132, 134, 137, 138, 139, 141, 143*

Clark v. Wells, 45 Vt. 4 (Vt.1872), *367*

Classified Parking Systems v. Dansereau, 535 S.W.2d 14 (Tex. Civ.App.-Hous. (14 Dist.) 1976), *212*

Cleve, State v., 127 N.M. 240, 980 P.2d 23 (N.M.1999), *44*

Cobb Coin Co., Inc. v. Unidentified, Wrecked and Abandoned Sailing Vessel, 549 F.Supp. 540 (S.D.Fla.1982), *62*

Cochrane v. Moore, 25 Q.B.D. 57 (1890), *274, 275, 276, 277, 305*

Cohn, In re, 187 A.D. 392, 176 N.Y.S. 225 (N.Y.A.D. 1 Dept. 1919), *282, 283, 284, 285*

Collins v. Lewis, 111 Conn. 299, 149 A. 668 (Conn.1930), *54*

Columbus–America Discovery Group v. Atlantic Mut. Ins. Co., 203 F.3d 291 (4th Cir.2000), *65, 66*

Columbus–America Discovery Group v. Atlantic Mut. Ins. Co., 56 F.3d 556 (4th Cir.1995), *65, 166*

Columbus–America Discovery Group v. Atlantic Mut. Ins. Co., 974 F.2d 450 (4th Cir.1992), *166*

Columbus–America Discovery Group, Inc. v. Unidentified, Wrecked and Abandoned Sailing Vessel, 742 F.Supp. 1327 (E.D.Va.1990), reversed Columbus–America Discovery Group v. Atlantic Mut. Ins. Co., 974 F.2d 450 (4th Cir.1992), *58, 59, 62, 63, 65, 66*

Columbus–America Discovery Group, Inc. v. Unidentified, Wrecked and Abandoned Sailing Vessel, S.S. Central America (E.D.Va.1989), *60*

Commonwealth v. _____ (see opposing party)

Coos Bay Oyster Co-op. v. State Highway Commission, 219 Or. 588, 348 P.2d 39 (Or.1959), *23*

Corbin, State v., 343 N.W.2d 874 (Minn.App.1984), *35*

Corliss v. E.W. Walker Co., 64 F. 280 (C.C.D.Mass.1894), *201*

Corliss v. Wenner, 136 Idaho 417, 34 P.3d 1100 (Idaho App. 2001), *154*

Cornelio v. Stamford Hosp., 246 Conn. 45, 717 A.2d 140 (Conn. 1998), *99*

Cowen v. Pressprich, 117 Misc. 663, 192 N.Y.S. 242 (N.Y.Sup. App.Term 1922), reversed 202 A.D. 796, 194 N.Y.S. 926 (N.Y.A.D. 1 Dept.1922), *216*

Cress v. Scott, 117 N.M. 3, 868 P.2d 648 (N.M.1994), *82*

Dado v. Jeeninga, 743 N.E.2d 291 (Ind.App.2001), *214*

Dalia v. Lawrence, 226 Conn. 51, 627 A.2d 392 (Conn.1993), *335*

Dapson v. Daly, 257 Mass. 195, 153 N.E. 454 (Mass.1926), *43*

Davis v. Davis, 842 S.W.2d 588 (Tenn.1992), cert. denied sub nom. Stowe v. Davis, 507 U.S. 911, 113 S.Ct. 1259, 122 L.Ed.2d 657 (1993), *101*

De Cicco v. Barker, 339 Mass. 457, 159 N.E.2d 534 (Mass.1959), *300*

DeHart v. First Fidelity Bank, N.A./South Jersey, 67 B.R. 740 (D.N.J.1986), *352*

Delaware v. New York, 507 U.S. 490, 113 S.Ct. 1550, 123 L.Ed.2d 211 (1993), *181*

DeWeldon, Ltd. v. McKean, 125 F.3d 24 (1st Cir.1997), *259*

Douglas v. Seacoast Products, Inc., 431 U.S. 265, 97 S.Ct. 1740, 52 L.Ed.2d 304 (1977), *40*

Dressel v. Weeks, 779 P.2d 324 (Alaska 1989), *76*

Durfee v. Jones, 11 R.I. 588 (R.I.1877), *145*

Dyste v. Farmers & Mechanics Sav. Bank of Minneapolis, 179 Minn. 430, 229 N.W. 865 (Minn.1930), *318*

Eads v. Brazelton, 22 Ark. 499 (Ark.1861), *2, 45, 46, 50, 52, 53, 54, 56, 57, 59, 63, 65, 67, 144, 152, 158, 164*

Edmonds v. Ronella, 73 Misc.2d 598, 342 N.Y.S.2d 408 (N.Y.Sup. 1973), *145*

Ehorn v. Sunken Vessel Known as the Rosinco, 294 F.3d 856 (7th Cir.2002), *165*

Elyachar v. Gerel Corp., 583 F.Supp. 907 (S.D.N.Y.1984), *304*

Epstein v. Automatic Enterprises, 6 Conn.App. 484, 506 A.2d 158 (Conn.App.1986), *75*

Erickson v. Sinykin, 223 Minn. 232, 26 N.W.2d 172 (Minn.1947), *157*

Estate of (see name of party)

Everitt v. Higgins, 122 Idaho 708, 838 P.2d 311 (Idaho App. 1992), *373*

Fairport Intern. Exploration, Inc. v. Shipwrecked Vessel, Captain Lawrence, 177 F.3d 491 (6th Cir.1999), *163*

Fairport Intern. Exploration, Inc. v. The Captain Lawrence, 105 F.3d 1078 (6th Cir.1997), vacated on other grounds 523 U.S. 1091, 118 S.Ct. 1558, 140 L.Ed.2d 790 (1998), later opinion at 245 F.3d 857 (6th Cir.2001), *162*

Faith Lutheran Retirement Home v. Veis, 156 Mont. 38, 473 P.2d 503 (Mont.1970), *280*

Farrell v. Coulter, 898 S.W.2d 139 (Mo.App. E.D.1995), *335*

Favorite v. Miller, 176 Conn. 310, 407 A.2d 974 (Conn.1978), *158*

Federal Ins. Co. I.C. v. Banco De Ponce, 751 F.2d 38 (1st Cir.1984), *75*

Felter, United States v., 546 F.Supp. 1002 (D.Utah 1982), *37*

Ferguson v. Miller, 1 Cow. 243 (N.Y.Sup.1823), *31, 32, 33*

First Wisconsin Trust Co. v. United States, 553 F.Supp. 26 (E.D.Wis.1982), *326*

Flax v. Monticello Realty Co., 185 Va. 474, 39 S.E.2d 308 (Va.1946), *157*

Fleet Bank Connecticut, N.A. v. Carillo, 240 Conn. 343, 691 A.2d 1068 (Conn.1997), *325*

Flying "W" Enterprises, Inc., State v., 273 N.C. 399, 160 S.E.2d 482 (N.C.1968), *56*

Ford Motor Credit Co. v. Caiazzo, 387 Pa.Super. 561, 564 A.2d 931 (Pa.Super.1989), *272*

Foulke v. New York Consol. R. Co., 228 N.Y. 269, 127 N.E. 237 (N.Y.1920), *50, 57*

Fuentes v. Shevin, 407 U.S. 67, 92 S.Ct. 1983, 32 L.Ed.2d 556 (1972), *81*

Fukida v. Hon/Hawaii Service and Repair, 33 P.3d 204 (Hawai'i 2001), *82*

Gaden v. Gaden, 323 N.Y.S.2d 955, 272 N.E.2d 471 (N.Y.1971), *300*

Ganter v. Kapiloff, 69 Md.App. 97, 516 A.2d 611 (Md.App.1986), *79*

Geer v. State of Connecticut, 161 U.S. 519, 16 S.Ct. 600, 40 L.Ed. 793 (1896), *41*

Ghen v. Rich, 8 F. 159 (D.Mass.1881), *14, 16, 357*

Gillet v. Mason, 7 Johns. 16 (N.Y.Sup.1810), *31, 33*

Gonzalez v. A–1 Self Storage, Inc., 350 N.J.Super. 403, 795 A.2d 885 (N.J.Super.L.2000), *231*

Goodard v. Winchell, 86 Iowa 71, 52 N.W. 1124 (Iowa 1892), *84, 86, 88, 89, 90, 158*

Gray's Estate, In re, 27 Wis.2d 204, 133 N.W.2d 816 (Wis.1965), *329*

Green, State v., 456 So.2d 1309 (Fla.App. 3 Dist.1984), *79, 147*

Griffin v. Nationwide Moving and Storage Co., Inc., 187 Conn. 405, 446 A.2d 799 (Conn.1982), *231*

Griffith v. Fowler, 18 Vt. 390 (Vt.1846), *251*

Gruen v. Gruen, 505 N.Y.S.2d 849, 496 N.E.2d 869 (N.Y.1986), *295, 296, 302*

Guth v. Freeland, 28 P.3d 982 (Hawai'i 2001), *91*

Hannah v. Peel, 1 K.B. 509 (1945), *154*

Harwood v. Smethurst, 29 N.J.L. 195 (N.J.Sup.1861), *80*

Haslem v. Lockwood, 37 Conn. 500 (Conn.1871), *68, 69, 70*

Hayes v. Alaska Juneau Forest Industries, Inc., 748 P.2d 332 (Alaska 1988), *90*

Hecht v. Superior Court, 59 Cal.Rptr.2d 222 (Cal.App. 2 Dist. 1996), *101*

Helmy v. Swigert, 662 So.2d 395 (Fla.App. 5 Dist.1995), *24*

Henderson v. First Nat. Bank of Dewitt, 254 Ark. 427, 494 S.W.2d 452 (Ark.1973), *338*

Hernandez v. Roberts, 675 F.Supp. 1329 (S.D.Fla.1988), *167*

Hessen v. Iowa Auto. Mut. Ins. Co., 195 Iowa 141, 190 N.W. 150 (Iowa 1922), *250*

Hi–Ho Tower, Inc. v. Com–Tronics, Inc., 255 Conn. 20, 761 A.2d 1268 (Conn.2000), *74*

Hochstadter v. H. Tarr, Inc., 188 Misc. 561, 68 N.Y.S.2d 762 (N.Y.Sup.App.Term 1947), *201*

Hodges v. Smith, 159 N.C. 525, 75 S.E. 726 (N.C.1912), *18*

Hoffman v. Eastman Kodak Co., 99 Cal.App. 436, 278 P. 891 (Cal.App. 1 Dist.1929), *215*

Hughes v. Cobb County, 264 Ga. 128, 441 S.E.2d 406 (Ga.1994), *155*

Hughes v. Oklahoma, 441 U.S. 322, 99 S.Ct. 1727, 60 L.Ed.2d 250 (1979), *41*

Hunziker v. State, 519 N.W.2d 367 (Iowa 1994), *155*

Hurley v. City of Niagara Falls, 53 Misc.2d 999, 280 N.Y.S.2d 182 (N.Y.Sup.1967), reversed 306 N.Y.S.2d 689, 254 N.E.2d 917 (N.Y.1969), *148*

Hydaburg, City of v. Hydaburg Co-op. Ass'n, 858 P.2d 1131 (Alaska 1993), *373*

Indian River Recovery Co. v. The China, 645 F.Supp. 141 (D.Del. 1986), *61*

Innes v. Potter, 130 Minn. 320, 153 N.W. 604 (Minn.1915), *288, 375*

In re (see name of party)

International Aircraft Recovery, L.L.C. v. Unidentified, Wrecked and Abandoned Aircraft, 218 F.3d 1255 (11th Cir.2000), *46*

Irons v. Smallpiece, 106 Eng.Rep. 467 (K.B.1819), *274, 276, 277, 280*

Isaack v. Clark, 80 Eng.Rep. 1143 (1615), *143, 186*

Isle Royale Mining Co. v. Hertin, 37 Mich. 332 (1877), *362*

J.A. Bel Lumber Co. v. Stout, 134 La. 987, 64 So. 881 (La.1914), *54*

Jamison v. Estate of Goodlett, 56 Ark.App. 71, 938 S.W.2d 865 (Ark.App.1997), *278*

Jefferies v. Great Western Railway, 119 Eng.Rep. 680 (Q.B.1856), *121*

Johnson v. Weedman, 5 Ill. 495 (Ill.1843), *77*

Johnston v. Atlanta Humane Soc., 173 Ga.App. 416, 326 S.E.2d 585 (Ga.App.1985), *26*

Jones v. Ross, 98 Ala. 448, 13 So. 319 (Ala.1893), *18*

K–B Corporation v. Gallagher, 218 Va. 381, 237 S.E.2d 183 (1977), *183*

Keeble v. Hickeringill, 103 Eng.Rep. 1127 (K.B.1707), *11, 12, 29, 52, 62*

Kent Storage Co. v. Grand Rapids Lumber Co., 239 Mich. 161, 214 N.W. 111 (Mich.1927), *370*

Kenyon v. Abel, 36 P.3d 1161 (Wyo.2001), *75, 245, 293*

TABLE OF CASES

Keron v. Cashman, 33 A. 1055 (N.J.Ch.1896), *145*

Klein v. Unidentified Wrecked and Abandoned Sailing Vessel, 758 F.2d 1511 (11th Cir.1985), *162*

Knight v. H & H Chevrolet, 215 Neb. 166, 337 N.W.2d 742 (Neb.1983), *211*

Knowles v. Gilchrist Co., 362 Mass. 642, 289 N.E.2d 879 (Mass. 1972), *213*

Kostin v. Mehlbaum, 24 Pa.D. & C.4th 30 (Pa.Com.Pl.1995), *197*

Krumsky v. Loeser, 37 Misc. 504, 75 N.Y.S. 1012 (N.Y.Sup.App. Term 1902), *217*

Lamare v. North Country Animal League, 170 Vt. 115, 743 A.2d 598 (Vt.1999), *25*

Lanfear v. Sumner, 17 Mass. 110 (Mass.1821), *236*

Lawrence v. Buck, 62 Me. 275 (Me.1874), *145*

Lewis v. Poduska, 240 Neb. 312, 481 N.W.2d 898 (Neb.1992), *295*

Liesner v. Wanie, 156 Wis. 16, 145 N.W. 374 (Wis.1914), *10*

Lindh v. Surman, 560 Pa. 1, 742 A.2d 643 (Pa.1999), *297*

Lipton v. Lipton, 134 Misc.2d 1076, 514 N.Y.S.2d 158 (N.Y.Sup. 1986), *297*

Little, State v., 400 So.2d 197 (Fla.App. 5 Dist.1981), *36*

Long v. Dilling Mechanical Contractors, Inc., 705 N.E.2d 1022 (Ind.App.1999), *67*

Los Angeles, City of v. Times–Mirror Co., 219 Cal. 198, 25 P.2d 826 (Cal.1933), *371*

Lowe v. Quinn, 318 N.Y.S.2d 467, 267 N.E.2d 251 (N.Y.1971), *297*

Lowry v. Lowry, 541 S.W.2d 128 (Tenn.1976), *334*

Maddox v. State, 252 Ga. 198, 312 S.E.2d 325 (Ga.1984), *42*

Maine, State of v. M/V Tamano, 357 F.Supp. 1097 (D.Me.1973), *41*

Malek v. Patten, 208 Mont. 237, 678 P.2d 201 (Mont.1984), *330*

Matter of (see name of party)

Maxfield, Matter of Estate of, 856 P.2d 1056 (Utah 1993), *314*

McAdoo v. Dickson, 23 Tenn.App. 74, 126 S.W.2d 393 (Tenn.Ct. App.1938), *289*

McAvoy v. Medina, 93 Mass. 548 (Mass.1866), *151*

McClain, United States v., 593 F.2d 658 (5th Cir.1979), *356*

McCune v. Brown, 8 Ark.App. 51, 648 S.W.2d 811 (Ark.App. 1983), *302*

McGlynn v. Parking Authority of City of Newark, 86 N.J. 551, 432 A.2d 99 (N.J.1981), *198, 199*

McKee v. Gratz, 260 U.S. 127, 43 S.Ct. 16, 67 L.Ed. 167 (1922), *35, 362*

MDM Salvage, Inc. v. Unidentified, Wrecked and Abandoned Sailing Vessel, 631 F.Supp. 308 (S.D.Fla.1986), *57*

Menzel v. List, 28 A.D.2d 516, 279 N.Y.S.2d 608 (N.Y.A.D. 1 Dept.1967), reversed on other grounds 298 N.Y.S.2d 979, 246 N.E.2d 742 (N.Y.1969), *350*

Metier v. Cooper Transport Co., Inc., 378 N.W.2d 907 (Iowa 1985), *40*

Michael v. First Chicago Corp., 139 Ill.App.3d 374, 93 Ill.Dec. 736, 487 N.E.2d 403 (Ill.App. 2 Dist.1985), *176*

Michigan Humane Soc. v. Natural Resources Com'n, 158 Mich. App. 393, 404 N.W.2d 757 (Mich.App.1987), *44*

Millbrook Hunt, Inc. v. Smith, 249 A.D.2d 281, 670 N.Y.S.2d 907 (N.Y.A.D. 2 Dept.1998), *27*

Millett v. Temple, 280 Mass. 543, 182 N.E. 921 (Mass.1932), *276, 283*

Mills, In re, 172 A.D. 530, 158 N.Y.S. 1100 (N.Y.A.D. 1 Dept. 1916), affirmed 219 N.Y. 642, 114 N.E. 1072 (N.Y.1916), *282*

Mohler v. Labor Day Committee, Inc., 443 Pa.Super. 651, 663 A.2d 162 (Pa.Super.1995), *44*

Molenda v. Simonson, 307 Mich. 139, 11 N.W.2d 835 (Mich. 1943), *275*

Mondragon v. Austin, 954 S.W.2d 191 (Tex.App.-Austin 1997), *83*

Moore v. Regents of University of California, 215 Cal.App.3d 709, 249 Cal.Rptr. 494 (Cal.App. 2 Dist.1988), affirmed 271 Cal. Rptr. 146, 793 P.2d 479 (Cal.1990), *91, 92, 97, 98, 99, 100, 101, 102*

Morgan v. Kroupa, 167 Vt. 99, 702 A.2d 630 (Vt.1997), *24*

Morgan v. Wiser, 711 S.W.2d 220 (Tenn.Ct.App.1985), *154, 160*

Morrison v. United States, 203 Ct.Cl. 692, 492 F.2d 1219 (Ct.Cl. 1974), *156*

Morton, Estate of, 241 Kan. 698, 769 P.2d 616 (Kan.1987), *337*

Mucha v. King, 792 F.2d 602 (7th Cir.1986), *352, 354*

New England Box Co. v. C & R Const. Co., 313 Mass. 696, 49 N.E.2d 121 (Mass.1943), *121*

Newman v. Bost, 122 N.C. 524, 29 S.E. 848 (N.C.1898), *286*

New York City Friends of Ferrets v. City of New York, 876 F.Supp. 529 (S.D.N.Y.1995), *42*

New York, State of v. Seventh Regiment Fund, Inc., 746 N.Y.S.2d 637, 774 N.E.2d 702 (N.Y.2002), *245, 339*

Nicholaides v. University Hotel Associates, 390 Pa.Super. 112, 568 A.2d 219 (Pa.Super.1990), *234*

Nissho Iwai American Corp. v. New England Warehousing & Distribution, Inc., 650 F.Supp. 147 (D.Mass.1986), *211*

Noble v. Moistner, 180 Ind.App. 414, 388 N.E.2d 620 (Ind.App. 4 Dist.1979), *126*

North Carolina v. Armistead, 19 N.C.App. 704, 200 S.E.2d 226 (N.C.App.1973), *169*

O'Connor's Adm'x v. Clark, 170 Pa. 318, 32 A. 1029 (Pa.1895), *253*

O'Donnell v. Slack, 123 Cal. 285, 55 P. 906 (Cal.1899), *91*

O'Keeffe v. Snyder, 83 N.J. 478, 416 A.2d 862 (N.J.1980), *347, 349, 352, 353, 354, 355, 357*

Oregon Iron Co. v. Hughes, 47 Or. 313, 81 P. 572 (Or.1905), *90*

Outlaw, State v., 485 So.2d 217 (La.App. 2 Cir.1986), *34*

Owens v. Sun Oil Co., 482 F.2d 564 (10th Cir.1973), *292*

Owsichek v. State, Guide Licensing and Control Bd., 763 P.2d 488 (Alaska 1988), *43*

Pagliai v. Del Re, 2001 WL 220013 (S.D.N.Y.2001), *205*

Pahanish v. Western Trails, Inc., 69 Md.App. 342, 517 A.2d 1122 (Md.App.1986), *18*

Pangburn v. Partridge, 7 Johns. 140 (N.Y.Sup.1810), *79*

Paset v. Old Orchard Bank & Trust Co., 62 Ill.App.3d 534, 19 Ill.Dec. 389, 378 N.E.2d 1264 (Ill.App. 1 Dist.1978), *150, 158, 171*

Peet v. Roth Hotel Co., 191 Minn. 151, 253 N.W. 546 (Minn. 1934), *209, 210*

People v. _____ (see opposing party)

Phelps v. McQuade, 220 N.Y. 232, 115 N.E. 441 (N.Y.1917), *265*

Pierson v. Post, 3 Cai. R. 175 (N.Y.Sup.1805), *2, 7, 8, 9, 10, 12, 14, 29, 35, 45, 49, 51, 52, 53, 54, 72*

PJ–GO, Inc. v. R.V. Hopkins, Inc., 2002 WL 576127 (Iowa App.2002), *78*

Pollard v. Photographic Co., LR 40 Ch.D. 345 (1888), *201*

Price v. Brown, 545 Pa. 216, 680 A.2d 1149 (Pa.1996), *209*

Propst, Estate of, 268 Cal.Rptr. 114, 788 P.2d 628 (Cal.1990), *325*

Pyle v. Springfield Marine Bank, 330 Ill.App. 1, 70 N.E.2d 257 (Ill.App. 3 Dist.1946), *149*

Ray v. Flower Hosp., 1 Ohio App.3d 127, 439 N.E.2d 942 (Ohio App. 6 Dist.1981), *151*

Ray v. Ray, 270 N.C. 715, 155 S.E.2d 185 (N.C.1967), *376*

Richard v. Massachusetts Port Authority, 2 Mass.App.Ct. 826, 310 N.E.2d 146 (Mass.App.Ct.1974), *197*

Riesinger's Jewelers, Inc. v. Roberson, 582 P.2d 409 (Okla.App. Div. 1 1978), *347*

Ritz v. Selma United Methodist Church, 467 N.W.2d 266 (Iowa 1991), *154*

R.M.S. Titanic, Inc. v. Haver, 171 F.3d 943 (4th Cir.1999), *165*

Robinson v. Delfino, 710 A.2d 154 (R.I.1998), *333*

Rubenstein v. Rosenthal, 140 A.D.2d 156, 528 N.Y.S.2d 539 (N.Y.A.D. 1 Dept.1988), *304*

Russell v. Hill, 125 N.C. 470, 34 S.E. 640 (N.C.1899), *119, 122, 123, 124, 129, 134, 141*

Sanders v. Mincey, 317 Ark. 398, 879 S.W.2d 398 (Ark.1994), *23*

Sanders, People v., 182 Ill.2d 524, 231 Ill.Dec. 573, 696 N.E.2d 1144 (Ill.1998), *43*

Scherer v. Hyland, 153 N.J.Super. 521, 380 A.2d 704 (N.J.Super.A.D.1976), affirmed 75 N.J. 127, 380 A.2d 698 (N.J.1977), *308*

Schley v. Couch, 155 Tex. 195, 284 S.W.2d 333 (Tex.1955), *152*

Schreiner Farms, Inc. v. Smitch, 87 Wash.App. 27, 940 P.2d 274 (Wash.App. Div. 3 1997), *42*

Scott v. Shuffler, 269 Md. 432, 306 A.2d 531 (Md.1973), *374*

Sea Hunt, Inc. v. Unidentified Shipwrecked Vessel or Vessels, 221 F.3d 634 (4th Cir.2000), *66*

Sergey, People v., 137 Ill.App.3d 971, 92 Ill.Dec. 695, 485 N.E.2d 506 (Ill.App. 2 Dist.1985), *77*

Shamrock Hilton Hotel v. Caranas, 488 S.W.2d 151 (Tex.Civ. App.-Hous. (14 Dist.) 1972), *234*

Shaw, State v., 67 Ohio St. 157, 65 N.E. 875 (Ohio 1902), *12*

Skyways Motor Lodge Corp. v. General Foods Corp., 403 A.2d 722 (Del.Supr.1979), *235*

Slaton v. Davis, 118 Okla. 92, 246 P. 863 (Okla.1926), *236*

Sloin v. Lavine, 11 N.J. Misc. 899, 168 A. 849 (N.J.Sup.1933), *297*

Smith, In re Estate of, 694 A.2d 1099 (Pa.Super.1997), *309*

Society Nat. Bank v. Jacobson, 54 Ohio St.3d 15, 560 N.E.2d 217 (Ohio 1990), *376, 377*

Solomon R. Guggenheim Foundation v. Lubell, 567 N.Y.S.2d 623, 569 N.E.2d 426 (N.Y.1991), *355*

Solomon R. Guggenheim Foundation v. Lubell, 153 A.D.2d 143, 550 N.Y.S.2d 618 (N.Y.A.D. 1 Dept.1990), *354*

South Staffordshire Water Co. v. Sharman, 2 Q.B. 44 (1896), *153, 156*

Southview Associates, Ltd. v. Bongartz, 980 F.2d 84 (2nd Cir. 1992), *44*

Sparrow v. Airport Parking Co. of America, 221 Pa.Super. 32, 289 A.2d 87 (Pa.Super.1972), *197*

Sponseller v. Meltebeke, 280 Or. 361, 570 P.2d 974 (Or.1977), *368*

Squires, State v., 108 Ohio App.3d 716, 671 N.E.2d 627 (Ohio App. 2 Dist.1996), *25*

State v. _____ (see opposing party)

State Highway and Transp. Com'r v. Edwards Co., Inc., 220 Va. 90, 255 S.E.2d 500 (Va.1979), *372*

State of (see name of state)

Stay, People v., 19 Cal.App.3d 166, 96 Cal.Rptr. 651 (Cal.App. 2 Dist.1971), *176*

Steed, Matter of Estate of, 521 N.W.2d 675 (S.D.1994), *332*

Stewart, State v., 40 N.C.App. 693, 253 S.E.2d 638 (N.C.App. 1979), *42*

Stokes, Matter of Estate of, 747 P.2d 300 (Okla.1987), *337*

Stone v. Livingston, 222 Mass. 192, 110 N.E. 297 (Mass.1915), *370*

Tannenbaum v. New York Dry Cleaning, Inc., 2001 WL 914272 (N.Y.City Civ.Ct.2001), *211*

Teaff v. Hewitt, 1 Ohio St. 511 (Ohio 1853), *370*

Terk v. Ruch, 655 F.Supp. 205 (D.Colo.1987), *43*

Terry v. Lincscott Hotel Corp., 126 Ariz. 548, 617 P.2d 56 (Ariz.App. Div. 1 1980), *235*

Terry v. Lock, 343 Ark. 452, 37 S.W.3d 202 (Ark.2001), *151*

Texas, State of v. State of New Jersey, 379 U.S. 674, 85 S.Ct. 626, 13 L.Ed.2d 596 (1965), *180*

Texas Diamond Intern., Inc. v. Tiffany and Co., 47 S.W.3d 589 (Tex.App.-San Antonio 2001), petition for review denied (2001), *205*

Thomas, State v., 8 Ohio N.P. 653 (Ohio Com.Pl.1901), *13*

Thompson, State v., 136 Idaho 322, 33 P.3d 213 (Idaho App. 2001), *42*

Thummel v. Krewson, 764 S.W.2d 700 (Mo.App. S.D.1989), *213*

Tom Growney Equipment, Inc. v. Ansley, 119 N.M. 110, 888 P.2d 992 (N.M.App.1994), *362*

Totten, In re, 179 N.Y. 112, 71 N.E. 748 (N.Y.1904), *335*

Treasure Salvors, Inc. v. Unidentified Wrecked & Abandoned Sailing Vessel, 640 F.2d 560 (5th Cir.1981), *46, 47*

Treasure Salvors, Inc. v. Unidentified Wrecked and Abandoned Sailing Vessel, Nuestra Senora De Atocha, 546 F.Supp. 919 (S.D.Fla.1981), rehearing denied and affirmed in part and reversed in part Florida Department of State v. Treasure Salvors, Inc., 629 F.2d 1350 (5th Cir.1980), *164*

United Farm Family Ins. Co. v. Riverside Auto Sales, 753 N.E.2d 681 (Ind.App.2001), *208*

United States v. _____ (see opposing party)

Unknown Silver Coins, Matter of, 418 N.W.2d 317 (S.D.1988), *175*

Upman v. Clarke, 359 Md. 32, 753 A.2d 4 (Md.2000), *289*

Wallander v. Barnes, 341 Md. 553, 671 A.2d 962 (Md.1996), *120*

Waltham, City of v. Tukay Furs Service Co., Inc., 6 Mass.App.Ct. 864, 374 N.E.2d 347 (Mass.App.Ct.1978), *216*

Wetherbee v. Green, 22 Mich. 311, 2 Mich.N.P.Supp. 84 (Mich. 1871), *359, 360, 361*

Whatley v. Mitchell, 24 Ga.App. 174, 100 S.E. 229 (Ga.App.1919), *280*

White v. Finch, 3 Conn.Cir.Ct. 138, 209 A.2d 199 (Conn.Cir.Ct. 1964), *299*

White v. White, 769 A.2d 617 (R.I.2001), *319*

White Birch Farms v. Garritano, 233 N.J.Super. 553, 559 A.2d 481 (N.J.Super.L.1987), *81*

W.H.V., Inc. v. Associates Housing Finance, LLC, 43 S.W.3d 83 (Tex.App.-Dallas 2001), *371*

Wilcox v. St. Mary's University of San Antonio, Inc., 497 S.W.2d 782 (Tex.Civ.App.-Austin 1973), *356*

TABLE OF CASES

Williams v. Armroyd, 11 U.S. 423, 3 L.Ed. 392 (1813), *251*

Williams v. Williams, 20 Ch.D. 659 (Eng.1882), *91*

Willsmore v. Oceola Tp., 106 Mich.App. 671, 308 N.W.2d 796 (Mich.App.1981), *149, 170*

Wilmore Coal Co. v. Brown, 147 F. 931 (C.C.W.D.Pa.1906), *56*

Wilson, Estate of, 183 Cal.App.3d 67, 227 Cal.Rptr. 794 (Cal.App. 1 Dist.1986), *337*

Winkfield, The, (1902) P. 42 (C.A.1901), *116, 192*

Wolfenbarger v. Williams, 826 F.2d 930 (10th Cir.1987), *130*

Worth, Commonwealth v., 304 Mass. 313, 23 N.E.2d 891 (Mass. 1939), *42*

Wyoming State Farm Loan Bd. v. Farm Credit System Capital Corp., 759 P.2d 1230 (Wyo.1988), *370*

Young v. Hichens, 115 Eng.Rep. 228 (Q.B.1844), *11, 54*

Young v. Young, 240 Va. 57, 393 S.E.2d 398 (Va.1990), *293*

Yukon Recovery, L.L.C. v. Certain Abandoned Property, 205 F.3d 1189 (9th Cir.2000), *65, 164*

Zander v. Holly, 1 Wis.2d 300, 84 N.W.2d 87 (Wis.1957), *329*

Zendman v. Harry Winston, Inc., 305 N.Y. 180, 111 N.E.2d 871 (N.Y.1953), *260, 261*

PERSONAL PROPERTY

IN A NUTSHELL

Third Edition

*

CHAPTER I

WILD ANIMALS AND FIRST POSSESSION

The study of the law of property generally commences with the subject of personal property as opposed to real or land-related property. The explanation lies in the students' likely familiarity with personalty as opposed to realty: although some students will come to law school owning land or their own homes, all will own their wristwatch or some other form of personal property. "Owning" a thing is of course an all-encompassing term; what it encompasses, what its features are, is the subject of this book.

The study of the law of personal property in turn often commences with cases involving the hunting of wild animals. Our common law early accepted the Roman law idea that a wild animal (*ferae naturae*) is the common property of all, hence no one's personal property. For this reason, these cases present a unique factual situation because in them the wild animal usually has never previously been anyone's property. No prior possessors claim it. When one stops to think about it, the absence of a prior possessor and a chain of title is really quite unique. Most every chattel (the law's generic term for an object of personal property but etymologically rooted in the word "cattle") has been owned by someone at sometime. Occasionally, a chattel which has once been owned is then abandoned by its owner and reverts to being unpossessed. *Eads v. Brazelton* (1861). It is with previously unpossessed chattels that this chapter first deals.

I. THE LEADING CASE

In *Pierson v. Post* (1805), Post, with hounds and upon uninhabited and unpossessed wasteland, started to hunt a fox; Pierson, knowing Post was in pursuit and in order to prevent Post's capturing the pursued animal, killed and carried it off. Post was probably livid at having his hunt spoiled by that spoil-sport Pierson. So Post sued Pierson.

Post styled his complaint as a request for a writ of trespass on the case. Trespass, applied to personal property, is an action to recover damages for any willful injury or harm done by defendant to a chattel where the plaintiff had a present right to possession and the defendant interfered with this right. Trespass thus covers only willful or forcible acts. Where the acts of the defendant were unaccompanied by direct or immediate force and were the indirect cause of an injury and where defendant was not willful, but negligent in his actions, trespass on the case is the proper cause of action. This common law writ, often abbreviated as "case," covers a much wider area than does simple trespass. It is premised on a defendant's duty to respect the plaintiff's right, a breach of that duty and some subsequent harm caused the plaintiff.

The advantage of this latter writ, from Post's viewpoint, is that he did not have to show that he had possession of the fox, as obviously he did not. But this only allowed Post a bit of breathing space since he still had to define the nature of his claimed "legal right," even if it did not amount to a right of possession. Basically Post still had to plead his case in such a way as to emphasize his rights rather than the wrong committed by Pierson. Alternatively, Post could have pled his case in tort, emphasizing that Pierson interfered with his hunt rather than with Post's own right to the fox. It is reasonable to assert that Post's attorney should have pled his client's case using this alternative or tort basis for his complaint.

Why would Post's attorney plead as he did? Perhaps it was done in an effort to avoid having to show an injury (as would be required in a tort action) or under a commonly-used judicial rule of thumb that if possession were shown, so would an injury to Post's right. Remember that from the facts it would appear that the injury had been to Post's pride, not his pocketbook. His attorney did not want the court to dwell on the petty nature of the suit and so pled that his client's rights were injured.

From Post's perspective, then, interference with the lawful activity of hunting, rather than a legal right to the fox, is the gist of the action complained of. It is also probably what made Post angry enough to bring suit. Pierson, to legitimatize his own actions, is interested in focusing the court's attention on the fact that Post had no right to possession of the fox and, this being so, Pierson had as much right as Post to kill it. The writ sued for (trespass on the case) is broad enough to allow both parties ample play at trial; it after all concerns an infringement of a right and thus contains both tort (infringement) and property (rightful possession) elements.

Post won both a jury verdict and the judgment of the trial court. Pierson, however, sued out a writ of certiorari, thus getting himself listed first in the case name that comes down to us. Certiorari permits an appellate court to review the matters of law involved in the case tried below. Indeed, an appeal using this writ is limited to those matters.

The result of this appeal was a reversal of the judgment obtained by Post. Why? Because, the appellate court said, Post's complaint did not state a cause of action. This legal conclusion was just what Pierson wanted and perhaps could not have been obtained in the forum below because if Pierson had there demurred to Post's complaint, he would have only succeeded in getting Post to amend it. So tactically suing out a writ of certiorari was preferable to demurring below.

The decision of the appellate court could not have been an easy one. As of 1805, there was no case-law binding the court. A decision for neither party was compelled by New York precedents. Indeed, the appellate court cites none; it cites no American cases but does cite and distinguishes some English ones where a similar dispute arose on private land. It also cites some seventeenth-century European natural-law treatise writers much in vogue at the time of the decision. It cites the Emperor Justinian whose jurists in the sixth century A.D. wrote a passage which supports but does not compel its holding. It further anglicizes these continental writers by references to Fleta and Bracton. However, all this discussion really shows that the court was free to decide for either party.

What did it decide? Its holding, read most narrowly, is that Post did not state a cause of action. This says little of value as a precedent; it is only in the court's discussion of why Post fails that it makes statements giving any precedential value to the opinion.

But how important is this case anyway? The issue presented to the court is novel and interesting, but not much seems at stake here. Much if not all law, however, follows from procedure and much law in its incipient stages closely reflects procedural rules. So it is here.

Another reason for stating the holding in procedural terms is the notion that though in some nonlegal sense Post deserves the fox, he should not get it because this will encourage other people to bring such petty disputes to the courts. However, this aim probably was not uppermost in the court's

mind because limiting litigation and protecting the
docket was not accomplished in the cleanest possible
way with this opinion. It would have been far
more effective just to deny certiorari. Likewise, the
objective of limiting litigation assumes that parties
to future disputes will read and, even more unlikely,
act on the basis of the opinion in the present
case. Moreover, the facts of future cases may well be
easier to decide if some substantive rule of law is
laid down and used. Each of these rationales seems,
finally, judicially self-serving to some degree and so
might naturally be downplayed, particularly by
courts in the early years of the Republic, when the
role of the judiciary was not firmly established.

What more disinterested and useful statements of
the holding might be gleaned from this opinion?
From the facts, it is clear that Post was in pursuit
of the fox; the court concludes that he acquired no
rights in the creature. So the narrowest substantive
holding is that pursuit alone gives rise to no rights
in the fox.

Like the procedural version of the holding, this
statement may be too negative. True, it helps to
answer the plaintiff's question as to whether he has
a cause of action but it will probably not be very
interesting to the population as a whole. People are
seldom interested in learning about rights which
they don't have; rather, they are interested in those
rights they do have. On the other hand, a court will
not be too interested in explicating rights in a
lawsuit which it thinks is petty, breeds unnecessary
litigation, or is of first impression (when later cases

in the same vein may present unforeseen issues or not reach the courts at all).

In any event, will the facts of similar future cases be easier or harder to decide if a rule based on pursuit is used? Probably harder, because disputes will likely arise where there is more than one party in pursuit. Dwelling on the fact of pursuit will either make two or more pursuers indistinguishable as litigants before the courts or force the judges to rely on distinctions as to the types of pursuit. Either result is unsatisfactory. To avoid both, the appellate court in *Pierson v. Post* went on to state that a right in a wild animal arises only (1) when a person intends to control the animal and (2) when that person gains possession of it. Pursuit is a factual component of this rule. It shows the requisite intent while possession is shown by control of the animal.

Post, by pursuing the fox, showed his intent to control it, but the very fact which showed this intent also showed that he lacked control and hence possession of the animal. Thus he failed to show a sufficient possessory right to the fox and failed to state a cause of action.

From the court's viewpoint, a rule based on intent, pursuit, capture, and control provides an easier standard to apply to future cases. Why? Because the first appropriator or possessor of a wild animal has distinguished himself from a "mere" pursuer of game. This implies that the facts of these cases should be allowed to develop or "sort themselves out" sufficiently to provide a court with the grist to elaborate on their legal ramifications. How much development the facts of a particular case need before a court can usefully intervene in a dispute is a matter about which judges and lawyers develop a capacity for determining. This capacity is, needless to say, a high art.

An additional benefit of this rule is that with the standard clearly enunciated, it may discourage disappointed pursuers of game from bringing this type of suit to the courts. However, if this opinion is a search for a definition of possession of the fox, then it is important to recognize the premises and the logic used in conducting the search. The majority assumes that in the future hunters, after learning how and why the majority decided for Pierson, will hunt more furiously than ever in the knowledge that they must become the first possessor of the fox. The dissenting judge in *Pierson v. Post* looks at the case very differently. He wants to encourage fox hunting; horseback riding in the fresh air does not serve his purpose, unless it is done with the aim of killing those noxious beasts. In this, he assumes that foxes are bad, that hunters will hear of the court's decision and that they will be encouraged to hunt. People need to be encouraged to hunt, to start the fox, in order that they might kill it. The law should not rely on the chance interloper (such as Pierson) but upon the hunter whose intent it is to rid the countryside of foxes.

Pierson v. Post has been cited by courts, state and federal, down to the present day.

A. CONTROL

No rule of first possession (or of law) can be inflexible. If it were to be (say it required that to acquire a right in a wild animal, that animal must be dead), what of the many forms of live traps for wild animals and the rights of trappers? To obtain the right to a wild animal, a hunter must assume a degree of control which deprives the animal of its natural liberty and which must inevitably result in possession. Just wounding the fox is insufficient; as is pursuit. In *Pierson v. Post,* it would not matter if Post had caught up with the fox, seized it manually, and was about to put it in a cage when the fox bit his hand and escaped. *Buster v. Newkirk* (1822).

In *Buster v. Newkirk,* op. cit., the plaintiff was a hunter who with his . dogs wounded and was in pursuit of a deer; he gave up over the pursuit as night descended, but his dogs kept on. In the morning, the plaintiff resumed pursuit and came to the door of the defendant's house, where the deer had been killed the previous night. The defendant alleged that the deer had been shot at by an unknown party just before the defendant killed it and that he had cut its throat just as the plaintiff's dog laid hold of it. (The court wisely ignores the tale about a third party and keeps its focus in this opinion on the two parties before it.)

The trial court, in an action for the monetary value of the animal, gave the plaintiff judgment for seventy five cents, judged to be the value of the skin. The slight value of the judgment is perhaps testimony to the defendant's willingness to compromise: the defendant had offered the plaintiff the venison, but not the skin, and plaintiff sued for the latter. This judgment was reversed in favor of the defendant. Even though the plaintiff's giving up the chase for the night argues abandonment, the continuous use of the dogs negates an intent to abandon pursuit. The facts, however, highlight again the thin line between a rule against interference and a rule of capture—between a tort rule and a property rule. The *Newkirk* opinion relies exclusively on *Pierson*. Its language is replete with many of the latter case's words of art. As to the pursuit, for example, that the plaintiff did not deprive the deer of "its natural liberty" before the defendant seized it, disposes of the case for the court. Its result is further testimony to the unforgiving, winner-take-all nature of the rule of capture.

However, if a wounding is followed by active pursuit the hunter who (1) closes in on his prey and who (2) is about to administer a fatal wound, has a right to do so without interference. This infliction of the mortal wound must be inevitable in order for the hunter to be protected from the interference of interlopers. For example, if Post had placed the fox in the cage referred to earlier and if Pierson had opened the cage door and let it escape, Post would recover from Pierson on a tort theory of interfering with Post's possession. *Liesner v. Wanie* (1914).

What, however, if the hunter has no opportunity at all to inflict a mortal wound or capture the animal? Will the writ of trespass on the case still serve him? Another leading case, *Keeble v. Hickeringill* (1707) says yes. In this English case, the hunter (Keeble) was a landowner who maintained his decoy pond in a meadow. The defendant fired a gun off on his adjoining land and scared the ducks away from the plaintiff's pond. The plaintiff could not in all likelihood show what his damages were because he did not take possession of the ducks, and he could not do so because of defendant's interference. This interference alone was held actionable, using the writ of trespass on the case. We will have occasion to return to the *Keeble* case to discuss the fact that in this case the hunt took place on private property.

In another context—fishing—fish in a weir which remains open may still be captured by another fisherman. A question of fact must usually be settled to decide these cases: the net or trap may be substantially closed (say with the fish being 60–70% encircled by the net), but the remaining gap may be large enough (say, 50 feet) for another fishing boat to enter and throw its own net. These were the facts in *Young v. Hichens* (1844). Whether the second fisherman damaged the net of the first, will be relevant if the tortious aspects of the case are dispositive; they will be less so if the possessory aspects are emphasized. In *Young,* the first fisherman had driven the fish against his net by beating on the water with oars and throwing the fish into flight against the net. This served to deprive the fish of their natural liberty, but because beating the water with his oars also meant not closing the gap in the weir, it diminished the inevitability of the first fisherman's taking the catch on board his boat.

Still, with careful pleading to emphasize the negligent interference of the interloper, the first fisherman might prevail with a writ of trespass on the case. Trespass, however, will not work as well for him, since to use it he must show a willful or forceful interference with the rights of the first fisherman. (To establish these rights, the damage to the first's nets or violation of local ordinances would be crucial.) Trespass on the case, however, requires only that the plaintiff make the easier showing of recklessness or negligence in the conduct of the defendant. Young's attorney pleaded in trespass. That was a bad mistake. It also denied him the use of *Keeble* and *Pierson* as precedent.

Finally in this discussion of control, what about the fisherman who, using another's nets which have confined fish so that escape is possible, but have made their capture practically inevitable, takes these confined fish for his own? Is this larceny? That is a statutory crime involving the carrying away of a chattel in the possession of another. In one court, when charged with larceny, such a fisherman's conviction was upheld. *State v. Shaw* (1902). Considering the presumption of innocence that attaches to criminal defendants and the policy of construing criminal statutes narrowly, this result may seem surprising. When the uncertainty in the concept of possession is taken into account, it is even more surprising that a decision in a criminal case would turn as it did in this case on a finding that the first fisherman had taken possession of the fish in spite of the fact that they were in an unattended net. However, even in a criminal case, possession is a relative concept: the first fisherman has possession as against the secretive defendant who trespasses on another's nets and interferes with another's efforts. Trespass on and interference with a line of actively worked traps would yield the same result, also sustaining a criminal conviction.

One later criminal case took a balanced view of the amount of control necessary over fish in a net; talking about a two and a half foot wide opening, from which some, but not the majority of fish caught, would escape, the court said: "Very likely it would be going too far to say that escape must be rendered impossible under all circumstances.... But the avenues of escape must be closed, and the chance at least reduced to a minimum." *State v. Thomas* (1901), quoted in *People v. Burtt* (1980).

B.　CUSTOM

Possessory intent and a possessory act are the two requirements for gaining rights to a wild animal. The second—the possessory act—may in some instances be modified by custom so that a person need not gain actual control over the animal.

The leading cases on custom arose in the whaling industry. O. W. Holmes, *The Common Law* 167–68 (1881) (M. Howe ed., 1963). Herman Melville, in *Moby Dick* (1851) (W.W. Norton & Co., 1967), at

331–334, summarizes the industry's customs. Where a whale is harpooned by a bomb-lance identifiable as a particular whaler's, the persons who find the whale washed ashore dead cannot take possession of it without paying the whaler the market value of the whale. The courts use the custom of whalers, that "the iron holds the whale," to decide for the first harpooner. *Ghen v. Rich* (1881). So where a live fox in a trap, a fish in a net, or a harpooned whale on the beach, are customarily regarded by other trappers, fishermen or whalers as already "reduced to possession," the courts will take the custom as controlling.

Proof of a custom requires a showing of a shared set of values between the parties to the litigation. No such thing was present in *Pierson v. Post,* for example, and similarly, custom would not control a case between one set of whalers respecting the rights of the first harpooner to hit the whale and another set who require a fatal harpooning. Custom is confined by circumstances and is not therefore as broadly applicable as a basis for judicial decision as is a rule of first possession. In some instances, however, it remains a doctrinal substitute for actual control.

The facts of *Ghen v. Rich,* op.cit., provide a good illustration of the limitations of this doctrine. The plaintiff sought to recover the value of a fin-back whale. The custom of fishermen from Provincetown, Massachusetts, was to pursue such whales in open boats launched from shore, shooting them with bomb lances fired from guns expressly made for this hunt. Fin-backs swim too swiftly to be pursued with harpoon and line, in the usual fashion of whale hunts. Once lanced, the whales sank and were recovered later, when floating in the sea or washed ashore. A person coming upon a lanced dead whale customarily towed it or got word of the dead whale's location to Provincetown, receiving a salvage award for his services, and the lancer went to it and removed the valuable blubber.

The whale in question was lanced, killed immediately and sank, coming three days later to rest on a beach seventeen miles away. The defendant bought its carcass at auction from the finder. The plaintiff, however, proved that the custom among whalers in this region was that the lancer who shot and killed a whale was its owner and that the subsequent finder was obligated to send word of its carcass' location to Provincetown. "I see no reason why the usage proved in this case is not as reasonable as that sustained in the cases [involving other whaling regions]. Its application must necessarily be extremely limited, and can affect but a few persons. It has been recognized and acquiesced in for many years. It requires of the first taker the only act of appropriation that is possible in the nature of the case. Unless it is sustained, this branch of industry must necessarily cease, for no person would engage in it if the fruits of his labor could be appropriated by any chance finder." The judge, saying this, found the custom valid and the property of the whale in the plaintiff.

Ghen has some interesting aspects—the failure of more widely-used whaling techniques, and specialized, bomb-lance technology among them. However, the dispositive feature of the custom sustained here is that the custom is absolutely necessary, in the court's view, to the continuance of this type of whaling. Preservation of the whaler's economic incentives to engage in the hunt is important, but more important is the continuance and organization of the whalery itself. (This decision occured, of course, at a time when that whalery was in decline.)

There is no mention of the finder's occupation. Was he a competitor, or not? In the cases cited by the court, the facts seem to indicate that the disputes were between whalers all bound by the customs of the ground. Was the defendant here so bound, or was he bound to know of the custom by being not far distant from the place of the kill?

The procedures involved in the custom sustained here are somewhat vague. The lance attached to the beached dead whale was not so distinctive that it could readily be identified as the plaintiff's. If this case represents more than the law applicable to the tip of Cape Cod, this lack of identifying marks might well make a difference to the outcome of the case. Any system of property rights depends in part on assigning those rights to a person readily identified as their holder—and later their vendor, so that purchasers of those rights can be secure in the knowledge that they are buying from their true owner and not some pretender. Again, we see that the writ of custom does not travel well.

C.　WILD AND DOMESTIC ANIMALS

Usually the intent and actions of the parties have been the dispositive factors in hunting cases. In some instances, however, the type of animal involved may make a difference.

Animals are customarily (and the word, you can now see, is not used lightly) classified by the law as either wild or domestic—*ferae naturae* or *domitae naturae*. A deer, moose, or elk will be wild. Wild animals which are subject to the rights of hunters are not just the noxious ones such as foxes, but food-producing ones as well. On the other hand, sheep or cattle are domestic. These classifications will hold even if an elk has been raised for food on a farm and the sheep strayed from its flock. That is, the classification of an animal as wild or domestic is by species and not according to the wildness or tameness of a particular animal.

The owner of escaped wild animals is absolutely liable for the trespasses and damages caused by such animals. For domestic animals, the English rule was similar: an owner was absolutely liable for trespasses of domestic animals likely to escape and do damage and he was under a duty to restrain or to enclose them. The liability for failing to do this was very early rejected as contrary to the customs of many American states, but was (in many states, again) reenacted in statutory form. Ternus, "Liability for the Escape of Animals," 30 Drake L.Rev. 257 (1980). Thus an owner may be liable either in strict liability or negligence. An owner was strictly liable when he or she knew or should—with the exercise of reasonable care—have known that the animal had a propensity to cause the particular type of damage or injury suffered by a plaintiff. When unaware of a propensity of an animal to mischief, an owner is liable in negligence when failing to exercise reasonable care in preventing the plaintiff's damage or injury. See e.g., *Pahanish v. Western Trails, Inc.* (1986); *Hodges v. Smith* (1912) (involving the sale of a vicious horse sold as a gentle one); *Jones v. Ross* (1893) (involving the sale of a horse whose viciousness was unknown to the seller).

Stray cattle or sheep will not become property of the hunter who takes possession of them. The elk, deer or moose will. Why? Because the domesticity of the sheep puts the hunter on notice that there exists a prior possessor with rights superior to any which he might acquire. This notice does not pertain to the deer, moose or elk; no one would reasonably be expected to know that they were domesticated if found in their natural environment, unless their actions and movements provide reasonable notice.

Where there is agreement in a community as to the classification of an animal as either wild or domestic, classifying an animal as one or the other helps to answer the question of whether a second captor ought to know of (and so respect) the rights of a prior possessor of the animal. If domestic, the second captor is on notice of such rights. If wild, no notice is given.

No matter which label is used, prior rights in any animal can often be deduced from the type of environment in which the animal is found. Cows in a pasture belong to the farmer who owns the pasture. Deer in an undeveloped forest (as opposed to a game preserve) are fair game.

By the same token—and to carry this line of reasoning to its final conclusion—if a wild animal was wounded by a hunter, but rose and escaped with the hunter on its back, the hunter has not reduced the animal to possession, but any interloper would certainly know of the hunter's pursuit and be bound to respect it.

Besides providing notice, the hunter's ride may also show an act of taming or hunting the animal so as to exclude others from doing the same. This is an argument to the effect that the rider has a degree of control over the animal sufficient to possess it.

A less fanciful set of cases illustrating this same reasoning involve animals formerly wild, but then domesticated, only to escape later. Here again, a common law policy of encouraging the domestication of wild animals and a concept of notice underlie judicial decisions in this area. However, some state statutes may alter this policy by prohibiting the keeping of wild animals and/or by requiring the domesticator to secure a permit before doing so. If an animal has regained its freedom, it usually has no intent to return (*animus revertendi*) to its first captor. Actions in line with an intent to return will reflect its prior training by the first captor, as in the instance of a carrier pigeon or a hunting falcon. Such animals exhibit behavior linking them to their first captor.

In another instance, a wild animal may have escaped, but not yet regained its native habitat when set upon by a hunter. Once the hunter recognizes that the animal is not native to his hunting ground, such an animal, too, remains the property of its first captor.

By extension, it is possible that an escaped wild animal may have made it back to its native heath, but retains some identifiable features (a clipped wing, a band, etc.) which link it to its first captor who would again be able to reclaim it.

The same result may obtain when the first captor has expended considerable effort in raising the animal, but this is not compelled unless that effort would be obvious to its second captor.

In summary, if a wild animal has escaped, has no intent to return, and is found in its native habitat, then it is the property of its next captor. However, if the animal has not returned to its native habitat and has identifiable features or exhibits behavior that link it with its first captor, its ownership stays with the latter.

When a formerly wild animal escapes from its domesticator, a second captor may wound or kill it in defense of his property. The farmer who kills an obviously rare and valuable fox about to enter his chicken coop may use whatever means are necessary to protect his chickens, but if killing force becomes necessary, he will have to return the fox's pelt or carcass to its first captor.

Although the law speaks of the *animus revertendi* of a single animal, rather than of a species, this *animus* is an awkward legal concept because it is hard enough to fathom the human mind with its capacity for speech, let alone an animal's, lacking human capacity. Thus it is preferable to deal with once-tamed but escaped wild animals in terms of the notice of previous rights which the escaped animal in particular surroundings gives to a potential second captor. If the underlying policy is to encourage the taming of wild animals, one way to do this is to return escaped animals to their first captor.

Thus judicial attitudes toward the rights of first and subsequent captors of animals depends on an interplay between the actions of the animal and the habitat in which it is found. This interplay is illustrated—with the habitat aspect of the case replaced by a factor of land ownership—in cases involving bees.

Where bees swarm, the owner of their hive has the right to possess their honey; he has this right not because he has taken possession of every bee in the hive, but because his possession of the hive gives him as much control of the bees as he can reasonably be expected ever to have. As such, he has a qualified right to these bees even if they go onto the land of another. The qualification is that he must pursue them there or keep them in sight (if he cannot go onto another's land). So the owner of the land on which the bees swarm a second time has a right to them when they are unreclaimed. Although the original hive owner has a right in them, that right is defeasible upon his failure to pursue or keep them in sight.

At this point we can ask whether the second landowner does not have a right superior to the first after the bees have swarmed upon the second parcel of land, for then having the hive on his land would seem to give him present control. The prior right controls, however; the concept of prior possession is one to which we will return in the next chapter. For now, it is enough to recognize that the first possessor of a previously unclaimed animal (or chattel) will be preferred; this is particularly so if, up to the time his right is disputed, he has labored to make sure that bees build their hive and give their honey on his land.

One final context in which there is authority for classifying an animal as either wild or domestic is in a condemnation case. Where private submerged land is condemned when being used as seeded or planted oyster beds, shall the owner be compensated for their loss? Oysters in their natural habitat are classified as wild. If, however, they are seeded where they do not naturally grow—on posted beds—they are domestic and subject to private control. They stay put but are not rooted in the bed; they get their food from the water and not the bed. On this basis, one court has ruled them to be personal property, not real property, and denied their owner compensation for them as part of the award given for the taking of his real property. *Coos Bay Oyster Cooperative v. State Highway Commission* (1959).

As realty or personalty, however, oysters can be carried off the bed with larcenous intent. Control of them may not be actual but, like the bee-keeper, so long as the possessor of the beds has done all reasonably expected of him to indicate an intent to possess and control them, interference with his beds can lead to a charge of larceny.

1. Estray Statutes

Providing for the treatment of an escaped, domesticated, animal, more than forty states have statutes that prohibit owners from letting domestic animals run free and also permit others to take any such escaped animal—or estray—into his possession and work him as is customary. *Sanders v. Mincey* (1994). Usually he must register his find with a public official; sometimes criminal penalties are provided for failing to register. The original owner has the right to reclaim it within a short period of time. In this sense, these statutes amount to a very short statute of limitations for the recovery of possession of estrays. When reclaimed, the finder can recover the cost of the animal's keep from its owner, set off by the value (if any) of working the animal as his own while it was in his possession. This recovery is enforced by means of a lien on the estray that, if foreclosed, permits the animal to be sold. If unclaimed after the statutory period has passed, the animal can be sold (and the proceeds used to satisfy the claim for costs). See e.g., Mich.Comp.Laws Ann. §§ 433.15–433.18 (1991). At common law an estray was, and is still in some states, an animal subject to the foregoing type of lien.

Such statutes have two legal consequences. First, the finder of the unclaimed estray obtains title to it after a report of the find and the passage of the required amount of time, whereas the common law would provide him only with a right to possession. Second, these statutes provide a rule of liability for the owner or the keeper of estrays by either (1) making any owner of estrays strictly liable for property damages done by the animal, and in the case of an escaped wild animal, for personal injury as well, or (2) making the negligent owner liable for "reasonably foreseeable injury" by the estray if the estray was fenced, but imposing strict liability on the owner when the estray was unfenced. The person with a claim for damage done by an estray is also typically given a lien on the animal for payment of the claim.

Finally, where the estray statute was found only to apply to agricultural animals and other "beasts," one court held that after a finder of a lost dog diligently searched for its true owner, the finder may be awarded possession as against its owner when the latter later claimed it over a year later. *Morgan v. Kroupa* (1997).

2. Stray and Lost Pets

Pets are generally classified as personal property. *Helmy v. Swigert* (1995) (involving a dog), 197 So.

2d 329, 331 (Fla. App. 1995). A stray pet must first be found to be lost or abandoned (as opposed to mislaid) in order to have the right to its possession transferred to its finder. Lost dogs, cats, and other pets are numerous and must, for various reasons, be impounded by animal control officials. Special statutory treatment is often provided for such animals, permitting their sale or transfer to a private adoption agency. *Lamare v. North Country Animal League* (1999) (reviewing recent cases from several jurisdictions). Dogs running loose and injuring other domestic animals may subject their owners to a statutory liability for damages. See e.g., N.H.Rev. Stat.Ann. 466:19 (Butterworth 1991).

One example of the classification of a pet as personalty is that dog owners may, by statute in about 20 states, be liable for injury to people or property from dogs running free. *State v. Squires* (1996). Many states have also enacted "dog bite statutes." These typically impose liability regardless of the dog's former viciousness or the owner's knowledge of the dog's viciousness. Ariz.Rev.Stat. § 11–1025 (Michie 1991); Rev.Code Wash.Ann. § 16.08.040 (West 1991). They repeal the popular notion that "every dog gets one bite." Other such statutes impose liability in damages for owners of dogs biting a person on public or private property, including the owner's [Mich.Comp.L.Ann. § 287.351 (1991)], liability for biting without provocation a person who, like the postman, has a right to be or is required to be where he is when bitten [Ala.Code § 3–6–1 (Michie 1991); Ind.Stat.Ann.

§ 15–5–12–1 (Burns 1991)]—or some combination of these terms. See e.g., Calif.Civ.Code § 3342 (Bancroft–Whitney 1992). Some of these statutes incorporate, *sub rosa*, a rule that trespassers may be bitten. See Mass.Ann.L. ch. 140, § 155 (Lawyers Coop 1992) (excepting trespassers and persons teasing, tormenting, or abusing the biting dog).

A trespassing animal of either type may be distrained or seized by a land owner suffering damages and held until the damages are paid or the animal is sold in order to pay them. In addition, a state or local government may have statutory powers to impound a lost or stray animal and hold it, eventually offering it for adoption and transferring all rights in it from its prior owner or possessor to a new one. *Johnston v. Atlanta Humane Society* (1985).

D. LANDOWNERS AS FIRST POSSESSORS

Landownership gives a defeasible or qualified right to take the wild animals, birds, and bees, into the owner's possession. Owners do not have possession itself, and their right to take possession exists generally only so long as the animals remain on their land or until they wander or fly away, unpursued.

More generally, a qualified right of possession, which arises out of the ownership of the land on which a wild animal is found, is called the *ratione soli.* It is an English doctrine, never very popular in the United States because it smacks of the hunting rights of the English landowning families who used it to make poachers out of England's yeomen. *The Case of Swans* (1592). American courts make grudging use of it. The doctrine legitimizes the use of one's lands to hunt and take possession of the wild animals found there. However, only a right to pursue wild animals arises from landownership *per se.* Ownership of the animals themselves does not arise as an incidental right of landownership. The right to hunt, even on one's own land, is in this country a qualified right—and, as we shall see, *infra*, this Chapter, it is regulated as that account, while in contrast, as we have seen, wild animal ownership arises only by pursuit (possessory intent) and capture or control (a possessory act). However qualified and regulated, the right to hunt on one's land is assignable. *Milbrook Hunt v. Smith* (1998) (fox hunt club's assertion of such a right on the land of another). If the animal in question were not likely to flee, as are wild animals, ownership of the land might more easily be equated with possession, as in the case of minerals on the land.

A hunter must, however, have a chance to commence hunting before he can reap its rewards. If H is a trespasser, starts an animal on O–1's land and kills it there, H acquires no rights to the animal and it is O–1's property. This result obtains even though a court could hold that H owns the animal but is liable to O for the trespass; a principle of judicial economy to avoid rights which are not reduced to judgment or perfected and the avoidance of multiple suits dictates this result. O–1 has "constructive possession." See Chapter IV, section III *infra*.

In another instance, if H starts a wild animal on O–1's land but pursues it onto the land of O–2, the logical extension of the first rule is to deny H any rights in this situation too. However, with two landowners involved, both have claims based on *ratione soli*. O–1 will argue that the animal was naturally on his land and his right to pursue it was cut off by H; O–2 will argue that, though this is so, O–1 had no intent to capture it and anyway his right to capture it was terminated when the animal left his land. O–2 further argues that because possession of the animal was not achieved when the animal crossed the boundaries of his parcel and death occurred on his land, only there was possession of the animal achieved.

If the litigation over the animal only involved H and O–1, H might be tempted to argue that O–2 has a better right than O–1 to the animal. This argument is the defense of *jus tertii*. Few courts would permit this, on the theory that one must argue the strength of one's own claim, rather than the weakness of an opponent's.

If both O–1 and O–2 were present, H would argue that O–1 lacks a possessory intent and that O–2 has no control and so did not completely take possession whereas he (H) has both. However, to permit H to put these two weaknesses in O–1 and O–2's claims together to establish a claim of his own, is to allow

a two-time trespasser to gain property by crossing a
boundary and committing a second trespass. Thus a
court, without deciding which owner has constructive possession of the animal, would reject the trespasser's claim to it in both instances just discussed.

Now consider a slightly different situation—a variation on *Pierson v. Post*. What would be the result
if O–1 had been hunting on his own land when H
(Pierson), observing the hunt in progress from adjoining wild lands, shot the fox as O–1, like Post,
pursued it? Under these facts, H was not trespassing on O–1's real property when he shot the fox
(although perhaps he will have to do so to recover
its dead body). Peering over the boundary into O–
1's land at the ongoing hunt, however, H started on
a course of action which no less than before interfered with a legitimate use which O–1 was making
of his land. O–1 was in the course of exercising his
right to hunt (*ratione soli*) in a setting in which he
would not reasonably expect such interference.
Thus the facts now emphasize the maliciousness of
H's acts and one need be less concerned with O–1's
rights to the wild animal. If H is liable for a
trespass in these circumstances, O–1's and Post's
attorney would have been well advised to argue
from this position, rather than attempting to prove
his client's right to possession of the fox. *Keeble v.
Hickeringill* (1707).

The *Keeble* case was even easier to decide for
persons like Post. In that case, Keeble, like our O–1,
improved a duck pond, maintaining it with decoys
and taking the ducks with nets "and other ma-

chines." He was, the court concluded, "in the trade of seducing ducks to come there in order to be taken" and when O–2 (which stands for Hickeringill here) fired a gun from his neighboring land and scared off the ducks before O–1 could capture them, O–2 was liable for hindering the trade of the plaintiff. Whether the benefit claimed by the plaintiff is premised on his ownership of the pond or his rights as a hunter, is a question to which we should now turn.

O–1's ownership is not the basis for the decision. It is, however, a precondition. If O–1 was hunting on his land profitably while O–2 passed up a similar opportunity, this difference makes the protection of O–1's decoy pond as a man-made improvement on his land all the easier for a court. The facts that both parties are landowners with similar opportunities highlights the industriousness of O–1 and makes the interference of O–2 seem more malicious. The fact that the two are neighbors puts the interloper among them on notice of O–1's intent to capture the ducks decoyed to his pond. This reenforces the idea that malice underlies the interference. O–1 thus in the law's eyes becomes a hunter whose landownership and improvements give him protection from the interferences of interlopers disturbing his hunt. Turning O–1's freedom from interference into an affirmative right, one might say that a landowner has the right to exclude others from his land in this situation. After an act of possession with an intent to possess, an intent to exclude others from the benefits of property is often thought to be a third crucial attribute of property as an institution.

E.   MORE BEE–HIVE CASES

The keeping of bees has spurred several puzzling, important personal property cases. Marking a bee-tree was not sufficient to vest a right in the honey. *Gillet v. Mason* (1810) [hereafter *Gillet*]. This is so because the finder at least needs possession of the hive to have a right to the honey. Cutting down the tree is likewise insufficient. Id., citing *Ferguson v. Miller* (1823) [hereafter *Ferguson*].

Gillet was decided in 1810. It was an action in trespass for cutting a tree with a bee-hive and carrying away the hive and the honey. The honey was worth ten dollars. The tree was blazed by the plaintiff (Gillet), who was the son of the deceased landowner on whose land the tree was located. Plaintiff's blazing the tree was insufficient to establish a right to the hive or the honey. The court stated: "Marking the tree did not reclaim the bees, nor vest an exclusive right of property in the finder, especially in this case, against the plaintiff in error, who, as one of the children of Timothy Gillet, (who does not appear to have made a will,) must be considered as one of the heirs, and, as such, a tenant in common in the land." Thus the presence of other holders of the title to the land was important to the outcome of the case. Blazing the tree was insufficient to extinguish the claim of the co-tenants of the plaintiff and so was likewise insuffi-

cient against the defendant. Then, in dicta, the
court states that seizing the hive is—according to
that powerful trio of treatise writers, Justinian,
Bracton, and Blackstone—the minimum that would
be necessary.

Ferguson, decided thirteen years later, was also a
trespass case. Plaintiff claimed a license to go on
the land of another and cut down a bee-tree. Plaintiff marked the tree with his initials, but did not cut
the tree. Meanwhile, the defendant paid the landowner fifty cents for the same license, removed
plaintiff's mark, substituted his own, cut the tree
and carried off the hive. In the court's short opinion, the rule of capture was but one ground on
which the court based its decision. The other was
the matter of the licenses. The plaintiff's first oral
license was without consideration. This lack of consideration rendered the license revocable. Construing the license as a right to cut the tree and reduce
the hive to possession, the court reasoned that
under the license's terms, the landowner retained
the right to capture the hive himself. Reserving this
right, he also must have reserved the right to assign
his right of capture, which assignment he proceeded
to make to the defendant. This second license, the
court said, "may have been a revocation of the
former license. But suppose it was not, then the two
parties stood on an equal footing; and he who first
reduced them (the bees) to possession became the
owner". Here the rule of capture looks like a device
for filling gaps in the record about the licenses. In
Ferguson, then, the rule of prior possession is an

afterthought and dicta, the conveyancing rules of the common law having already disposed of the case.

More generally, in both *Gillet* and *Ferguson,* the right of the landowner figures in crucial portions of the opinion. However, even the rights of the landowners in these two cases do not amount to a right to prevail in trespass against the possessor of the hive. In a sense, the landowner does not have "possession" (here constructive possession) of the hive merely by holding title to the land on which the hive is located. That is not possession sufficient to bring trespass successfully. Neither the land title, nor the marking or blazing of the hive tree, is sufficient for this purpose. A policy of actual possession or use of the hive is thus encouraged and its user preferred over the holder of the passive asset— the title. Here neither landowner shows either that he holds the land as a repository for the hives on it or that he has, for example, some special way of processing the honey and needs all the honey from his hives to sustain this process. Absent such a "honey farm" showing, mere title is insufficient grounds for obtaining a trespass judgment.

F. MORE ON *RATIONE SOLI* IN THE UNITED STATES

The rights of landowners to exclude hunters was well-settled in England, where the land tenure pattern was one of large estates. In this country, on the other hand, the tenure pattern involved many smaller land-holdings. If H starts a fox on O–1's land, the fox is before long being pursued on O–2's land. O–2 would not have the benefit of *ratione soli*—the fox not being naturally on his land, and O–1's right is lost, so H is free of both landowners' claims if he is not trespassing.

In England, though Blackstone argued against this hunting monopoly, English statute extended the privilege of hunting only to those of "substantial means". This meant landowners in an age when most wealth was land-related. In the United States, these rights of landowners were suspect from the start. They smacked of a royal prerogative so recently overthrown.

The law of trespass, as we have seen in instances just discussed, still had the potential for excluding hunters from private lands. Early in our history, however, this threat was countered by state legislatures' enactment of statutes allowing entry by hunters on undeveloped lands. This put the burden on the landowner to enclose his lands, post a "no hunting" notice, or otherwise put them to use. *State v. Outlaw* (1986).

Judicial emasculation of the law of trespass also occurred. The courts made an owner show a property right in the animal claimed—possessory intent and a possessory act are not usually shown by the observation of game on one's land. Even if they are, the trespass may be found to be without injury. (Today, an owner claiming a similar right to photograph wildlife would probably be treated similarly.)

For policy reasons, the courts may wish to steer clear of silly, petty suits over game. Even if Post were to be found to have a claim to his fox, the court in *Pierson v. Post* may have wanted to give judgment for the Piersons of the world as a way of discouraging petty suits such as this.

From the early days of the Republic, hunters were regarded as foragers controlling "noxious" beasts. Foragers could wander freely, unless they were warned off undeveloped land by means of a posted notice. Early statutes required them to respect the boundaries of agricultural land or land otherwise enclosed or developed (what the common law called a "close"). These statutes gave rise to the presumption that they could go elsewhere without fear of being charged with trespass. Other statutes permitted hunters to retrieve wild, wounded game animals from agricultural lands. See e.g., *State v. Corbin* (1984). Custom also fostered a presumption that land owners welcomed hunters on their unposted, unenclosed, and undeveloped lands. *McKee v. Gratz* (1922) (Holmes, J.). Such a rule rather than a strict adherence to the English law of trespass was more suited to the American wilderness, over which " ... it is customary to wander, shoot and fish at will until the owners see fit to prohibit it. . . . " Id.

In the context of the criminal law, these statutory provisions may be encapsulated in one word— "poaching." It is made a crime in many a state's criminal code—and refers in this country either to hunting in violation of a landowner's posted notice not to hunt or to hunting out of the state's hunting season. It is not constitutionally void for vagueness when applied to a hunter (1) trespassing upon another's land (2) ignoring a landowner's posted prohibition on hunting. *Cabot v. Thomas* (1986); *State of Florida v. Little* (1981).

Posting land both protects the landowner from intrusion and permits hunting on unposted lands. See, e.g., Neb.Rev.Stat. § 37–213.02 (1991) (recognizing both purposes). It must be done by the owner or his agent. Simple posting procedures to prohibit hunting on many types of land (e.g., cultivated or agricultural, fenced or enclosed, farm or ranch lands) are perhaps the most numerous type of statute in this regard. Although some states require a "conspicuous posting" [N.J. Stat.Ann. 23:7–1 (2002)], some dictate the dimensions of the sign [Ariz. Rev. Stat. § 17–304 (2002)], and more recently some states have enacted statutes requiring that permission to hunt on any land, posted or not, be express or in writing. See Ga.Code Ann. § 27–3–1(a)-(b) (2002) (providing that permission be obtained or, when land is posted, in writing if a law enforcement agency is first informed of the posting). With the advent of the environmental movement, other legislatures have, as previously noted, heightened the permission requirements needed in order to hunt on the land of another.

A special category of hunters in recent years are Native Americans asserting tribal hunting rights. Such tribal rights are held by the entirety, that is, collectively by the whole tribe, and not as a collection of individual rights held by members of a tribe. Thus a Native American holds a use right to hunt derived from the tribal right. See e.g., *United States v. Felter* (1982). This tribal right may pre-empt a duty to procure a state hunting license.

II. GOVERNMENT AS FIRST POSSESSOR

The opening section of this chapter recited the maxim from Roman law that a wild animal is no one's personal property and hence the property of everyone living in the commonwealth. This statement must now be qualified to some degree and its implications discussed. Wild animals are everyone's property, as we have seen, only in the sense that everyone has an equal opportunity to reduce them to his or her possession. Alaska Const. Art. VIII, § 3 ("Wherever occurring in their natural state, fish, wildlife ... are reserved to the people for common use."). As one Chesapeake Bay waterman reportedly said, looking over one of the Bay's oyster beds: "The Bible says the Lord's a cheerful giver, and He put those oysters there for me to take." But wildlife is everyone's property in another sense as well: that is, every citizen (and so the government) has a collective interest in seeing that wild animals are conserved and protected so that they can continue to be reduced to private possession. As a trustee for the rights of its citizens, the government acquires an authority to protect every citizen's hunting rights. See e.g., Ohio Rev. Code § 1531.02 (Baldwin 1991) (codifying the trust); and see, *State v. Bartee*

(1994). This is a sovereign power, so labeled in an age when the sovereign was someone who might actually want to do some hunting!

The government is said to have proprietary or ownership rights as well: it is in this sense that the law refers to a "wildlife trust" and the government's having title to wildlife for the benefit of its citizens. See Hope Babcock, *"Should Lucas v. South Carolina Coastal Council Protect Where the Wild Things Are? Of Beavers, Bob-o-Links and Other Things that Go Bump in the Night,"* 85 Iowa L. Rev. 849, 883–889 (2000). Consider a chemical spill by a private company into public waterways. If a large fish kill results, can the state bring a suit in trespass, trespass on the case, or trover for compensation for the damages wrought on local fisheries? If the state has to show that it had the fish in its possession, its suit will fail; instead, the state will have to argue that its suit is necessary to protect the fishing rights of its citizens and that such suits are a precondition for the fisherman's initiative and the functioning of the private law governing this resource. One court has rejected this argument. See *Commonwealth v. Agway, Inc.* (1967), which held that the state did not have possession of the fish and so could not maintain a suit in trespass.

What effect will such a suit have? If the state sends its agents out to clean up the dead fish, and so takes possession of them, would it have sufficient possession then to maintain a suit? Any possession it has lacks the utility of a fisherman's (the dead fish cannot be used for food) and so the government is not standing in the same position that its citizens would wish to be. On the other hand, if the company got to the fish first, it might preclude the state's suit by becoming their first possessor. In this situation, the company still would not have the possession of a hunter. If we asked whether the company in cleaning up had acquired such possession of the fish that would give title to the animal, the answer would be "no": the state can regulate the taking of wild animals, and the company "took" them by poisoning them. No method of taking possession that spoils their utility to a fisherman is one authorized by regulation. More particularly, the company will normally not have a fishing license. In any event, it acquired no title. On the other hand, if the company's "possession" were found sufficient to award it the status of a first possessor, the system of private law surrounding wild animals would have at least encouraged the cleaning up of the waterway.

There is, then, a conflict between the public regulation and the private acquisition of wild animals. That is, the state's public law seeks to conserve animals so that its citizens may acquire them, but there are no comparable incentives in the private law to spur conservation: acquisition of possession as quickly as possible is the effect of a rule requiring first possession.

If the state is to gain rights to preserve fisheries and wild animals, its right must be premised on an encompassing right to preserve them in trust for its citizens, not as an extension or modification by regulation of private law governing the hunting of wild animals. The terms possession and ownership must be understood to have shifting connotations. A government may have enough ownership to regulate the taking of wild animals, but would surely not be strictly liable for their trespasses onto private lands and the damage they might do there. A government's ownership is no more than a legal conclusion pending its showing a strong interest in preserving and protecting an important resource and subjecting it to "skillful capture" by its citizens. *Douglas v. Seacoast Products, Inc.* (1977); cf. *Metier v. Cooper Transport Co.* (1985) (state's ownership interest does not impose liability on it for deer colliding with motor vehicle on highway).

Thus the trust theory of state ownership should be sufficient to sustain a state's trespass action against a person polluting an environment and so destroying fish or wildlife. The weight of the case law supports this proposition in the case of either a negligent destruction of fish or wildlife, or illegal hunting and fishing. *Attorney General for the State of Michigan v. Hermes* (1983). See also, Idaho Code 405736–1404 (1991) (providing for damages against a person for illegal waste of animals, birds, or fish). Nonetheless, because a state's interest in fish and wildlife is either a trusteeship or the result of its police power, state officials must plead their interests in the alternative and appear as owners, trustees, regulators, and generally as guardians, of the state's wildlife. While courts scrutinize the interests asserted by the states, most of them have upheld the state's right to bring an action for damages as an assertion of its *parens patriae* guardianship. See, e.g., *Maine v. M/V Tamano* (1973). There are cases to the contrary (e.g. *Agway*), but they constitute a distinct minority. Bean, *The Evolution of National Wildlife Law* 13–20, 34–45 (1977). Moreover, in twenty-five states, statutes permit public officials to sue to recover damages for the loss or destruction of fish and wildlife. F. Halter and J. Thomas, *Recovery of Damages for Fish and Wildlife Losses Caused by Pollution*, 10 Ecol.L.Q. 5, 9 (1982). Federal and state endangered species acts provide further authority for such actions when such species are involved.

A. STATE HUNTING REGULATIONS

In the absence of such legislation or a possessory interest in fish or wildlife, state officials have predicated such damage suits on a claim to act as a trustee for the public, or as the guardian or *parens patriae* of the fish or wildlife. Nineteenth century cases accepted the proposition that the state had a property interest in wildlife that by definition no individual citizen can own without capturing. *Geer v. Connecticut* (1896). More recently, courts have also emphasized the importance of the state's role in regulating the capture of wild animals as an exercise of its inherent police power. *Hughes v. Oklahoma* (1979). Today one implication of this regulatory power is that, when one plans to raise for profit a fish or animal labeled wild or "wildlife" by statute, the permission of the state should first be procured. *Maddox v. State* (1984). So it may be a misdemeanor for a farmer to raise elk or deer, or catfish or trout, on private land without a license. *Schreiner Farms, Inc. v. Smitch* (1997). Even rescuing and raising a baby racoon or squirrel is illegal, and the animal subject to seizure. *Bilida v. McCleod* (1999); and see also, *New York City Friends of Ferrets v. City of New York* (1995), (upholding ordinance prohibiting keeping wild animals as pets).

Regulation over the time, place, and methods of hunting are routinely sustained in the courts. *Burns Harbor Fish Co. v. Ralston* (1992) (sustaining ban on gill net fishing); cf., *State v. Stewart* (1979) (invalidating overbroad regulation prohibiting the use of automobile headlights to immobilize wildlife at night). So there commonly are, for example, different hunting seasons for rifle and bow hunters. Likewise, prohibitions on hunting or killing wildlife out of season, even on one's own land, and even (absent a statute to the contrary) to prevent the wildlife from eating one's garden plants, are valid. *State v. Thompson* (2001) (shooting a deer out of season a misdemeanor). Even an animal unintentionally killed by one's automobile is possessed unlawfully and subject to seizure. *Commonwealth v. Worth* (1939). So too, possessing a wild buck's carcass without a license is a regulatory violation, even after being attacked and killing it with one's bare hands: a person has every right to defend himself, but no right to the unlicensed possession of the animal. However, regulation of the number of hunters is often a subject of controversy. *Terk v. Ruch* (1987) (bighorn sheep permits). And one attempt to assign exclusive territories to hunting guides was invalidated under a state constitutional provision intended to insure broad public access to hunting. *Owsichek v. State, Guide Licensing and Control Board* (1988).

There is no such controversy over whether the state may require every hunter to obtain a hunting or fishing licence. Today no one may assert the common law rights of a hunter without holding a license. *Dapson v. Daly* (1926) (holding in the alternative). A hunting licence does not confer a right to trespass or ignore posted property. However, by statute in some states, no person may interfere with or harass a licensed hunter's taking possession of a wild animal during an otherwise lawful hunt. See, e.g., Mich.Comp. L.Ann. § 300.262a (1991); N.J. Stat. Ann. 23:7A–1 to–3 (2000). These statutes are aimed at controlling anti-hunting protests, protecting hunters from intentional interference, and so indirectly protecting their right to hunt. For example, statutes prohibit driving or disturbing animals in the path of a hunter, or interjecting oneself into the hunter's sight line. Compare *State of Connecticut v. Ball* (2002) with *People of Illinois v. Sanders* (1998) (both cases involving harassed hunters in state forests, Connecticut upholding and Illinois reversing convictions under its hunter harassment statute, and discussing protester's free speech rights). Wildlife particularly subject to such protests include endangered species, such as bighorn sheep, wolves, moose, or wild animals with a symbolic meaning, such as American eagles. *Mohler v. Labor Day Committee* (1995) (involving a pigeon shoot); *Michigan Humane Society v. Natural Resources Commission* (1987) (involving a hunting season for mourning doves, characterized as birds of peace).

State anti-cruelty statutes also protect both wild and domestic animals against killing, torture, or intentional neglect, and often specifically prohibit practices such as cockfighting or bear-baiting. Often however, these statutes contain express or judicially implied exceptions for a person's acting to protect his property. *State v. Cleve* (1999).

Where the regulatory or trust powers of the state are invoked, they trump the claim of a private landowner that property has been "taken" (in the Fifth Amendment sense) for a public use and that compensation is payable. An owner's rights are not infringed if nothing is taken from him, and nothing is taken if the state had ownership rights in the protected wildlife to begin with. *Southview Associates, Ltd. v. Bongartz* (1992) (rejecting a takings claim when owner prohibited from building over a winter deer yard). The common law protecting wildlife is thus an implied limitation on private land titles.

CHAPTER II

POSSESSION AND THE FORMS OF ACTION FOR PERSONALTY

The rules discussed in the first chapter, having to do with wild animals, present a particular instance of the law's sanctioning a person's acquisition of a property right in a chattel (meaning any piece of goods or personal property). However, a wild animal is not the only type of personal property which can be acquired by a person who becomes its first possessor. Any chattel, even one as insignificant as a seashell, a nut, or fruit, is equally subject to capture and control when found on lands open to the public (the foreshore of the beach or a public highway), or on private lands entered with permission—the chattel having not previously been claimed as the property of another, or having been abandoned by its owner.

I. ANOTHER LEADING CASE: *EADS v. BRAZELTON*

Eads v. Brazelton (1861), is a Mid–South variation on the themes of *Pierson v. Post*. It tells the story of the retrieval of a cargo of lead from the bed of the Mississippi River. Something of value, other than a hunter's wounded pride, is at stake.

A. THE CONTROVERSY

The lead plaintiff, Brazelton, having been informed of the wheareabouts of the wreck of a Mississippi River steamboat, America, proceeded to the site in the River. He blazed trees on the shore to help him locate the spot, and fastened a buoy to a weight that rested upon the wreck to mark the spot, but a combination of bad weather (it was January, 1855), the need to repair his equipment, and the press of other salvage[1] business, forced him to cease operations over the boat. Brazelton left his buoy and blazed trees to mark his effort and help him relocate the wreck.

One month later—in February, 1855— come the defendants,[2] who finally, on September 28, 1855,

1. The law of salvage, a traditional body of federal admiralty law, permits a volunteer to save a vessel or its cargo, once in peril, and recover a fee for doing so. The presence of a maritime peril, the voluntary nature of the service, and its success, are the three elements entitling a salvor to a fee award. Salvage fees range from 20–70 percent of the cargo raised. There is a presumption that a salvor's assistance is wanted by the owner of the vessel or cargo, absent its clear and timely rejection. *International Aircraft Recovery, L.L.C. v. Unidentified, Wrecked and Abandoned Aircraft* (2000). More on salvage law appears infra, Chapter IV.

2. One case subsequently citing and relying upon *Eads* makes much of this "race to the wreck." See *Treasure Salvors, Inc. v. Unidentified Wrecked and Abandoned Sailing Vessel* (1981) ("Brazelton was, however, first, distracted from this task by another salvage operation and then, disabled from the undertaking by a rise in the river which made it impossible for his salvage vessel to pursue the project. In the fall of 1855, Brazelton again headed toward the site of the sunken barge (sic). On the way,

with "Submarine No. 4,"[3] raised the cargo. They located the America independently of the plaintiff's earlier effort, including the blazed trees. Eads was shown to have known the wreck's location as early as 1843 and persons who lived along the River both at the time of the sinking and also while the defendants were locating the wreck, directed their efforts. Pilots along the River also had provided information on the location. The court stated: "Neither the sinking of the America nor its locality seems to have been so obscurely remembered as the bill [of the plaintiffs] supposes." The defendants' independent grounds for knowing of the location is important in characterizing their efforts as not building upon or taking advantage of the plaintiffs' labor. The defendants were thus able to place Submarine No. 4 over the wreck and began to raise the remaining cargo of lead—worth $4,507.96. They even raised the wreck's boilers.

Plaintiffs sued for an injunction against further work by the defendants. As the remedy indicates, this suit was in equity. It was brought in this manner because of the uncertainty of the plaintiffs about their legal (as opposed to their equitable) right to possession of the cargo and the wreck.

however, he was passed up by a swifter vessel belonging to Eads.") *Treasure Salvors* was a suit in which the petitioner obtained an injunction against rival salvors operating on the site of the wreck of a Spanish galleon for 2,500 yards on either side of the wreck site.

3. This "Submarine" was a double-hulled, wooden catamaran, with a deck bridging the hulls, and above the deck masts and rigging for hoists and tackles. In the deck was an opening through which a diving bell was raised and lowered.

Plaintiffs brought the suit this way to protect their work in progress.

1. The Decision

The Supreme Court of Arkansas stated that "the principal ground of controversy ... is Brazelton's right of occupancy of the wreck by finding, and ... that may depend upon its possession." This statement of the issue emphasizes the difference between finding a thing and assuming possession of it. The act of finding does not by itself confer any legal right to a thing. What is important is what happens after that. This latter focus is necessary because possession requires an intent to reduce a thing to possession, plus an act amounting to possession. Brazelton had shown the intent, but not the act. Judgment reversed, for defendants, on the issue of possession.

Even though plaintiff Brazelton marked the wreck's location with buoys and blazed trees, the court found such actions insufficient to establish possession of the wreck. These actions were at most only one component of a salvage operation leading to possession. In effect, they show that Brazelton's complaint pleads facts insufficient to show possession and that he was in the process of taking possession, but that process remained incomplete when he pulled his boat off the site. Because the plaintiffs had not acquired possession of the wreck, it was available for capture by the defendants.

The court said, however, that a decree should be entered for the recovery of the thousand dollars, with interest, that were assigned to Brazelton as "his damages for being obstructed by the defendants in his work upon the wreck after the service of the injunction upon the defendants...." The opinion expresses a willingness to let the fine stand if it was intended to punish Eads' employees' disobedience to the process of the court.

Brazelton eventually did choose to remove his boat. His reasons for doing so were several. One reason is that he had difficulty with his rig and had to make repairs in it. Brazelton looks like the possessor of old technology for raising cargoes, while the defendants have the latest gear. Eads' firm was running a fleet of at least four steam-powered salvage boats, each one more up to date than the last. They could hold a position in the swiftly moving main channel of the River. (Eads later developed an interest in the River's hydraulics.) This meant that the operation did not completely depend on lines slung from shore to keep the boat over the wreck. The court said: "If Brazelton's boat had been accompanied with steam-power as was the Submarine No. 4, the rise of the water in June, or the season of floating boats and rafts, would not have been uncontrollable obstructions to his desire to save the lead of the America...." So in part, when Eads is given judgment, the appellate court is protecting the most efficient salvor and the trial court is reversed because it attempted to protect the least efficient one. This is just the sort of efficiency which the rule of *Pierson v. Post* was meant to promote.

Yet efficiency is not dispositive in this opinion. Another reason Brazelton chose to remove his boat from the site of the wreck was that he had to attend to other business. Reasons of efficiency aside, the court might also have chosen with its decision to protect the first salvor to complete the salvage operations, regardless of the efficiency of the successful operation.

Why protect the first salvor to complete the job? Because the speedy removal of the wrecks from the main channel of so large a waterway as the Mississippi serves an important public interest in safe navigation. Recall that the River was awash in wrecks. The court might as well have put the question before it this way: do we want to encourage people to start to search for wrecks, or do we want to encourage them to take possession and remove them? The latter best serves the interests of commerce.

Abandonment by the owners—actual abandonment, plus an intent to abandon the wreck and its cargo—ends their rights. "Abandoned property is owned by him who takes it into his ownership." *Foulke v. New York Consol. R. Co.* (1920). This is the most cited rule of *Eads*. Fascinating questions, however, can be asked about what the situation would be if the owners had not abandoned and if further, the ingots Eads recovered identified them. If the true owners of the cargo were known Eads might then have had the obligation to search for them and, if and when he found them, return the chattel, accepting a reward for his efforts at least

sufficient to recover his expenses in taking possession. Information about the true owners might,
arguably, have made a significant difference to the
outcome of this case.

Why does the law often distinguish between commercial and non-commercial parties? To take account of expertise, to protect investment, labor, and
effort, and to regulate competition—all are possible
rationales for the distinction. In addition, there are
judicial process rationales of inducing flexibility and
fact specificity into the law.

Thus the case illustrates the rule of capture formulated in *Pierson,* but used here to resolve a
commercial dispute. Several points can be made.
First, the citation of *Pierson* illustrates the judicial
urge to have one rule for all types of litigants.
Whether a case involves two hunters or two commercial salvors makes no difference, because relatively, the parties in each dispute have the same
status inter se. A second point shows one result of
the rule of capture. After the decision in *Pierson,*
one might expect that each of the hunters would
hunt more furiously. This might mean one of two
things; either they modify their hunting practices—
honing their marksmanship, shooting at random, or
more wildly and frequently, in the hope of hitting
the game—or they will invest in better hunting
equipment—a better gun, a faster horse, etc. In the
commercial case, the litigants will already have
modified their practices, i.e., honed their skills until
they are of professional quality. Thus, if the rule of
capture is still to control their actions, they will

have to invest more heavily in the technology of their trade. The heavy investor captures the prize! This is surely a second lesson of *Eads.*

A corollary lesson is that old technology and less investment loses. However, the talk of technology blurs the human facts of *Eads.* The defendants' boat was able to hold its position in the current, close to the wreck, but also close to the plaintiffs' boat, which, being the more technologically backward, had to have more room to maneuver and eventually, had to back off. The newer technology interfered with the old, in the sense that it lets the defendants bully the plaintiffs into backing off from the wreck, ostensibly to pursue other salvage work. The line between a malicious interference with a competitor and the use of a technological advantage over him will thus be a thin one. [An easier case would involve the interference of one neighbor with another. *Keeble v. Hickeringill* (1707).]

Eads thus plays out some consequences of the rule of capture designed in *Pierson.* In so doing, it raises a question about the extent to which courts should interfere in commercial endeavors. Favoring old technology is not this court's way. Its opinion is supportive of legal rules that encourage investment in new inventions and the accumulation of capital, rather than individual initiative unsupported by capital investments. We do not know much about the investments and capital of Eads' competitors, so the contrast between these competitors is not conclusively shown here, but it is apparent that Eads was interested in putting his own and others' capital to work.

The rule of capture, formulated in *Pierson,* was applied there to settle a dispute between two equally equipped hunters; in *Eads,* the opinion of the court gives us good reason to think that the court did not believe both parties equally equipped. Thus the question arises: why does the court apply a rule, meant to settle a question of use, occupancy, and possession, in such a way as to reward the accumulation of investment capital in Ead's inventions? The probable answer to this question is that the writer of the *Eads* opinion did not recognize the change as such. The protection of capital was too new a thing. The shift from protecting use to protecting capital was too gradual to notice. In any event, whose capital was being protected? That of Ead's employers, if he had any, or Ead's own property in his inventions. The shift from protecting the hard-working inventor, to protecting his financial backers, is only faintly present.

B. ACTUAL POSSESSION

However, "Brazelton's act of possession need not have been manual." What does this mean? The court explains that "[p]lacing his boat over the wreck, with the means to raise its valuables and with persistent efforts directed to raising the lead ... would have been such acts of possession as the law would notice and protect." Such acts might have sufficed on two grounds. First, they would have provided notice to interlopers like the defendants. Second, they would have been, as the court recognized elsewhere in the opinion, in accord with the custom of salvors on the River, a signal to other salvors and thus provided the plaintiffs with a right to complete the operation free of further interference.[4]

C. CITATIONS TO *EADS*

Since the *Eads* case was decided, it has been most frequently cited, not for its rule on establishing possession, but for its rule on the abandonment of personal property by a former owner. Just as does possession, the abandonment of property has two elements: an intention to abandon, and action (or inaction). *Collins v. Lewis* (1930) (abandonment requires an intent to abandon as well as physical abandonment). The inaction of a former owner, over a long period of time, gives rise only to an inference that an owner intends to abandon. This holding is the title-clearing portion of *Eads*. It justifies the rule of capture's amoral tone, because it defeats the possibility that the true owner of the property is losing his right or title as a result of the later capture.

A good example of this use of *Eads* is *J.A. Bel Lumber Co. v. Stout* (1914). This Louisiana opinion involved the recovery, from the depths of the bay-

---

4. By way of analogy, one can compare the *Eads* opinion on this point with the dissent by Judge Livingston in *Pierson v. Post*, or to the custom of the fisherman in the Bay of St. Ives in Young v. Hichens (1844). See *supra*, Chapter I.

ous of the lower Mississippi River, of logs lost while floating from the logging site to the saw-mill. The lost logs, known as "sinkers," sank during a log drive. Ten percent of the logs in a typical drive were lost in this manner. They were often marked with a brand by either the loggers or the mill-owner, who might have bought them in mid-drive. Branded, they rested on the bottom of the bayou until raised. Their wood remained sound for an indefinite period, making it difficult to distinguish a sinker lost ten years ago from one lost for fifty years. Sinkers were not raised in great numbers until the loggers ran out of prime timber and began harvesting smaller and inferior logs. Of the smaller, inferior logs, a greater number (approximately 20 to 30%) became sinkers and never made it to the mill. Thus the value of the sinkers rose as the loggers shifted into secondary operations.

Eventually salvage operators began to raise all the sinkers. The plaintiff's mill began to buy them and to employ others to raise them. Other mill-owners published a notice warning everyone to respect the brands on sinkers. However, the plaintiff continued to buy sinkers with many brands on them after the publication of this notice. Because the brands were often used by more than one logger and some logs were sold in mid-drive after branding, the court states: " ... the mere fact that a 'sinker' raised from the bottom of a stream, bears the brand of a logger falls considerably short of proving that it belongs to him, or belonged to him when it sank." So the brands were of little use in sorting out the conflicting rights of loggers and millers. No notice of a right to possession—no constructive possession—could be justified by the registry or presence of a brand.

The court declared that the renewed actual possession of the sinkers trumped their branding. Were it otherwise, confusing disputes over ownership would add to the costs of acquiring the sinkers, while benefitting only owners whose efforts are exerted in litigation. So, by "common understanding" the court found that the sinkers were abandoned. This is not as clear a use of custom as in *Eads*. The court vindicated the plaintiff's rights to secondary recovery. Clearly this is a useful holding, since it kept the local logging industry in business for a longer period than would otherwise have been possible. A similar value might be assigned to the lead cargo involved in *Eads*, raised years after peak production of lead from the mines in the region, and probably more valuable on that account. As the rule of capture is a result-oriented rule, its result, possession, is all important—not the manner, the effort, or the time spent achieving it.

Over the years since *Eads* was decided, citation to it has been sparse, but frequent enough so that two types of citations are discernable. The first is as an authority for clearing title. Here its use as authority meant a reference to its rules of abandonment.[5] The

5. See e.g. *State v. Flying "W" Enterprizes, Inc.* (1968) ("It is well-settled law that the owner of sunken or derelict vessels or their contents may abandon them so effectively as to divest title and ownership."); *Wilmore Coal Company v. Brown* (1906), economic utility of such authority is most evident in cases authorizing secondary or scavenger recovery of a resource, such as sunken timber or "sinkers," and functioning to place goods back in circulation that were previously not valued sufficiently to be marketable.

A second use is the more recent. As salvage operations became more sophisticated (and expensive), the rule of capture came back into vogue, particularly in shipwreck cases. Much is at stake here: much investment is required both to stake the claim, establish a field of operations by constructively taking possession of the stake area, and then seize the stake. *MDM Salvage v. Unidentified, Wrecked & Abandoned Sailing Vessel* (1986) [refusing to grant exclusive salvage rights to a Spanish galleon driven over a mile-long shoal during a hurricane in 1733, the shoal dismembering the galleon as the boat scraped across it, leaving objects strewn along a long swath of the sea bed, this court stating: "The law of finds ... dictates that the finder of abandoned property must continuously possess or be in the process of reducing to possession the property which he has found." (citing *Eads*)].

The rule of capture in *Eads* has again proven adequate in this second context. It brings both the need for inventions and investment, as well as the need to use them actively, to a court's attention. In

(abandonment "is the voluntary throwing away or forsaking of property, leaving it open to be appropriated by the first comer."). But see, *Foukle v. New York Consol. R. Co.* (1920) (holding personalty found in a railroad car cannot be presumed abandoned).

shipwreck treasure cases it is used, not just to protect individual effort, but effort backed by considerable capital. In these cases, the investors are passive, energizing with capital the effort of others, often over long periods of time.

II. A RECENT SHIPWRECK CASE: *THE CENTRAL AMERICA*

Recent advances in the technology available to salvors have made their work feasible in deep-sea locations which previously would have defeated their efforts. In particular, the location and recovery of wrecks of archeological, cultural, and monetary value has become possible through the use of new sonar and remote television cameras mounted in small, unmanned, robotic, radio-controlled submarines. An example is the opinion in *Columbus-America Discovery Group, Inc. v. The Unidentified, Wrecked, and Abandoned Sailing Vessel* (believed to be the S.S. Central America) (1990), [hereafter *Central America*] (an admiralty action involving the contents of a wooden-hulled, side-wheel, luxury steamboat, awarded by the District Court to its finders, the plaintiffs in this action).

In 1857, the Central America was plying a course between Panama and New York City when it sank, one hundred sixty miles east of Charleston, South Carolina, in the Atlantic Ocean. The ship had encountered a September hurricane and, after a leak disabled its boilers, sank, with many lives lost. Many of the passengers were prospectors returning from the California gold-fields. Their lost possessions included several hundreds of thousands of dollars in gold. Lost as well was a large, insured cargo of gold; it was worth $1.6 million in 1857 and shipped from California merchants, banks, and express companies to New York. Many passengers survived, reached shore with harrowing tales (making the sinking famous at the time), and reported the loss of their gold, giving the wreck further notoriety.

Plaintiff's efforts to locate the wreck spanned ten years and expended over ten million dollars—"[u]tilizing numerous written accounts, oceanographic, meteorological and other data, modern search theory mathematics, advanced technology and equipment, along with the services of numerous experts ..." The technology employed in the search was described as "side-scan sonar, satellite navigation, tele-operated deep-sea equipment (submersible with stereo camera and robotic arms) and computer modelling software," all on a specially-outfitted ship. In this case, the equipment operated at ocean depths a mile and a half beneath the surface.

Plaintiffs in the *Central American* litigation learned one of the lessons taught by the *Eads* litigation: that is, they filed to protect their search efforts from the interference of rival search parties. They sought protection of the admiralty jurisdiction of our federal courts in doing so. That jurisdiction is in rem, against the cargo of the Central America, as well as in personam against potential rivals. In their complaint, they asked for a temporary restraining order against their rivals. Once the order was granted, in successive complaints, they enlarged the search area to which it applied. Enlarging the area in which rivals were enjoined from working had two consequences: it both baffled their rivals as to the wreck's location and freed the plaintiffs from further interference and surveillance.

The basis for the injunction was the remote television pictures taken of the wreck by a submersible robot. These pictures were sufficient for the issuance of the injunction, for the enlargement of the area covered by it, and the finding of civil contempt made by the court against parties violating the injunction. The right to work the site of the wreck, free of competitors, was granted on the basis of what the court dubbed "tele-presence"—that is, the presence of the remote, unmanned vehicle. "Effective possession of an object is attained in this unique environment by: (1) locating the object searched; (2) real time imaging of the object; (3) placement or capability to place teleoperated or robotic manipulators on or near the object, capable of manipulating it as directed by human beings exercising control from the surface; and (4) present intent to control including deliberately not disturbing the location of the object (so-called 'telepresence' or 'telepossession'." *Columbus—American Discovery Group, Inc. v. The Unidentified, Wrecked and Abandoned Sailing Vessel, S.S. Central American, in Rem (1989).* Not quite a new legal basis for establishing possession, it is as close as the court can come to one and a doctrine that should probably be used only when a manned presence is impossible.

Here the use of the temporary restraining order, available under the law of salvage, aids the salvor in the early establishment of a right to pursue possession of the sunken cargo under the law of finders. Salvage law is administered by federal courts asserting admiralty jurisdiction. That type of jurisdiction has the saving of the cargo or wreck uppermost in mind, but if the true owner of the cargo does not appear, the court can later order the cargo's title transferred to the finder. 28 U.S.C.A. 40571333 (1991). Thus skillful pleading by the person whose initial rights are those of a salvor, seeking only a salvage award from the owner, can turn control of the wreck site gained through a restraining order, into possession, and then into title to the cargo or wreck. The exclusive right to continue working the wreck site modifies the unforgiving nature of the law of finds, protecting investment, effort, and continuous work—taking an equitable right to an injunction and ripening it into a possessory right.

The requirement of actual possession traditionally serves only the aims of individuals, but sometimes serves group aims as well. In *The Indian River Recovery Company v. The China* (1986), the court denied the claim of a professional treasure hunter and instead awarded concurrent possession to a group of local charter boat captains and divers, conducting amateur diving trips over a wreck of an eighteenth century ship loaded with dinner plates and recovering the cargo slowly in the course of operating local charter and diving businesses.

This said, however, the *Central American* opinion is nonetheless reminiscent of the case of *Keeble v. Hickeringill* (1707) (protecting the owner of a decoy pond from a neighbor's firing a musket frightening away waterfowl from the pond in an action in trespass on the case). The *Keeble* opinion emphasizes the control of competition: the neighbor with the gun could set up a competing decoy pond and fire a musket in order to reduce the fowl to possession by killing them, but could not fire the musket to scare away the fowl from the neighboring pond. A similar control of competition is evident in the law of salvage when considering the issuance of a temporary restraining order. "The 'finder' or salvor is entitled to protection of the Court to continue working a wreck as long as he exercises such complete and continuous possession as the circumstances dictate and demonstrates reasonable success in saving the valuables from their peril." *Cobb Coin Company, Inc. v. Unidentified, Wrecked, and Abandoned Sailing Vessel* (1982).

The *Central American* opinion provides a right to take possession, not by physically seizing the cargo, but by the remote location of it, with television and robotics. Location and continuous working of the site, by remote control, becomes the basis for a right to possess the cargo. Indeed, the plaintiff's crew was locating, and then having the robot relocate, some of the cargo to a central location near the wreck, but still on the ocean's bottom. This comes as close to physical, manual seizure of the cargo as is possible if technology, seen as an extension of the human arm, is the means employed in the seizure. The interesting point about the opinion is that the court is willing to envision the plaintiff's technology as just this sort of extension.

The plaintiff's effort was not the end of the story of the Central American's gold. In *Eads,* the true owners of the lead ingots never stepped forward to claim them; indeed, the court found that they had abandoned their claim. Lapse of time, during which the owners asserted no right; the removal of the boilers and other valuable objects, followed by further neglect, caused the court to infer abandonment. This is one advantage of the law of finders as opposed to the law of salvage. The salvor is presumed to be working for the owner, while the finder works in the absence of an owner. Salvage law preserves the true owner's claim by requiring clear and convincing evidence of abandonment.

In the *Central American* case, in contrast to *Eads*, several types of putative true owners appeared. There were, for example, the alleged insurers of the wreck, who claimed to have paid the claims of some owners and now further claimed, in their own right, to be subrogated to those owners' rights. There was no dispute that the wreck was long lost and that only the plaintiff could now produce a map of its location. However, shortly after the sinking the insurance companies entered into a salvage contract, agreeing to give the salvor seventy-five percent of whatever he recovered. However, nothing ever came of this salvor's efforts. The next effort at recovery on the insurers' part was more than a century later when, in 1979, another salvage contract was executed. Meanwhile, the insurers had thrown all of their claims records away. Their payments were proven by newspaper accounts of the claims at the time they were made and paid. Neither were the insurers were able to produce invoices, cargo bills of lading, packing lists, or insurance policies. The destruction of the claims and payment-related documents would seem, by the same token, to destroy the subrogation rights of the insurers. While there was no evidence that they hoped to locate or recover the cargo, neither was there evidence of those documents' intentional destruction. In addition, the insurers did produce: (1) minutes of their Boards of Directors meetings discussing the claims, as well as (2) Board resolutions to pay them; (3) an insurance industry study on the sinking; and (4) the 1858 salvage contract.

These insurers made no effort to use technology akin to the plaintiff's once it was available. When offered a chance to participate in a search in the early 1980s, they made no investment. For the Court of Appeals, however, a lack of recovery activities by the insurers and of investment in various salvage operations presented to them, is inconclusive on the issue of abandonment. Before finding an abandonment, two elements must appear: first, taking no action to recover the cargo and, second, a relinquishment of the right to recover it. The court found a century of inaction, but refused to find that the right of recovery had been relinquished. Inaction, even a failure to appear in a related law suit, is not the equivalent of abandonment. *Yukon Recovery, L.L.C. v. Certain Abandoned Property* (2000). The insurers took no action when they had no hope of recovery, but once hope returned, they exhibited a care never to deny or relinquish their right in more than a decade of correspondence with several salvors, including the plaintiffs. *Eads* was thus distinguishable, as a case in which the ingots' true owners had already performed whatever salvage operations were of benefit to them.

The *Central American* court found that the vessel, the uninsured cargo, and the passengers' possessions, had been abandoned, but that the insured cargo of gold had not been. The insurers' rights in the insured gold remained intact, subject to the awarding of a salvage fee that, the court said, should be "by far the largest share of the treasure"—including perhaps an award in specie. When there is evidence that there is enough specie to affect gold and precious metals' markets, the salvor may additionally be awarded the exclusive right to market it in order to effect a unified marketing plan and to assure a maximum return. *Columbus America Discovery Group v. Atlantic Mutual Ins.Co.* (1995). Moreover, in the interests of further protecting its market value, the specie and artifacts awarded a salvor may remain under seal over the objections of the owners. *Columbus America Discovery Group v. Atlantic Mutual Ins.Co.* (2000). Further cases have held that salvage of a vessel's hull is not a conversion of its cargo. *Adams v. UMS Generali Marine S.P.A.* (2000).

The *Central American* opinion also held that the law of salvage, where the title to the cargo remains with the true owner, should be applied unless an abandonment is found; after an abandonment is found, finder's law should be applied. Only for an ancient and long-lost shipwreck should abandonment be inferred by lapse of time. Commercial record-keeping can otherwise preserve a claim never formerly relinquished until there is a practical hope of recovery. True owners of personal property have durable and long-lasting rights; in the *Central American* case, the insurers were able to step into the shoes of some of the cargo's true owners.

Thus, when an owner appears in court and asserts ownership of a shipwreck, and there is no evidence of express abandonment, the ownership of and title to the shipwreck remains with the owner. Long lost property, involuntarily taken from the owner, is no basis for inferring otherwise. *Columbus America Discovery Group v. Atlantic Mutual Ins. Co.* (2000)

A further example of the difficulty of proving abandonment occurred in the case of two Spanish naval ships, wrecked in the territorial seas off the Virginia coast in 1750 and 1802. *Sea Hunt, Inc. v. The Unidentified Shipwrecked Vessel or Vessels* (2000). The state of Virginia granted salvors permission to recover artifacts from the wrecks, but in the course of protecting their search efforts from interference, the salvors were required to notify the government of Spain. As a result, Spain appeared in court. The salvors' rights were trumped by its ownership claims, asserted through the foregoing common law rules about abandonment (none found) and treaty rights to its sovereign vessels. Abandonment of ownership claims to North America by Spain in treaties were not (this court held) an abandonment of vessels entitled to sovereign immunity at the time of their sailing a state's territorial seas, particularly when recognition of such seas did not gain legal currency until after the shipwrecks were in place. Likewise, the treaties' failure to impose any deadline for removal of Spanish effects from ceded lands, guaranteed a right of removal irrespective of the time elapsed.

III. TRASH AND POSSESSION

"Property is said to be abandoned when it is thrown away...." *Eads v. Brazelton* (1861). Thus there is a strong presumption that personal property discarded as trash or waste is abandoned. When trash is placed in a trash bag, bin, or dumpster, left unlocked and accessible, its former owner loses his rights in it. Trash is trash, and its appropriation, for recycling for instance, is not a misappropriation of the former owner's rights. It removal is not theft, nor criminal trespass, even if it is removed (without further injury) from private land. A person generating trash and intending to retain ownership or control of it must take affirmative steps to do so; no constructive possession is retained until it is hauled away or destroyed. So a celebrity with a drinking problem should not put the empties in the trash, for fear a journalist will go through it. Likewise, a business should not put its customer list in the trash, for fear a competitor will get hold of it. *Long v. Dilling Mechanical Contractors, Inc.* (1999) (involving employee list put into trash and procured by union organizers).

An example of the foregoing rules was played out in a famous nineteenth century case: horse manure left on a town's street has also been abandoned, but once raked into a heap, it might be defensible personalty again. In *Haslem v. Lockwood* (1871) the plaintiff assembled heaps of scattered manure worth $6 and left on a public road, intending to remove the same to his own land a day later. The next day the defendant removed the heaps. Neither the plaintiff nor the defendant had permission from the town owning the roadway to remove the manure, although the town's health and appearance benefitted from the removal. As the plaintiff claimed, because the manure was abandoned personal property, it became the property of its first subsequent possessor, and after a person has actual possession, he may lose the right to possession by not using it. If after discovering something and doing nothing to enhance its value, upon leaving the property as found, the right is lost. If, however, the plaintiff substantially adds to its value after its discovery, leaving it as he enhanced it—as with the manure gathered into heaps—preserves his right as against a later possessor doing nothing further to it. Possession then gives notice of his claim: his right is preserved for the time necessary to take it away for his use. The period of time allowed is subject to a rule of reason, and increases according to the value added. So, in *Haslem*, the plaintiff was allowed a little more than a day to return and remove the heaps from the roadway, and was allowed to recover the value of the manure from the defendant, described as a wrongdoer by the court. This recovery is the proper outcome for the case: like Eads holding his boat over the wrecked steamship, the heaps of manure themselves give notice that the plaintiff is asserting a right to possession, and further acts to provide notice to third parties—having a teamster immediately put the heaps in a wagon, enclosing or fencing the heaps, or hiring a guard to watch them—would only have added to the plaintiff's costs without providing a clear benefit to anyone else. Richard Posner, *Savigny, Holmes, and the Law and Economics of Possession*, 86 Virginia L. Rev. 535, 562 (2000) (commenting on *Haslem*).

No public official claimed the manure in *Haslem*. The town's claim, had it acted as did the defendant, might be on a different footing from the defendant's. Removal of the manure from the street would arguably be the control of a health hazard. This suggests that, as to the generation of toxic or otherwise hazardous trash or waste, the owner might be said to be in constructive possession of the waste until it is hauled off. The law doesn't protect one's trash because its presumptive fair market value is zero, but a toxic's negative value to the community gives its disposal a positive value for its former possessor and justifies a finding of at least constructive possession.

IV. OTHER FIRST POSSESSORS AND THE FORMS OF ACTION

Rules like those found in the *Haslem* opinion may be modified by statute. For example, in Georgia, pecans are big business. When Georgia pecans are grown on private property in a tree overhanging a public highway, any pecans falling on the road remain the property of the owner of the tree until the end of the harvest season. Thereafter, anyone may remove them from the roadway. Official Code Ga.Ann. §§ 44–12–241 to 44–12–243 (1992).

Much like Georgia pecans are standing timber and growing crops of various types. They have not been previously possessed but because they are normally grown on private lands, any claim to them must take into account the ownership of the land on which they are located. At common law, the right to harvest and profit from a growing crop is called an emblement; it is not a right to the crop itself, but is a right to harvest it where, for example, a lease to agricultural lands expires during the growing season and after the tenant has sown the leased ground.

Chattel which are attached to real property and intended to be permanently attached or annexed to it are called fixtures. They are personal property before attachment and real property thereafter, being then considered part of the realty on which they are located. Immature crops are often classified as fixtures to prevent their being levied on by a farmer's creditors before they are ready for harvest. However, marijuana plants growing between rows of crops in a field are the personal property in the possession of a grower, though he is not in possession of the field, for purposes of enforcing the criminal laws' prohibition against possessing marijuana. When crops are severed from the land—cut or harvested—they are no longer fixtures, but become personal property. As the basis for legal action, the crop or timber is probably more valuable as personal property and so whatever cause of action is brought to protect them after a wrongful severance, its objective will be to assert rights in what is now personalty. Even if an original or prior possessor has treated a chattel as real property, his seeking to assert rights to it in its present form allows him to bring an action that relates only to personal property. And, in any event, the defendant will have treated it as personal property and is in no position to assert that, as to any rights that he claims to it, it is not personal property.

A further objective in this chapter is to review the choices that must be made when deciding what type of lawsuit should be filed to enforce claims relating to personalty.

A. THE FORMS OF ACTION

In discussing wild animals, we considered trespass, the oldest form of action pertaining to personalty. An unauthorized and intentional taking or
interference with the possession of a chattel of
another is a trespass to that personal property. A
trespass may be under a mistake of fact or law, but
still be intentional. The intent necessary for the
action does not require wrongful motive.

The trespass must also result in more than nominal damages. In this regard, and recognizing some
conflict in the authorities, the loss of possession is
generally of sufficient value to satisfy the requirement of actual damages. (Where the damages were
immediate, trespass lies; where they were conse-
quential or indirect, *trespass on the case* was the
proper action to bring and the particular circumstances causing the damages had to be spelled out
in the complaint.)

The objective of an action for trespass has always
been to protect the possession of the disputed chattel as it was at the time of the trespass. *Pierson v.
Post* (1805). This requirement of a present right to
possession has been expanded somewhat over the
years by allowing the action for a plaintiff not in
possession at the time but having a present right to
possession. (Indeed, this is another way of restating
the issue in *Pierson*.) A still further modification in
this line of reasoning extends the action to one with
a present right to future possession—as with a

bailor of chattel presently in a bailee's hands. Finally, because it is possession (and not title) to the chattel which lies at the heart of the action, the defendant cannot set up the rights of a third party as superior to the plaintiff's—i.e., the defense of *jus tertii* (law Latin for the rights of a third party) is unavailing.

Conversion has today largely replaced trespass as the basis for most causes of action involving personal property. It is the wrongful exercise of dominion or control over personalty rather than (as with trespass) the interference with another's rights in personalty. *Chiappetta v. LeBlond* (1986) (conversion action for the return of a TV from a repair shop). It is completed by any distinct act of control, whether by way of assumption, use, detention of, or interference with personalty. It does not involve the wrongful taking of a chattel (as would trespass) but looks instead, later in time, at a wrongful exercise of control over the chattel. That exercise is taken to be a denial or repudiation of another's (the plaintiff's) right to the property. Originally this action was intended to lie when a finder of lost chattel did not return it to the true owner or prior possessor but instead used it as his own or, worse yet, sold or disposed of it to another. If the personal property allegedly converted is afterwards incorporated into real property, an action for conversion based upon its use thereafter will not lie.

Thus a conversion occurs when a person—without authority—assumes, uses, and exercises possession, or the right to possess personal property, to the exclusion of the rights of another. For purposes of this action, the personalty involved must be tangible. Intangible property has not traditionally been subject to conversion, except for those intangible property rights that are evidenced by a document—and then, of course, the document itself is the personal property involved. *Hi-Ho Tower, Inc. v. Com–Tronics, Inc.* (2000). Thus a bank account's passbook can be converted, but not the right to draw on the bank's funds on account, as can a corporate share certificate, though not the part ownership of the corporation it represents.

It is easier to say that a conversion occurs than to state what it is; courts have found it virtually impossible to agree on a definition. It has both property and tort aspects. Although conversion may involve a tortious taking, so that the possession is initially wrongful, how personal property came to be where a plaintiff locates it is often not susceptible of proof. Because of this evidentiary problem, conversion in the taking is presumed: it is the use or exercise of another's right when the possession, initially authorized, becomes wrongful by reason of the property's detention, persisting even in the face of a demand for the property's return. There need be no allegation that the defendant refused upon demand to return it when the initial taking can be proven. (That taking then becomes the conversion of the property to the use of the defendant.) Without this proof a demand and refusal is a necessary allegation of the complaint because it shows that notwithstanding the manner of acquisition, or more precisely, the plaintiff's failure to allege a wrongful acquisition, the defendant wrongfully withholds its possession from the plaintiff. *Epstein v. Automatic Enterprises* (1986).

This act of control is the basis for the last, most important, allegation in a complaint in a cause of action called *trover* (or trover and conversion), to wit, that the defendant "converted the thing for his own." It originally was preceded by allegations that (1) the plaintiff was in possession of a chattel, (2) he lost it, and (3) the defendant found it, (4) refused to return it upon demand, and finally (5) "converted it to his own use." This last allegation long ago became the only one that the plaintiff had to prove— the rest were either surplusage (following as they did from the conversion) or fictions (the original possession, the subsequent loss, and the defendant's finding) that the defendant was not permitted for historical reasons to deny. *Federal Ins. Co., I.C. v. Banco De Ponce* (1984) (reviewing this history). That the conversion was the cause of some injury or damage to the plaintiff is often a sixth allegation required. *Kenyon v. Abel* (2001).

As the focus of trover became the last conversion, other allegations fell away in many jurisdictions, and trover and conversion loomed larger in the mass of litigation over personal property, until they drove trespass from the field in all cases in which there was no forceful taking of the chattel by the defendant. It being easy to be stealthy in acquiring personalty, or any force or violence in its acquisition being dissipated or forgotten over time, proof of how the defendant acquired the chattel was often unavailable to the plaintiff. Thus much litigation centers quite naturally around its later conversion.

The theory of trover is different from that used in trespass actions. In trespass, the title is assumed to stay with the plaintiff, but in trover, the defendant is assumed to have acquired the title from the plaintiff. (At least the plaintiff does not contest the acquisition of title, and might be said, by reason of the conversion, to be estopped to deny it.) The plaintiff's bringing an action in trover is like an offer to sell the chattel and a judgment for the plaintiff in trover confirms this sale and transfers the title to the chattel to the defendant. Thus trover is in effect a "forced sale" of a chattel. With this theory in place, plaintiffs had an economic incentive to use trover instead of trespass. They can recover a larger measure of damages in so doing. Trespass gives them a recovery for any damages done to the chattel and the value of their lost possession for the time during which the defendant has the chattel, but trover allows them to treat the chattel as already sold to the defendant, and so the measure of damages is the value with which the plaintiff parted—the full fair market value of the chattel.

Generally, trover and conversion are described as so serious an interference with the rights of another in personalty that the defendant may justly be required to pay its full fair market value. *Dressel v. Weeks* (1989).

Courts will then impose this measure of damages when the exercise of control over another's chattel is a serious interference with the plaintiff's rights. One young attorney, Abraham Lincoln, convinced an Illinois court that taking someone else's horse for a fifteen mile ride was not so serious as to warrant liability for a conversion. *Johnson v. Weedman* (1843). The seriousness of the interference is a matter of degree involving many factors, including the extent of the damages done to the chattel, the loss or inconvenience caused the plaintiff, and the extent and duration of the defendant's exercise of control.

In evaluating seriousness, the bad motive or the intent to interfere will be taken into account as one of the many factors considered. *People v. Sergey* (1985) (involving a criminal conversion of an automobile and comparing the facts—no intent to interfere with another's rights, no damage, and the owner's recovery of the auto—to Lincoln's case in *Johnson v. Weedman,* op. cit.). If good faith is present, the measure of damages may be reduced by any amounts expended by the defendant to protect, maintain or improve the chattel. On the other hand, when personal property in which another has an interest is sold without authority, the full measure is imposed, particularly if the authority should have been discovered by resorting to official records. *Bank of Landisburg v. Burruss* (1987) (a trover and conversion suit for selling a farmer's cattle and giving the $24,000 proceeds of sale to the farmer, instead of the bank with a recorded security interest for $46,000 in the cattle).

As in trespass, a defendant can lack a motivation to interfere with plaintiff's rights and still have the requisite intent to convert another's chattel.

While the carrying away of a chattel may not constitute a conversion when it is done without serious consequences, even a verbal assertion of ownership can be sufficient for a conversion when serious consequences are present. In this type of lawsuit, most important as a matter of proof is the defendant's refusal to return the chattel upon demand. This refusal is *prima facie* evidence of conversion. No wonder the demand and refusal counts of the original action in trover were added with time! When a plaintiff attempts self-help, these counts are absorbed into proof of the conversion itself which takes place at that time if no wrongful taking or earlier act of dominion is provable.

Often, then, the time of the demand and refusal is the time of the conversion. Likewise, the statute of limitations on the resulting cause of action runs from the time of the refusal. The place of the conversion provides the law applying to the incident.

Finally, using the cause of action in *replevin,* a plaintiff can physically recover a lost chattel. This action is designed to recover the possession of a chattel wrongfully detained by another, restoring it to one entitled to its immediate possession. *PJ-GO, Inc. v. R.V. Hopkins, Inc.* (2002). It is not necessary that the plaintiff know how the chattel came to be lost, or came into the hands of the person having present possession of it. *Ganter v. Kapiloff* (1986) (involving postage stamps thought to be in the plaintiffs' possession until they were found in the defendant's). This action does not lie against a person in possession in *custodia legis*—that is, in possession of a chattel subject to a judicial proceeding, as (say) the police might be, holding a chattel pending prosecution of a person accused of stealing it.

The property sought must be tangible personal property. Fixtures permanently attached to real property do not qualify, although items such as a tenant might remove at the end of a leasehold do. Conversely, a landlord seeking replevin of property removed from premises while a tenant was in possession, would have to allege and prove that the tenant had abandoned his or her right to it. *State v. Green* (1984). Crops and timber severed from the land are also proper subjects for replevin.

Replevin is based on an ancient writ. Its original use in feudal England was to permit a tenant to recover a chattel distrained by the lord of the manor for non-payment of rent. The writ was never widened much beyond this original use in England, so that Blackstone could correctly say, when he wrote his commentaries on English law in the 1770s, that the writ was limited to cases of distraint. American judges quickly rejected this limitation and extended it to any unlawful conversion of a chattel. *Pangburn v. Patridge* (1810). Thus the trespasser and convertor, as well as the distrainor, could be defendants in suits involving this writ. It became the most widespread form of action for the specific or in kind recovery of personal property wrongfully taken by a defendant.

Our law also extended the writ to cover instances in which specific recovery was sought for a chattel not necessarily wrongfully taken but wrongfully detained. (The common law writ in such a situation was called *detinue*.) Some courts, however, refused to extend the writ. *Harwood v. Smethurst* (1861). State legislatures stepped in to do the job and the writ of detinue was subsumed in our writ of replevin. Then a new controversy sprang up, for if replevin was available when there had only been a wrongful detention of the chattel, some argued that the taking could be constructive or ignored altogether, while others said that both a wrongful taking and detention were required. Legislatures stepped in again to solve this second problem and provided that a wrongful detention shall be deemed an unlawful taking. So replevin lay for a taking and/or a detention of a chattel. One recent example of the end-product of this process is N.J.Stat. § 2A:14–1 to–5 (2002).

The theory of replevin is that, through all the facts alleged in the complaint, the title to the chattel remained with the plaintiff. This has one very important procedural consequence: unlike a suit in conversion or detinue, the plaintiff, after posting a bond and a preliminary hearing, becomes entitled to possession of the chattel and the sheriff takes possession of it for him shortly after the cause of action is filed. The bond is usually for double the value of the chattel. Until recently in many jurisdictions, posting the bond was the only requirement plaintiff had to meet before the sheriff took possession of the chattel and delivered it to him. The bond was intended to indemnify the defendant in case the chattel was damaged or destroyed while in the hands of the plaintiff and it turned out that the defendant was entitled to its possession back.

Recently, however, a second requirement, that of a preliminary hearing to determine whether the plaintiff should get immediate possession of the chattel, has been imposed by the courts. This change is an attempt to provide due process before transferring possession of the chattel between the parties. The mandate for it is a constitutional one. *Fuentes v. Shevin* (1972); *White Birch Farms v. Garritano* (1987) (holding a procedure for a private sale of a horse under a stableman's lien statute unconstitutional when there is no notice and hearing with regard to the sale). Many state legislatures have responded to these and other cases by incorporating a preliminary hearing on the right to possession into replevin procedures in state codes. Some state codes permit the defendant to post a bond for the value of the chattel in lieu of delivering it over to the sheriff. McKinney's—N.Y.Civ.Prac.Law § 7102(e)(1992).

So the imposition of a bond or a preliminary hearing, conducted by a judge or magistrate, has been one response to the constitutional due process problems with replevin statutes. Another has been a statutory limitation on the instances calling for the initial seizure of the chattel by the sheriff: in some states, this initial seizure is only possible when the goods have been the subject of a felonious taking, are in danger of destruction, or are property of a particular type—e.g., a credit card.

Still another response has been to abolish replevin altogether. Virginia has adopted this course of action. Va.Code § 8.01–218 (1992). This course of action may leave common law detinue in place (although Virginia had also codified the action). Detinue requires only a showing of the wrongful detention of a chattel.

At the hearing and trial in a replevin action, the plaintiff seeks to justify his taking of possession through the sheriff. He may also seek any damages caused by the wrongful taking or detention. These "loss of use" or lost opportunity damages will, under the traditional rule, be limited by the fair market value of the chattel. *Cress v. Scott* (1994). The assumption is that if a chattel is totally destroyed, it will be immediately replaced and in trover and conversion, the judgment will be for its fair market value; in contrast, if, in a replevin action, the chattel is returned in a damaged condition, its repair will take time and that lost time is compensated with a judgment for damages. *Fukida v. Hon/Hawaii Service & Repair* (2001). The implication of this assumption is that, for instances of total destruction, loss of use damages are not traditionally available, although this implication has been rejected in some recent cases. *Mondragon v. Austin* (1997).

For the defendant's part, he seeks to show that he had been rightfully in possession of the chattel. He cannot show (and barring this defense may partly account for replevin's wide use) that the title to the chattel lay in another, not a party to the action. Our courts rejected the defense of *jus tertii* (right of a third party) during the course of the nineteenth century. Finkelstein, *The Plea of Property in a Stranger in Replevin*, 23 Colum.L.Rev. 652 (1923). Absent a statute to the contrary, prior possession alone will support the cause of action. (At a later stage of the proceedings, when the court considers the matter of measuring damages, the *jus tertii* defense may be considered by the court. In the context of the awarding of damages, a lesser award may indeed be appropriate (1) if a plaintiff has a right to possession without having title or (2) if he sues and wins in trover, but the defendant still faces the possibility of a later lawsuit by the true owner.)

As with trover and conversion, the statute of limitations for replevin does not begin to run until there has been a demand and refusal. *Choice Hotels Internat'l, Inc. v. Manor Care of America, Inc.* (2002). Replevin lies so long as the chattel can be identified and until the doctrine of accession (See *infra*, Chapter X) cuts it off. Thus if the identity of the chattel is substantially altered or its value has become an insignificant portion of the value of another chattel, the doctrine of accession cuts short the right to a specific recovery of the original chattel. Likewise, a defense of of adverse possession (See *infra*, Chapter IX) may cut off the plaintiff's recovery rights.

V. A THIRD LEADING CASE: *GODDARD v. WINCHELL*

An example of the uses of replevin is the case of *Goddard v. Winchell* (1892). Imagine that a meteorite drops to earth, embedding itself in the soil. It contains valuable minerals. The land on which it fell was rented prairie, the grazing rights of which were leased; the lessee allowed H to enter the premises and dig the meteorite up. H sold it to B, against whom the owner of the land brings suit to replevy it.

In an action for replevin, the complaint must allege (1) some immediate right to possession of or title to the chattel; (2) a wrongful taking or detention of the chattel by the defendant; (3) defendant's retention of it at the time of the suit and after the plaintiff demands it back and the defendant refused to return it; and (4) damages. When the complaint is filed or after a preliminary hearing, the chattel is transferred to the plaintiff pending the outcome of the suit or else the defendant must post the bond in the amount of the value of the chattel for which recovery is sought.

B is the present possessor of the chattel. His rights in this litigation will depend on H's right to the meteorite. No possessor's right can rise any higher than those of his transferor and when H dug up the meteorite, the issue becomes whether the labor he expended on another's land gives him any rights superior to the owner of the land on which he is digging.

First consider H's status on the land while he dug up the meteorite. H is not like the trespassing hunter pursuing a wild animal onto the private lands of another. Why? Because the tenant of the owner invited him onto the land. Because H did not trespass, a court is freer to decide that his rights in the meteorite are superior to the landowner, O, unless there is some crucial difference between the meteorite and a wild animal. And there is an obvious difference: the animal is not part of the ground, while the meteorite is found embedded in it.

Next consider the expenditure of effort and labor involved in the digging. Does that avail H? When compared to O's non-existent efforts, it might, but its legal effect still depends on (1) whether a court will treat the meteorite as it would a wild animal, subject to a rule of capture and control, and also (2) whether H's labor was expended at a time before the rights of others arose; in other words, on whether H is the first possessor.

The court held that H was not the first possessor of the meteorite. Replevin lies only for the recovery of personal property; so the appropriateness of the landowner's suit is initially judged by the type of property sought at the time that the lawsuit is brought. The meteorite was clearly personalty when the complaint was filed, so bringing an action of replevin is proper. However, this classification of the meteorite as personalty is for the sole purpose of judging the adequacy of the complaint. On the merits of the case, the issue of whether H is the first possessor turns again on the classification of the property. If it is part of the land in which it is found, it is real property and so possessed by the owner of the realty. If it is not part of the land, no one can claim to have "possessed" it before H dug it up and he becomes its first possessor. The status of the meteorite at the time H dug it up, is therefore important to the case's outcome on the merits. Because the meteorite was embedded three feet into the soil, and because its components were no different from other elements found in the earth in nature, the court in *Goddard* has a basis for concluding (and did conclude) that it was a part of the real property when the defendant first interfered with the landowner's rights.

So the meteorite is realty when in the ground, but this status is not immutable. After it was dug up it was personalty, and so when it was sold to B, it remained personalty. Why is this close attention to the time-warp of the facts important? Because the sale to B will be governed by different rules of law depending upon whether the thing sold is realty or personalty. For example, in a sale of personalty, there may be an implied warranty of title. B might reasonably expect that H owned the object which he offered to sell and by offering an object for sale, H implicitly represented that he had title to what he offered. Such a warranty is absent in sales of real property—*caveat emptor* being the rule there. When B is forced to give the meteorite to O, once the court decides that it is real property, he (B) will certainly want to explore the possibility of suing H. What he (B) knew about H's title (or lack of title) will be important to the outcome of this second suit, but as a preliminary matter, he will surely have to show that, at the time H sold the meteorite to B, it was personalty and so sold with a warranty of title.

Because it was real property before H dug it up, and only upon its severance from the soil did it become personalty recoverable thereafter in replevin, the landowner O became its first possessor. He not only had the right to dig it up and reduce it to possession, but also an ownership right in the thing itself. This is *ratione soli* (discussed in Chapter I) in the rawest and broadest form. These initial rights, conferred by the meteorite's status as real property, is what H interfered with. Answering the definitional question of what type of property it was when H thwarted these rights, permits the court to award possession of the meteorite to O.

How did the court justify this result? By asking questions about the consequences of deciding otherwise. Were the law otherwise, would not the industrious H's of the world be able to mine the sand, stones, and gravel on another's land with impunity. The rubble made by glaciers eons ago broadly speaking arrived on a particular parcel of land by the same forces of nature sending the meteorite to earth. Unless a court could say that the owner of the land is less likely to make good use of the minerals in the meteorite than he would of this glacial debris, the owner becomes the first possessor of it recognized by the law and occupies a special place in the law. If he can show that he had first possession, his title to the meteorite remains intact regardless of the number of persons into whose hands the thing later passes. Absent an intentional transfer of his title, the title of the first possessor also remains intact regardless of the good faith of subsequent possessors.

Thus where objects are found embedded in the soil, their possession is to be awarded to the owner of the soil on the basis that his possession of the soil carries with it possession of whatever is found therein. The landowner's possession is thus said to be constructive. To deny him this meteorite would call into question his right to other components of his land and eventually his title to the land itself. This is a path down which the law should be hesitant to move. There is a heavy burden of persuasion on one asking the courts to move away from upholding the right of the first possessor. This burden is considerable because to have it otherwise also calls into question the titles of those who purchase or improve the property of a first possessor.

However, the *Goddard* court chooses to protect the first possessor without a detailed discussion of the problems of doing so. There is some question as to the good faith of the purchaser raised by the facts of the case, but the opinion makes nothing of this. Why? Because O never intended to transfer the meteorite to either his lessee, H, or to B. Apparently the good faith or bad faith of the subsequent possessor of a piece of property makes little difference to the court. It isn't nearly as important as possession of the meteorite. This is a judgment rooted in an overly-broad conclusion. Society as a whole has a stake in firmly grounding the title to a chattel in the first possessor in order to protect subsequent ones, but it also and equally has a stake in overseeing a smoothly-running economy, which requires that trade be maintained and titles to things remain fungible and negotiable. Perhaps protecting the first possessor's title is at the same time to protect society's interest in later trade and to foster that trade, but whether this is so is a question that would seem to merit some extended discussion by the court. In some instances, the rights of a first possessor underlie, not just a chain of transactions, but institutions vital to society. Landownership seems to be such an institution. Epstein, *Possession as the Root of Title*, 13 Ga. L.Rev. 1221, 1238–43 (1979). First possession, and its second-best alternative, prior possession, protects the institution that has grown up in its wake. The rights of a first possessor has both a transactional and an institutional justification. This has proven an unbeatable combination no matter what cause of action—trespass, conversion, trover, detinue, or replevin—he brings to protect himself against convertors.

The legal path followed by the meteorite in *Goddard* from real property to personal property is not a one-way street: property classified as personal property may again become real property. For example, consider the tailings of a gold or coal mine, once thought not to contain enough minerals to justify further processing, but, with the rise in mineral prices, justifying a reconsideration of this matter. When the holder of the realty is not the holder of the personalty around the mine—as when it is owned by one and operated by another—the title to the tailings may become unclear. *Hayes v. Alaska Juneau Forest Industries, Inc.* (1988). This issue must be settled before further processing is likely to start up.

Finally, more on meteorites. Less complicated than the dispute between private parties over the meteorite in *Goddard,* is the tale of the largest meteorite ever discovered in the United States. The site of the 1902 discovery was Oregon's Willamette Valley, on land relinquished by treaty in 1857 by the Clackamas Indian Tribe. The bell-shaped, mostly iron rock weighs 16 tons. It was found by a miner who, with the aid of his family and a horse, dragged it from the land of the Oregon Iron and Steel Company to his own. There he exhibited it, charging a quarter for admission. His exhibit came to the attention of the Company. It filed a replevin suit against the miner and won. *Oregon Iron Co. v. Hughes* (1905) (using *Goddard* as controlling authority, even though the rock was not embedded and local Indians used it in religious ceremonies). The Company then exhibited the meteorite at a World's Fair, and it was bought by New York City's

Natural History Museum for its collection. Later Oregon school children unsuccessfully asked for the meteorites' return to their state, and the Tribe sued for its recovery, claiming it as an object sacred to their culture. The Museum resisted the claim, arguing that the Tribe had never "owned or controlled" it (a statutory phrase from the federal Native American Repatriation Act) by possessing (in the common law meaning of the term) the discovery site. Stephen Weil, *The New Millennium Cloning and Copyright*, 19 Cardozo Arts & Ent. L. J. 137, 142–144 (2001) (reporting the tribal action).

VI. PROPERTY IN ONE'S BODY: *MOORE v. BOARD OF REGENTS*

Time was, casebooks and courses on property often began with a discussion of cases dealing with rights in a person's dead body[6] or cadaver. Although courts recognize no property rights in a cadaver, a quasi-property right to possession for purposes of burial or cremation is recognized. *Guth v. Freeland* (2001) (negligent mishandling of a dead body not actionable); *Williams v. Williams* (1882) (right of burial actionable); *O'Donnell v. Slack* (1899) (decedent's body not the property of his estate, but testamentary disposition of body permitted). Thus, absent statutory authorization, rights in a cadaver exist only for purposes of burial or cremation. A

6. A near-death body has value, i.e., the transplantation value (to donees) of organs from a comatose, brain-dead body, but is not property.

cadaver was, and is, not subject to replevin, cannot be the subject of common law larceny (special statutes prohibit grave robberies) or a gift *causa mortis*, nor can it be held for security for funeral costs. However, cadavers are an important source of medical knowledge.

Biotechnology merged with medicine today makes the living bodies of a physician's patients an even more vital source of knowledge and litigation. See *Moore v. The Regents of the University of California* (1988). In 1976, John Moore was first diagnosed as having leukemia. A month later, he sought a second opinion, which confirmed the first, from a specialist at the University's medical center. The cancer affected Moore's bone marrow, spleen, liver, and peripheral blood. The cancerous cells in Moore's blood had a rare type of white blood cell that produces a protein regulating the immune system. This protein could sometimes be reproduced in large quantities through recombinant DNA techniques.

The physician attending Moore at the University hospital recommended a splenectomy to slow the cancer's progress. In preparation for this surgery Moore signed a consent form. The form authorized the surgery and provided for the disposal of severed tissue by cremation. The attending physician, however, obtained tissue from Moore's spleen from the pathologist. With it, he and a colleague established a Mo cell line—Mo referring to Moore—capable of reproduction indefinitely and producing proteins with great commercial value.

Some five years after taking Moore's spleen tissue, the physicians filed for a patent on the Mo cell line, along with the method for producing the proteins as well as isolating and cloning their DNA genetic information. The patent was granted in 1984 and was assigned to the University. Agreements for the cells' commercial development were then executed with pharmaceutical firms. The physicians were paid stock rights and over $400,000 for the exclusive rights to the cells and research performed on them. The value of the products that might be developed from the line was estimated at three billion dollars.

Moore returned to the University hospital several times during the years 1976–1983. In April, 1983, he executed another consent form, this one authorizing the use of his blood in research and granting the University all rights he or his heirs may have in any cell line or any other potential product made from it. He was told that the form was standard and necessary for continued treatment. Several months later, he was presented with an identical form, but refused to sign it after inquiring about the commercial value of his blood, which was not disclosed to him. He was told instead that the form was a formality. A month later, his physicians published their findings concerning his cell line in a well-known science journal.

In 1984, he brought suit, alleging 13 causes of action and seeking a share of the profits derived from the use of his cells. The primary cause of action was conversion because it formed the basis of most of the other causes of action, although some others were based on lack of consent and breach of fiduciary duty. No matter what the basis of each action, the defendants (the two physicians, the University, and the pharmaceutical firms) demurred to all of them.

The trial court upheld the demurrers, the intermediate state Court of Appeals reversed, and the California Supreme Court affirmed in part and reversed in part. It overruled the demurrers as to the breach of fiduciary duty and lack of informed consent brought against the physicians. It also held that the complaint states no cause of action for conversion, stating that "the use of excised cells in research does not amount to a conversion."

Conversion is any wrongful act of dominion over another's personal property that is inconsistent with the other's rights therein. It is often thought of as a form of strict liability in tort and requires that the plaintiff (1) have a right to possess personal property, (2) that he loose it, (3) that the defendant find it and (4) convert it to his own use by either refusing to return it or disposing of it to a third party. Moore alleged an interest in the cells after their removal from his body: "He theorizes," the court states, "that he continued to own his cells following their removal from his body, at least for the purpose of directing their use...." The court states that finding such a retained interest required a balancing of two competing interests: (1) a patient's interest in personal autonomy, and (2) the right of a physician to engage in socially useful research free of the duty to search the pedigree of the cells used. Balancing these interests, the court thought that the utility of permitting any alleged conversion was outweighed by the chill on future research. Further, the court reasoned that, if such a retained interest is to be found, it was better that the California legislature do it. No precedent supported the claim of such an interest and the court found that the tort of privacy as well as consent requirements were sufficient to protect Moore.

The court's choice between tort and property protection is a basic one. We will return to it later in this section. Moore's allegation of a conversion raises another basic issue involving the pleadings: when does the conversion occur? There are two possibilities: it occurs either after the cells' removal when the research takes place, or at the very moment of their removal. If the latter is chosen, that is a time when it is difficult to deny that Moore has possession of the cells. Moore's attorney may have mistaken the nature of the conversion and mispled this cause of action as a result.

A second issue of pleading is the nature of the property claimed. Moore alleged, the majority concluded, an interest in the genetic code for chemicals regulating the function of the immune system—a code which does not vary from individual to individual—and thus pleaded too broadly. On this point, the court "refused to hold that excised cells can never be property for any purpose whatsoever." Narrower pleading may well in the future encourage some court to find a property right in human cells.

As to the temporal aspect of Moore's right to possession of the cells, his counsel probably pled as he did because of several statutory restrictions: first, on a person's right to possess tissue removed from one's body and requiring sanitary disposal of such tissue; second, declaring that the procuring of blood is a service, not a sale; and third, regulating gifts of all or part of a body or its organs for specified purposes. "It is the specialized statutes, not the law of conversion, to which courts ordinarily should and do look for guidance on the disposition of human biological materials." Moore's property interest was rejected because these and other statutes drastically limited what may be done with bodily materials.

Moreover, the court found, the patent issued to the physicians and assigned to the University was a determination that the cell line was the product of invention, distinct from the tissue taken from Moore, and not occurring naturally. Thus, the lack of precedent, statutory limitations on the use of bodily materials, the patentability of the cell line, and policy considerations made the court reject Moore's claim of a property interest in the cells sufficient to sustain his action for conversion.

This rejection is unwise. First, just because the plaintiff asks the court for an unprecedented extension of the law to the facts of his case, is *per se* no reason not to oblige him; the common law has long adapted itself to new circumstances. That adaptation is one of its virtues. Second, no statute prohibits Moore's claim. Many of the statutes cited by the court are aimed at promoting research in which Moore is equally interested. In keeping with some of these statutes, Moore argued that he consented to research, but not to the commercial exploitation of his tissue and cells. Deference to statutes is arguably irrelevant to the scope of a common law form of action, unless the statutes are directly on point, expanding or limiting the action in some way. Third, the patentability of a thing is different from a determination of the basis for sharing the profits from it. Finally, biotechnology is an industry, not a guild of researchers in which information and research results are freely shared. Contracts, trade secrets, and patents are jealously guarded; indeed, the cell line's patentability undercuts the policy arguments for rejecting Moore's claim of a property interest in the cells; it instead recognizes a form of property in them.

Moreover, stating that the legislature is competent to act on this subject and enact statutes on it, is also to say that the legislature can act either before or after the courts decide Moore's claim, however they decide. Legislative competence is the same, no matter what the court decided. Deferring to it or anticipating it is really also a judgment, by judges, about their own capabilities, not those of the legislature.

The result in *Moore* is bolstered nonetheless by a fear that the sale of tissue is subject to abuse. Such abuse is historically represented by the 19th century trade in cadavers. A spectre of a poor person forced to sell his body's organs is haunting; market features, such as the highest bidder, the introductions of middlemen and brokers, tinge that spectre with exploitation, rather than economic opportunity. So some abuse is possible, but abuse can be separately regulated, either by the courts or the legislature. See e.g., *Brotherton v. Cleveland* (1991) (holding that the removal of corneas from body of widow's decedent requires pre-deprivation due process). For example, no sale of fetal tissue by a mother, imperiling the fetus, would arguably be countenanced by a contrary result in *Moore*. Any "used body parts" shops that did open for business would quickly come under the strictest regulation. See 42 U.S.C.A. § 274 et seq. (enacted 1984) (Congress' banning the sale of organs in interstate commerce). More than a dozen states ban the sale of fetal tissue and organs. Blood and sperm banks are also regulated, and the ability to contract for surrogate mother services are proscribed as well.

Many of the regulated activities involving bodily material involve healthy individuals, but Moore was far from healthy and was undergoing very expensive treatment. Indeed, his ill-health was the source of the uniqueness of his cells. This raises again the issue of whether Moore's cells fit the definition of personal property. (It also underlines the need for lawyers' and physicians' distinct expertise.) Should the uniqueness of the cells favor the recognition of Moore's conversion action, or more narrowly favor a recognition of the value of his cells as an offset to his medical expenses? If the result in *Moore* were otherwise, Moore might have offered his cells as collateral for a bank loan to pay his expenses. Immunizing the physician's profit from Moore's conversion action may be to ignore the patient's financial needs. Health costs are a national concern. Shouldn't those entering the health care system for treatment be able to pay for that treatment through their bodily contributions to it, rather than spreading those costs around, ultimately to the public at large?

The majority's final point in *Moore* is that adequate alternative remedies exists. These, however, sound in negligence and normally will provide no crisp rule as to when they apply. Physicians will not know when they transgress, but will instead be subject to litigation, with attendant costs and uncertainties. See, e.g., *Cornelio v. Stamford Hospital* (1998) (pap smear slide not subject to replevin). A physician has a duty to disclose to a patient that the former will profit if a patient accepts treatment by purchasing a particular drug, but if a physician's research is on-going at the time the tissue is extracted from the patient's body, who is to say what profit there might be? Moreover, the patient as a negligence plaintiff will often have to show that, had full disclosure been made, consent would not have been given. For a cancer patient like Moore, consent to the surgery will typically be given, and only later would the extent of that consent become an issue; few triers of fact are likely to find that a patient would refuse treatment because the tissue extracted during the course of it might later be used in profitable research. The cost-benefit equation weighed by the patient whose health is at stake declares treatment worth the cost—particularly when "a reasonably prudent person," not an individual patient, is making the decision. Finally, the class of plaintiffs in this type of negligence action is limited to those to whom the physician owes a duty of disclosure—namely, to the formally-declared physician's patients as a group. Other parties need not bother to file!

Finding property rights is to declare settled expectations for which all parties can plan. Negligence actions are meant for situations in which expectations are unsettled. No settled rules there! Moreover, planning to win a negligence action is almost a contradiction in terms. Giving a patient the right to refuse consent, as *Moore* does, does not give him the right to consent on the condition that he share the profits of future research. A veto power is not a right to participate. It is just the reverse. A property interest, on the other hand, provides a right to participate and share in future profits; recognizing such an interest, Moore might have donated his organ, giving a gift conditional on the later sharing of profits.

The judicial choice in *Moore* was between tort and property causes of action. The court regarded that matter as the product of unsettled expectations, so that a tort or negligence claim best suited. When reading Chapter V, however, consider whether the law of bailments isn't adaptable to the problems Moore might have faced if a full disclosure of his physician's interest in his spleen had been made. You might also consider whether the difference in value between Moore's cells and the patented cell line might be subject to the law of accession. See Chapter X, *infra*. And whether Moore might be considered to have abandoned his spleen and its cells.

A. OTHER RELATED DISPUTES

As previously noted and as the court said, *Moore* falls far short of holding that excised human cells cannot be property. For example, frozen embryos held by an in vitro clinic may be subject to the law of bailments. See Chapter V, *infra*. Absent statutes dealing with them, the law of personal property will apply. Unused pre-embryonic material is the joint property of parental donors, but when disputes arise between donors, or husband and wife divorce, it may be destroyed if one spouse insists. *Davis v. Davis* (1992) (concluding preembryos are neither persons nor property). Female pre-embryonic material (ova) may be valuable, but have not been recognized as property. Frozen male sperm may be property for purposes of being counted as an asset of a decedent's estate and bequeathed, but not alienable otherwise. *Cf. Hecht v. Superior Court* (1996).

Likewise, a newborn might have a property interest in umbilical cord blood, valuable because it contains stem cells and can be used to restore the immune system. Likewise, when unused by the newborn at birth, the parents have an interest in donating or storing it, limited perhaps when they cannot agree on its use. Thereafter, any property rights recognized in them are subject to the same balancing of interests done in *Moore*.

VII. THE PLAINTIFF'S ELECTION

No matter which of the previously discussed causes of action—e.g., conversion, trover and conversion, detinue, or replevin—are brought, a plaintiff who proceeds to judgment in one of them is barred from bringing any of the others. The rationale is that a defendant should not be doubly vexed, or brought to trial twice, for a single trespass or conversion. A judgment in any of these actions is a bar to bringing any other against a defendant who at the time the judgment issues, is still in possession of the chattel.

This immunity from further suit gives the defendant, even though now a proven trespasser or converter, a kind of property right in the chattel. He is freed from suit, in much the same way he would be if the statute of limitations or an adverse possession period tolled on the other unused causes of action. Thereafter, creditors of the defendant convertor who retains the chattel can levy on it, and a purchaser from such a defendant, after judgment is given, should take a perfect title to it.

Further, when the defendant, before judgment, sells the chattel to a third party, the plaintiff's right to recover it is undiminished; indeed, the change of possession enlarges the number of the plaintiff's remedies in the sense that his new right to sue the third party purchaser (or third convertor or whomever) does not bar his rights against the defendant. The plaintiff can thus sue the third party using the same or any other available cause of action that he used against the defendant. He cannot, however, have both judgments satisfied on the theory that he should not receive double compensation for the same trespass or conversion.

Finally, when the plaintiff has a cause of action against more than one defendant, all of whom together deprived him of his possession or rights in a chattel, he may sue them jointly or severally. If he proceeds against each separately, he can pursue the others as well in the same or another available cause of action. He can, however, satisfy only one of the judgments received.

CHAPTER III

PRIOR POSSESSION

In this third Chapter we will broaden our treatment of the subject of possession with a discussion of the rights of prior possessors as well as first possessors. The term prior possessor includes any possessor of a chattel whose rights arise earlier than another's in the chain of possession or title to that chattel. The first possessor who was the focus of the last two chapters becomes one example of a prior possessor who holds the initial link in the chain.

Where the chain is a particularly long one, there will be many prior possessors having rights against those subsequent in the chain. To sort out their rights, the law needs a flexible rule because it would not do to decide any first case as if the state of the title were thereby definitively established. What if two other possessors litigated the same question separately? What if the winner was then sued by a possessor prior to him? The law would be a muddle of absolutist statements about who has title.

This sort of confusion is avoided by a more flexible rule regarding the title: not a rule that makes statements awarding absolute title, but a rule saying that, as between the persons now before the court, the judgment holder has the superior right to the chattel. This is the doctrine of the relativity of title.

This doctrine entered Anglo–American law at an early date. In 1722, a chimney sweep found a jewel in a setting. He took it to a goldsmith to have it appraised. The smith's assistant returned the setting, but, saying that the sweep was not the true owner of the jewel, refused to return it. In a case styled *Armory v. Delamirie* (1722), the sweep sued the goldsmith for damages and won.

I.   CHOOSING REPLEVIN OR TROVER

We dealt in the last chapter with the action of replevin. It was originally a common law writ, but is today a statutory action at law. Being an action for the recovery of possession, the defendant must be in possession of the disputed chattel at the time the action is commenced.

If a plaintiff like the chimney sweep does not wish to recover possession, the law offers him another option. He can bring a writ in trover. Trover is an action for the recovery of damages for a wrongful taking of a chattel. The wrongful taking results in an exercise of control over the chattel and, as previously discussed, is referred to as a conversion of it. If the plaintiff wins, he obtains a monetary judgment, not the chattel itself; if the defendant has it, he keeps it.

The possibility of the defendant keeping the chattel is all well and good when he has it. What, however, if he does not possess it? What then does he receive in return for paying the judgment? In the first place, he keeps the sheriff from his door, but with time, the courts came to regard the payment of this judgment as the completion of a sale of the chattel commenced at the time of its conversion. This sale has a fictional element to it. Because the purchaser was first sued and then compelled to pay the judgment against him, the sale must be regarded as a forced one.

Trover is an instance of the rights in or title to the chattel trying to catch up with its possession. What the plaintiff has is his prior right to the chattel. So payment of the judgment transfers the plaintiff's right to it. The plaintiff who pursues a trover action to judgment has in legal effect elected to give up his right to the chattel.

If an action in trover, pursued to a judgment for the plaintiff, is a forced sale, the question arises as to when the sale is effective. There are two possible dates to consider—the date on which the wrongful taking took place (when the sale supposedly commenced) and the date on which the judgment is paid (when it was completed). The former, or date on which the wrongful taking took place, is the one selected by the courts. Why? There are at least two reasons. First, an action in trover is one for damages, and the damage was done upon the taking of the chattel; on that date, the plaintiff/vendor had done everything he could do to effect the sale and the convertor had an unfulfilled obligation to pay for it. This was an obligation that the courts would enforce, so the sale can be regarded as complete, as far as the plaintiff is concerned, on that date. Second, because the defendant/purchaser through this forced sale acquires the vendor's right or title to the chattel and will be entitled to replevy it as against any subsequent possessor of it, he must acquire his rights before plaintiff chose trover over replevin and so limited himself by his own election to that type of recovery. In trover, the plaintiff's damages will be measured by the fair market value of the chattel taken. This value is computed as of the time of the taking.

This choice of dates matters when the chattel's value is not constant. Moreover, the choice of trover or replevin matters in the same way. If the chattel has after its conversion decreased in value, it is more advantageous to the plaintiff to sue in trover rather than in replevin. If, on the other hand, there has been an increase in value, replevin would be the preferred remedy for the plaintiff, provided that the party in current possession of the chattel can be located and brought within the jurisdiction of the court.

Not to put too fine a point on it, but replevin may still yield an equivalent benefit to the plaintiff when there has been a decrease in value caused by the defendant's wrongful taking. In that event, the successful plaintiff is entitled to (1) an additional monetary damage award for the decrease in value caused by the defendant and (2) still another award for the mesne or interim "lost of use" damages which he incurred because of his lost possession.

The possibility of the second award is useful where the decreased value was not caused by the defendant, but by the depreciating value of the chattel itself, in which instance the plaintiff would have sold the chattel and prevented further loss to himself. This second award is then measured by the value to the plaintiff of a lost opportunity to sell just after the wrongful taking.

Finally, where the chattel is still appreciating at the time of the lawsuit, a plaintiff is clearly going to prefer an action in replevin to one in trover. Getting the thing back will then be worth more than getting its value at the time of the conversion.

A. THE CONSEQUENCES OF CHOOSING TROVER

Originally the common law writ of trover lay in cases where the defendant found the goods of the plaintiff, refused to return them, and converted them to his own use. After the allegations of a loss and a finding became matters of fiction and then dropped away entirely, the action of trover was one for remedying any interference with or detention of the chattel of another. The plaintiff has to have a right to possession at the time of the alleged conversion, the chattel claimed must be tangible or specific enough to be identifiable, and the conversion must be wrongful.

As mentioned previously in the context of the doctrine of relativity of title, *Armory v. Delamirie* is the leading case in Anglo–American jurisprudence concerning trover actions. The facts have been simply stated, but they can be distilled still further: a finder gives an object to another for a limited purpose, and the latter refuses to give it back. Giving possession of a chattel to another without giving up whatever right or title one has in it is called a bailment (for more on this subject, see Chapter V, *infra*). A bailment is thus a transfer of possession of a chattel for a limited purpose. In *Armory,* it was for appraising the value of the chattel.

In *Armory,* the finder—the chimney sweep—won. Consider two questions. First, is this a fair result? It seems so until one stops to think that the finder had no title to the jewel, did not earn it, and gets a windfall if allowed to keep it. But, second, should we be thinking of these things in the context of a trover action between a finder and bailee? The true owner of the jewel, wherever he is, is not before the court. In a legal system such as ours, where the due process of law is constitutionally guaranteed, his rights are not affected by the present litigation.

So the answer to the second question is no, the true owner's rights are irrelevant to the trover action before the court. In awarding the finder damages, the *Armory* court was careful to make this point, "(t)hat the finder of a jewel, though he does not by such finding acquire an absolute property or ownership, yet he has such a property as will enable him to keep it against all but the rightful owner, and consequently may maintain trover."

As to the rights of finders, this principle of law is perhaps too broad. The court could have used tort rules to decide the case, because the goldsmith and his assistant had interfered with whatever rights the sweep had, and so committed a conversion of the jewel. It could also have used the contract of bailment (and if there was no actual contract, then an implied one), one term of which is implied by the law to the effect that the chattel be returned in the same condition in which it is tendered. Both of these tort and contract characterizations of the lawsuit would have allowed the court to decide a narrower legal question—because both exclude consideration of the status of the sweep as the finder of the chattel—and thus the case could have been decided with a narrower principle of law.

Ignoring these opportunities, the court used instead the rule that the finder of a chattel has the right to possess it against all but the true owner. By referring to the finder's "property" in the jewel, the court uses a phrase that encompasses the range of interests it means to consider—a range of persons wider than just those involved in the bailment contract or the tort of conversion but, instead, includes the interests of the "true owner" as well.

This means that if and when the true owner of the jewel sues the finder, he will have the right to recover what the finder has already recovered from the bailee. If, as happened in *Armory*, the finder's recovery lay in trover, then the true owner could recover the amount which the finder had already recovered (if the true owner was willing to accept the forced sale and loss of his rights to the chattel itself). When the finder took the jewel for appraisal, he was behaving as if he owned it—a conversion; when he sold it through the forced sale involved in a trover action, he again acted like its owner and so (again) converted the chattel, thus giving the true owner a basis for a suit in trover against him. The finder has transformed his legal status by suing for damages and so rendered himself liable to the true owner in trover.

While it might seem unfair to stigmatize the innocent finder as a convertor, it should also be remembered that at the same time the finder acts as if he owns the chattel he is also starting to run the period of time necessary to acquire title by adverse possession.

If the finder's lawsuit against the bailee had been in replevin, and the finder was successful and able to recover the chattel, then the true owner would have the option of bringing either replevin or trover against the finder. If the owner seeks replevin, then his complaint must be somewhat longer than it would be in trover. In addition to the finder's conversion of the chattel must then be added the allegation that his retention of the chattel at the time of the suit was wrongful as against the true owner.

The forced sale resulting from the trover action in *Armory,* gives the bailee the finder's right in it. Lawyers speak of this substitution of one person for another as a subrogation. The person who is substituted receives or "is subrogated to" the rights of the person who is replaced; they say, "the bailee is subrogated to the finder's right." This right, however, does not amount to unqualified or absolute title to the chattel; it is only as good an interest as the finder himself had to transfer. That right was subject to the rights of the true owner, should he appear. When he does, and chooses to sue the smith in trover, he alleges that the bailee has now converted his chattel by wrongfully withholding it.

If the true owner is allowed to prevail in this last-mentioned suit, the bailee will be forced to pay twice for the chattel. Double liability seems a harsh result, but on the other hand, the bailee who holds himself out as an appraiser, but does not supervise his assistant, is not a natural object of our sympathy.

Actually, the smith is first paying to acquire the finder's right in the chattel and when later sued in trover by the true owner, he will acquire the latter's interest as well. Strictly speaking, the two plaintiffs in these suits have different interests and are recovering for separate conversions, both arising out of the same incident involving the jewel. It is a case of one incident provoking two injuries.

There is no case law precisely on point, but the possibility of his paying twice exists because the rights which the bailee acquired from the finder will not protect him from a suit by the true owner. *Armory's* rule on finder's rights allows it to gloss over this double liability problem: better to emphasize the status of this plaintiff as a finder than to sort out the goldsmith's duties as a bailee and to try to resolve all possible law suits which might spring from this situation in advance of their actually being brought to court.

II. THE REACH OF THE *ARMORY* RULE

The reach of the *Armory* rule has proved its usefulness in many situations. In this regard, consider a situation in which there are multiple finders of a chattel. For example, O, a gardener, is hauling home a bag of mulch in his pick-up. The mulch falls off his truck and A finds it. A is hauling it home when it again falls into the street and B finds it there. B hauls it off, loses it again, and C finds it.

What are the rights of each party in trover? Under the *Armory* rule, both A and B are protected as finders against B and C respectively. Why? Because each is a "finder" as to a person subsequent in the chain of possession of the chattel.

What is presented then by the *Armory* rule are a series of relative rights, arising in turn in possessors immediately prior in the chain of possession. *Armory*'s is a rule of relative prior possession. (As we shall soon see, that same sort of relativism applies when defining the "rightful owner" or as referred to here, the true owner.) When the *Armory* court refers to finders and words its rule in terms of finders' rights, one might just as well, and logically read "prior possessor" for finder.

One further reason for reading the rule this way lies in the *Armory* rule's potential for holding the bailee liable twice, once to the finder and again to the true owner should he turn up. The rule's reference to finders is perhaps one way the court has of saying that it is unlikely that the true owner would ever trace the chain of possession through the finder to the bailee. The reference makes clear that double liability for the bailee was only a remote problem in *Armory;* when it is not so remote, then, presumably the rule of the case can be reformulated or the question of the defendant's possible double liability squarely faced.

III.　JUSTIFICATIONS FOR PROTECTING THE PRIOR POSSESSOR

With the substitution of "prior possessor" for "finder," the rule of the *Armory* case becomes that the prior possessor of a chattel has a right to it as good or superior to all but the rightful or true owner. The first advantage of such a rule is that it acts to discourage or prevent an endless series of conversions of the chattel once it comes into the hands of one who cannot prove title to it.

This first advantage, however, is not helpful in judging the issue of the *Armory* case (whether or not the bailee may be compelled to pay damages to the prior possessor for not returning the chattel). On this issue, however, the rule has a second advantage. It aids the enforcement of bailment contracts, particularly the promise of the bailee to return the chattel, and so encourages a business practice useful to the development of trade and commerce.

A third, related advantage is similarly utilitarian. There may also be, in the broadly-stated version of the *Armory* rule, a preference for keeping chattels in circulation. The finder was in the process of removing the chattel from the netherworld of lost objects and restoring it to a position in which it can once more be used and useful.

A fourth, and perhaps the most general, advantage of protecting the prior possessor is that, in so doing, ownership and title will be protected as well. The prior possessor will be in the best position, often, to locate or be located by the true owner— protecting the one protects the other.

IV. THE MEASURE OF DAMAGES

The *Armory* court awarded the full value of the chattel to the finder. Is this justified? When it is remembered that the finder did not prove full title to it, the award of full-value damages seems too much. Some reduction in the award might have been made in recognition of the fact that the finder does not have full title and that the true owner might someday show up and make the subsequent possessor or bailee pay twice. The latter parties' risk of double liability can be hedged somewhat by discounting the value of the chattel to the finder. On the other hand, if there is no liability to the true owner, then the full measure of damages—the total fair market value of the bailed chattel—might more equitably be given to the finder or prior possessor. *The Winkfield* (1901). There is no inherent problem of the bailee's paying twice for his conversion; both judgments will still hopefully deter wrongdoing. For example, the postal service can recover for a conversion of the mails, even though it has by statute no liability to persons who post letters. There is a strong policy to deter wrongdoing where the mail is concerned. Where deterring the conversion is the law's overriding goal, a bailee can recover the full value of the chattel even though the bailee has no liability even to his bailor. A bailment in which the public has an interest gets special protection.

V. THE *ARMORY* RULE IN REPLEVIN ACTIONS

1. Who Is the "True Owner"?

What if the prior possessor has found the party with possession of the chattel that he claims? A suit in replevin is likely to follow if the chattel has increased in value or when the prior possessor, for whatever reason, wants it back.

The *Armory* case was a trover action in which the plaintiff merely had to show his prior possession of the chattel to receive damages. If his suit had been in replevin, would he have had to make more than a showing of prior possession? In replevin, after all, he is asking to get possession of the chattel itself. To obtain possession, would he have to show title to the chattel?

To answer this question, one must resolve an ambiguity in the *Armory* rule to the effect that the prior possessor has a right to retain a chattel against all "but the rightful owner." What does the last, quoted phrase mean?

When the cause of action is in replevin, at least three meanings, two substantive and one procedural, are possible. (The two substantive ones are discussed in this section, the procedural one in the next.) First, that when two possessors or convertors of a chattel are litigating their rights, the prior possessor among them, although he recovers in the present litigation, would have to yield the recovered possession only to the person who can show title to the chattel. Such a result makes the phrase "true owner" the equivalent of any person who proves title to the chattel. Given the doctrine of relativity of right worked out for the phrase "prior possessor," however, it is inconsistent to make one part of the *Armory* rule a relative matter of prior right, referring to and protecting every prior possessor, and then give the phrase "true owner" an absolutist cast by saying that it refers to the one person who has a deed or bill of sale for the chattel.

Instead, it is wiser to keep these two parts of the *Armory* rule consistent, by assigning a second meaning to the phrase "true owner." That is, it means any person who has a right of possession arising prior in time to the two possessors or converters litigating their own rights; anyone in the chain of possession prior to them is a true owner as to them.

Not only is the second meaning in keeping with the doctrine of relativity of title or right, it also avoids a further difficulty, for, although there is some authority for the first meaning, its acceptance would mean that any later litigation in replevin—and even any second litigation between possessors of a chattel—might require a showing of good title, as opposed to a right of possession. This heightened standard of proof would not only be inconsistent with the relativity in the *Armory* rule, it would also make righting the converter's wrong that much harder. For that reason, the authority to support it is slight. Any possessor, whether a finder, bailee, or even a tort feasor, has a better right to the possession of a chattel than a person who converts or seizes it from him. If the law is to discourage an endless series of such seizures, it must respect the right of the prior possessor and validate those rights even when the latter cannot show good title. *Anderson v. Gouldberg* (1892).

These two different meanings can however be fused into one rule, using the mechanisms of modern pleading and a legal presumption. It is generally presumed that the prior possessor prevails over subsequent possessors because he holds the title of a true owner, but in a replevin action in which the defendant, although he is a person further along on the chain of possession than the plaintiff, can produce proof that he stands in the shoes of the true owner, or can interplead the true owner, the plaintiff's claim in replevin is defeated. Compare

Anderson v. Gouldberg (1892) with *Russell v. Hill* (1900), to which this discussion will soon turn.

2.   The Defense of Jus Tertii

The *Armory* court could thirdly have had a more procedural meaning in mind for the phrase "all but the rightful owner." It could have meant that its rule applies "except when the title to the chattel is at issue." This third meaning admits of the possibility that, if the state of the title is injected into litigation between possessors, such evidence is admissible.

What if the defendant can easily identify the true owner, and in fact produces a deed showing that the title to the chattel is in this true owner, who is nonetheless not before the court? In this instance, where the deed shows that the title is in another, but does not convey the chattel to the defendant, the deed should be inadmissible because it is irrelevant to the relative merits of the claims of two (or however many are litigating) possessors. To permit the latter type of deed to influence the outcome of a replevin action would be to allow a party to litigation to plead the weaknesses in his opposing party's claim, instead of doing what he is presumably best able to do: plead the strengths and merits of his own claim. Such an influence would be the legal equivalent of smoke and mirrors.

This inadmissible claim is known as a defense of *jus tertii,* a Latin phrase for "the right of a third party." It is the claim that neither party to the litigation, but rather an absent third party, is the true owner. However, the defense can only be considered when the true owner has a right to bring the same lawsuit which the plaintiff filed. Ruling the evidence of third party rights inadmissible is based on a rule of judicial prudence not to determine the rights of parties not before the court. Moreover, in our legal system, this prudence is constitutionally grounded in the due process clauses of Federal and state constitutions.

Rejecting this third meaning saves the proof of title for litigation in which the person with title is actually before the court. Moreover, questions of title to personal property typically present difficulties of proof. No title records are routinely maintained (automobile titles excepted) and proof depends on bills of sale, canceled checks, and the testimony of witnesses. Thus plaintiffs should be relieved, it is argued, of the burden of proving title in personal property cases.

Another historical reason for denying a defense of *jus tertii* has to do with theories of trover and conversion. The necessary allegations included one to the effect that the plaintiff, possessing a chattel, lost it. A person cannot lose a thing without first being in possession of it and so trover and conversion came to be called possessory actions—a remedy for an interference with possession, rather than title. *Wallander v. Barnes* (1996).

As previously noted, it is often said when rejecting a *jus tertii* defense, that possession is presumptive of title. What is meant is that prior possession is presumptive of title, and this in turn, typically means that the prior possessor is in the best position to settle or litigate title issues with the true owner should he appear. The prior possessor is also better positioned than a later possessor to know of the initial conversion that took the chattel away from the true owner.

Whatever the justification—and whether it is intended to protect the true owner, protect the courts from difficult choices, or simply to protect prior possession and keep the peace—a majority of American jurisdictions consistently reject the *jus tertii* defense: thus the defendant in replevin, trover, or conversion may not introduce evidence of a third party's title to converted chattels, unless that defendant is claiming rights derived from that third party. The weight of precedent for this rejection is overwhelming.

A famous 1856 English case has provided an illustration. *Jefferies v. Great Western Railway* (1856). It involves an action of trover "for trucks." Trucks are the frames with two pairs of wheels used to support one end of a railroad car. The plaintiff purchased the trucks from a bankrupt who, while still in possession of them, made a second assignment of his right to them to the defendant. The latter took them out of the plaintiff's possession and when sued attempted to argue that the creditors of the bankrupt were the true owners. The court rejected the defense: the defense of *jus tertii* is impermissible unless the defendant had evidence showing that his right derived from the creditors. *New Eng-*

land Box Company v. C & R Construction Co. *(1943) more recently illustrated the same ruling.*

A consistent rejection of the defense of *jus tertii* permits the standard for measuring the sufficiency of the complaint in both trover and replevin actions to remain constant. It also makes a virtue out of the problem in the two cases discussed in the next section.

3.   Two Leading Cases

When the *Armory* rule is stated more broadly, it is sometimes said that "possession gives rise to a presumption of title." North Carolina had such a proposition in its case law, derived from the case of *Barwick v. Barwick* (1850) (a trover action for chattel the plaintiff had purchased from a remainderman while the life tenant was still alive; the defendants claimed the same chattel under a later purchase from the remainderman; held, a jury instruction that prior possession in the plaintiff was sufficient to maintain the action was erroneous).

Having this broader statement of *Armory* in the case law, the later North Carolina case of *Russell v. Hill* (1900) concluded that, when the title to the chattel in dispute was shown to be in another, the plaintiff's action in trover could not be maintained. *Russell* concerned timber cut on land which had been sold twice, that is, granted to two adverse parties by the state land office. The parties' land grants, as shown on their respective deeds, overlapped. The plaintiff was a logger who had the misfortune to be logging with the permission of the second grantee. The first grantee was not a party to this litigation that the logger brought after the defendants not only took possession of the logs, but also sold them to a lumber company insolvent at the time of the litigation. The defendants were thus converters of the logs and lacked any title or right, from the first grantee or anyone else, to do what they did.

In *Russell,* the second grantee with whose permission the plaintiff logged the land, was not in possession of the land. (And no question of constructive possession was argued so far as the court opinion reflects—such an argument would have been a weak one in any event because the second grantee lacked priority of title under the state's recording act.)

At trial, "the defendant showed no title in himself, but proved the plaintiff's lack of title." There is no discussion of the *jus tertii defense* in this case, so that one can only assume it was not raised. Instead, the court defines the action in trover in terms of an analogy to the action of ejectment for real property. Both, it said, require title. Why? Because trover is a forced sale and the plaintiff has to have the title to sell when the judgment is paid.

There is much wrong with this analysis. First, the rule that "possession is presumptive of title" is not so much a rule as a rationale for a rule of prior possession that makes proof of who holds title irrelevant. Second, if trover is indeed a forced sale, it is the legal fiction and a slim reed on which to base a decision. Third, the analogy between ejectment and trover is questionable. Real property titles are more carefully researched, guarded, and are matters of public record than titles to many types of personalty. It is more reasonable to expect litigants to be conversant with the state of title to real property with which they are concerned than they would be with personalty.

But the final and dispositive argument for the *Russell* court is the possibility of double liability for the convertor who pays a trover judgment, receives the plaintiff's rights in the timber, but is still forced to pay the timber's value a second time to the true owner who later sues. Protection against double liability is the most used rationale for accepting a *jus tertii* defense.

A close reading of the *Armory* opinion provides another justification for this acceptance. There, the defendant produced no evidence identifying the true owner, so that accepting the defense is not prohibited by the opinion.

Under the facts of *Russell v. Hill,* the result there may be justified because the true owner is known. He was an attorney well known in the locale and the holder (as a trustee) of the legal title to adjoining land. Moreover, his intervention in earlier litigation between the parties in *Russell* makes the concern of the *Russell* court, and by extension the *Armory* court, a real one. See John Orth, *Russell v. Hill (N.C. 1899): Misunderstood Lessons*, 73 N.C. L. Rev. 2031, 2037 (1995).

Yet even if the court had a good reason for holding as it did, it did too much. Its holding (that trover requires proof of title) is overbroad. It need not have redefined the cause of action brought to accommodate its law to the problem of the defendant's possible double liability. All it need have done was to hold that where the true owner is reasonably certain to learn of the defendant's conversion (in this instance, through proximity or court records), the defense of *jus tertii* is permissible and proof of the state of the title admissible. This is a more functional rule; perhaps it is even more efficient, in terms of judicial resources. When combined with a procedural rule permitting interpleader of the true owner by the defendant, it will more completely adjudicate issues concerning the disputed chattel. If the defendant can have interpleader and fails to utilize it against a known true owner, a court might reasonably conclude that he has assumed the risk of double liability.

A final rationale for accepting a *jus tertii* defense may be found in a situation in which the police raided and searched a plaintiff's residence, finding stolen personal property in the process. When the police refuse to return it to its prior possessor, should they be permitted to prove that they know the true owner before retaining possession or being forced to respond to the plaintiff in damages for trover and conversion? (The latter action is unlikely to succeed when the police act under a proper search warrant and are otherwise immune, as agents of the state, from such judgments; so a replevin action is more likely.) One Indiana inter-mediate appellate court thought that the answer was yes and accepted a *jus tertii* defense from the police. *Noble v. Moistner* (1979). Perhaps, when possible under applicable procedure rules, a compul-sory joinder of the third party the police allege to be the true owner should also be ordered at the time a court accepts the defense. Note, *Jus Tertii As A Defense to Conversion Suits in Indiana—Towards A More Rational Approach*, 18 Val.U.L.Rev. 415 (1984).

In a replevin action in which logs were again at issue, but in which the land from which the logs came was unknown or in dispute, another court applied the *Armory* rule. *Anderson v. Gouldberg* (1892). This was litigation between two converters of ninety-three logs of branded timber. The plain-tiffs cut the timber. They never showed that they did so with permission. The defendants took posses-sion of the logs at a mill site in the name of (they claimed) their true owners. The court instructed the jury that even if the plaintiffs were trespassers when cutting the logs, they were entitled to recover them from later possessors, the true owner or one acting for him excepted. The court left it to the jury whether the logs were cut and claimed as defen-dants said. The jury found for the plaintiffs. The trial court denied a defense motion for a new trial.

The defendants appealed, but the Minnesota Su-preme Court affirmed. It held that the plaintiff's bare possession, "though wrongfully obtained," was sufficient to maintain replevin against a mere stranger who takes it from him.

The Minnesota court's version of the *Armory* rule slightly rewords the original. The *Armory* court never said anything about "wrongfully" obtaining the chattel. And its rule was used in a trover action, not (as here) replevin. But the second objection is a minor matter because if the Minnesota court is willing to grant judgment in replevin on proof of bare possession and one of its sister states is *not* willing to grant trover on similar proof, then something is wrong: it takes less to get the thing back than it does to sell it. This is a strange and inconsistent result.

One explanation is that in *Anderson* the true owner seemed remote and unlikely to sue while in *Russell* he was known and likely to find out about who damaged his land. The jury in *Anderson* found that the logs were not cut on the land the defendants claimed, but that jury never did say where the logs were cut. Their ultimate ownership remained undetermined.

Perhaps one can see the benefits of deciding as the *Anderson* court did if one assumes the worst. Let's do that. It is often said that the rule in *Armory* protects a chattel's "prior peaceful possession." What does peaceful mean? Would this reformulation deny the benefit of the *Armory* rule to a thief or other willful convertor of a chattel? Probably not. One must ask, "peaceful" as to whom? If the litigation is concerned with a dispute between two possessors, the first's possession is peaceful in relation to the second's conversion of the disputed chattel. There the "peaceful" repose of the chattel is relative and the word is superfluous in any re-statement of the rule of prior possession or the doctrine of the relativity of title.

But why should not even a thief have the benefit of the *Armory* rule if he can show himself as a prior possessor? On the equities, it is easier for a court to formulate a "prior possessor wins" rule for a prior possessor who is a finder—as in *Armory*—than it is to reach the same result when he is just as much a convertor of the chattel as is the defendant—as in *Anderson*. If O's chattel is converted by A, who is then subjected to its seizure by B, the two conver-sions present just the sort of successive seizures or uses of force that the *Armory* rule—read as protect-ing prior possessors and not just finders—was in-tended to prevent. *Anderson*'s reformulation of the rule makes this plain. In the hypothetical, A should have judgment against B. Better to deter the last conversion than to encourage both of the conver-sions involved.

What if in the last hypothetical, O leased the chattel to A for a year and six months later B takes (steals) it from A's possession? A's lease has sixth months to run, but under *Armory*, A could recover a judgment in trover and conversion for the full value of the chattel, or replevy it from B. A's judgment is really two things: it is (1) compensation for the six months loss of use, and (2) the excess (the judg-ment, less the amount of the "loss of use" compensation), representing the fair market value of the chattel. A holds the second component of the judgment for the benefit of O, but can keep the first, even when O shows up. Should O be barred from suing B in trover if O knows of A's having the money from his judgment? *Anderson* suggests the answer is no, *Russell* suggests it is yes.

If both A and B in the prior hypothetical are thieves, A's suit against B would end the same way, but is perhaps harder to justify. A jury or trier of fact might consider the first component of A's judgment small in comparison to the second if and when O shows up and sues for it, and it is doubtful that O would be barred from suing B the second thief. O is not likely to benefit from one or another of the two of them having possession (if the suit is in replevin). Nor is O likely to be injured by a sale of A's rights in the prior forced sale—in trover, fenced or "as is" goods seldom bring full market value, so the possible double liability is less injurious, and if B is a willful convertor or a thief, who cares whether a thief pays twice anyway? Moreover, if both A and B's conversions are criminal in nature, their thievery is the concern of the criminal law and so long as a rule of the civil law does not encourage crime, it should be enforced.

So even if a bad guy wants replevin, he should obtain it upon a showing of prior possession. *Russell* is aberrational, and is in fact a minority rule. *Anderson* seems the best use of the *Armory* rule and best result: a plaintiff can maintain both trover and replevin with a showing of prior possession peacefully maintained as against his defendant.

Anderson, however, has its limiting facts. It was a case between two converters—that is, between two persons equally in the wrong. That has turned out to be a rare situation in the annals of reported cases. R.H. Helmholz, Wrongful Possession of Chattels: Hornbook Law and Case Law, 80 Nw.U.L.Rev. 1221, 1225–1226 (1986) (discussing the cases and arguing that the true rule is: "What a man has acquired illegally he cannot replevy.").

A final, more general question arises as to whether the law should endorse a rule that appears amoral. A pawn broker should have a sufficient property interest to bring a replevin action and in it might use the *Anderson* rule to recover chattels, even though they have been reported stolen. *Wolfenbarger v. Williams* (1987). A gambler, however, probably cannot replevy illegal winnings seized by the police. *Helmholz,* op. cit., at 1125 (by the same token, nor could a thief replevy the property he stole, argues Helmholz). Likewise, the winner and the loser in an illegal gaming operation could not use the *Anderson* rule to settle their dispute over the winnings. They might indeed each have a property interest in the winnings, but only for the purpose of showing their participation in the illegal game and then their interest would become the basis of their conviction for violation of an anti-gambling statute, not a ground for the recovery of the property.

VI. THE PROBLEM OF SUCCESSIVE FINDERS

The earliest, leading American case reciting and applying the rule of *Armory* occurred in litigation between two finders of property. *Clark v. Maloney* (1840). There, the plaintiff found ten white pine logs floating in the Delaware Bay. This was like finding the logs on a public highway—no trespass would be involved in taking possession of the logs by the plaintiffs. Plaintiff made this find after a freshet—a sudden rise in the level of the Bay due to a flood, the melting of snow or ice, or heavy rains, often in the eighteenth and nineteenth centuries made worse by the deforestation of the land in the watershed. The plaintiff moored the logs with ropes at the mouth of Mispillion creek. The defendants later found the same logs adrift floating up that same creek.

With no explanation as to how the defendants came to take possession of the logs, the plaintiff sued the defendants in trover, premised on the defendants' conversion of the logs, rather than trespass, which would require that the plaintiff allege facts showing how the defendant came to take possession. So the plaintiff's choice of trover and conversion over trespass as his cause of action for the present facts seems right.

If the case is viewed in this light, and it is remembered that two finders are litigating their relative rights here, *Clark* is a better case for the application of the rule of prior possession than was *Armory*. The latter case, after all, involved a finder/bailor and his bailee and so the court could have fallen back on a contract of bailment as dispositive of the case before it. Here, where two finders are litigating and no proven facts link their possession of the disputed chattel, the rule of prior possession is necessary to dispose of the case. As between successive finders, the rule here is that the first prevails where the first has not abandoned the chattel in dispute. If there were an abandonment by the first finder or his transferee, the second finder would prevail.

The plaintiff, as the prior possessor of the logs, won the case. Why? Because "possession is *prima facie* evidence of property." The court means that possession creates a presumption that the possessor has the title to the chattel possessed. This presumption is a mandatory one when the only evidence introduced at trial establishes prior possession, but it is also a rebuttable one, and "may be rebutted by evidence of better title, but in the absence of better title it is as effective a support of title as the most conclusive evidence could be." Why so? Because of the *Armory* rule, which the court goes on to recite. In other words, this court's statement of the doctrine of relativity of title is phrased in terms of a legal presumption that in the context of this litigation, cannot really be rebutted and is justified by a substantive statement of the same doctrine. All this rephrasing amounts to a non-sequitur, not a justification. Or, to put this analytical process in its best light, it shows the close relationship between legal rules and legal presumptions. (This closeness we will discuss *infra*, Chapter V, on commercial bailments.) Unlike the *Russell* court, this court does not require proof of title to the disputed chattel in order to file a cause of action in trover. Its talk of "better title" can, as before, be recast into "relatively better title" terms and the doctrine of relativity of title.

Why does the court talk of a "property" in the logs? First of all, this word reflects the *Armory* rule, but the *Clark* court needs a word which encompasses both its talk of a "better title" and a "presumption of title" as well as a right of prior possession in the logs. This ambiguity may once more be evidence of a concern that the last finder may have a double liability: once as the defendant in this litigation and again when and if the true owner or possessor with rights prior to the plaintiff's finds out about his conversion and sues him for it. The word "property" avoids a clear reference to title, but may mean more than a right of possession. When it is remembered that this court restates the *Armory* rule in terms of a legal presumption of title, one reason for this rephrasing becomes clear. If a judgment in trover is a forced sale of the plaintiff's presumed title to the logs, and if it turns out that the plaintiff does not have title and the true owner shows up to sue the defendant again, he can use the plaintiff's warranty of title made or implied in the course of the forced sale as a basis for a suit against the first finder.

Maybe this double liability problem for the defendant did not in fact worry the court. There may be

some customary legal arrangements involving the
local logging industry at the time of the case that
would solve this problem. If the true owner of the
logs followed an industry practice of himself floating
the logs to the sawmill, then the problem remains.
But if the practice was otherwise and the true
owner had given possession of the logs to a river-
driving company, or they floated away from the
sawmill's holding pond, a quite different situation
arises. In each of the latter instances, the owner has
created a bailment with the river-driver or the mill
operator and can hold that party responsible for the
loss of the logs. Each of these bailees will be responsible for the conversion involved in his failing to
deliver the logs back to the bailor and because
bailor and bailee are by definition known to each
other, the true owner will in all probability be
compensated for his loss by a suit against his bailee
and be barred from any further recovery from the
defendant.

Defendants' counsel was evidently working on a
parallel argument and thinking in general terms
about the finder (any finder) as a bailee for the true
owner. He argued that, in the case of a "special
property, it must be accompanied by possession to
support trover." What was the plaintiff's "special
property"? That term was often used in the 19th
century and is still used today to denote the interest
of a bailee in the chattel entrusted to him by the
bailor, as opposed to the "general" property of the
bailor. So special property was a reference to a
bailee's limited rights in a chattel, while general

property is the bailor's title as well as his right to future possession.

If the first finder is the equivalent of a non-consensual bailee of the true owner, however, his trover suit against a second finder emphasizes his "special property" and the forced sale resulting from it is a conversion of the true owner's general property in the chattel, on the basis of which conversion the true owner can later sue. Moreover, if the first finder were viewed as a bailee, he cannot transfer any more than his "special property" to the second finder as the result of a trover suit. No such transfer of rights in trover will render the second finder immune later from the true owner's suit. The reference to a "special property" is thus a way of safeguarding the true owner's "general property" and his continuing right to sue both finders.

The second finder might also argue that he is as good a bailee as the first finder and as capable as the latter of holding the chattel for the true owner. The rule of prior possession will, however, lead a court to reject this argument since the first finder evidently crossed the track of the true owner at the location of the loss. This intersection might mean that the true owner was more likely to locate the first finder than he would any successor. But this "intersection" theory does not work very well here, where the logs are floating in a large tidal body of water. At this point the second finder might want to interject a factual note into his argument to the effect that few true owners, in fact, ever repossess their lost or misplaced chattel, and that letting the chattel stay with the last finder gives the true owner, if and when he ever does show up, a clear option of suing the last finder in either trover or replevin. This choice will be denied him if the plaintiff wins, unless the double liability of the last finder is still possible. With this, the defendant may have argued too much, having in the course of his argument justified his possible double liability as a means to protect the true owner.

After all, this double liability of the second finder is a method of protecting the true owner's title. The *Clark* opinion acknowledges as much: " ... it is a well-settled rule of law that the loss of a chattel does not change the right of property; and for the same reason that the original loss of these logs by the rightful owner, did not change his absolute property in them, but he might have maintained trover against the plaintiff upon refusal to deliver them, so the subsequent loss did not divest the special property of the plaintiff." This recognition that the true owner's title is not defeated by subsequent possessors—even sometimes when they possess in good faith—again leaves open the possibility that the defendant may be liable to the owner again, and be forced to give up the logs in a replevin action or pay for them twice if the owner brings trover.

In the end the court probably means to leave this question of double liability open, as it was not before the court and then as now no reported cases resolved the problem for finders. It also leaves open the status of a finder as a bailee, and one should not necessarily assume that the law limits bailment to consensual arrangements—as we will discuss in the next two chapters. In the context of the *Clark* case, assuming that a bailment arises is one way of protecting the true owner's rights because a bailment relationship between the owner and a finder would impose a duty of reasonable care of the found object on the finder. If (say) a boat, rather than logs were adrift in the Delaware Bay, the boat owner might well be presumed to be willing to pay for a finder's reasonable expenses in preserving the boat and the finder could presumably be given a duty to take reasonable steps to preserve the boat for its owner. So too with the logs.

One reason for keeping the possibility of double liability open for a future court is that different types of defendants might be accorded different treatment. In the case of finders, the finder who earnestly searches for the true owner might escape double liability, while the more secretive finder who conducts no search would not.

The defendants in *Clark* might still argue that one of the policies underlying a rule of prior possession is inapplicable as between two finders. That is, finders are seldom visible as such, particularly to other "finders" and would-be converters, except at the time and place of the find. Because finders do not stand out in a crowd, justifying a rule of prior possession as a way of avoiding an endless series of forceful conversions makes little sense. Indeed, the development of the forms of action from trespass to conversion underlines this point. In cases in which a crowd does not gather around the finder and threaten him or the public peace—and specifically in *Clark* where the logs are floating around the Bay and up an adjacent creek and are picked up at isolated locations—this justification for a rule of prior possession seems inapplicable. Applying the rule here will not prevent an endless series of muggings, and some less extreme justification must be sought. This search in *Clark* produced the idea that protecting the prior possessor protects a true owner's title and right.

1. The Measure of Damages in *Clark*

The measure of damages for a conversion is the value of the chattel converted, measured not only at the time and the place of the conversion, but also at the nearest market in which the chattel has a value. One question which the court might have asked itself is whether it would be reasonable for the true owner, in the process of floating logs to the sawmill, to sue the last known convertor of the logs. The measure of damages for trover will be the value of the logs at the nearest convenient market, less any cost of transportation to that market. The logs are, in other words, more valuable at the sawmill site or other marketplace, so that the amount of a judgment for which the convertor is liable to the true owner, decreases the further the place of a find, or the place the conversion takes place, is from the sawmill. This would mean that in the usual case the true owner would have a stronger incentive to sue either the log-driving company or the mill operator, the two bailees named previously, than he would to sue either of the two finders. This is economically rational because the bailees have a duty to deliver the logs from the bailment at the sawmill, a site at which the logs have a value higher than they do at a point of conversion more removed from the mill.

A second measure of damages issue is raised when one considers that the chattels involved are only identified as "ten white pine logs"—not an unusual type of wood and probably not so unique as to identify them as the property of any particular logger. If identification of the owner was possible from the type of log or from any distinctive marking on them, as in *Anderson,* the defendants' conversion of them would seem less innocent. Pointing to the lack of evidence of a fraudulent conversion of the logs and the fact that innocent defendants often are permitted a reduced measure of damages in some areas of law, the defendants might argue for a reduced measure of damages, using the value of the logs as standing timber. This argument would be rejected. Why? Because standing timber is part of the real property on which it is located and there can be no conversion of real property because by definition this cause of action applies only to personalty. Moreover, both finders treated the logs as personalty. So the measure of damages for a conversion would have to reflect the value of labor that converted this portion of the real property into personalty. Their value as personalty, then, provides the measure of damages for the defendant's conversion. This value is measured by the value of the logs at the nearest convenient market for such logs, less the cost of transporting the logs to that market from the site of the defendant's conversion of them. This is not the site at which the plaintiffs moored the logs, but the place at which the defendants took possession of them. It was at that point that they committed their conversion against the plaintiff.

2. Salvage Rights

If the creek up which the logs floated into the defendants' possession were navigable, then the defendants may assert a right of salvage. The salvor's status has been awarded to persons clearing logs out of a navigable waterway or harbor; it can here be used to reduce the damages payable by the defendants to the plaintiff by way of a set-off against the amount of the plaintiff's judgment. The rights of salvors are discussed infra, Chapter IV.

VII. CONCLUSION

In *Armory, Russell, Anderson,* and *Clark,* the holdings seem formulated in recognition of the fact that the true owner is not deprived of his right or title no matter how many converters subsequently possess the chattel. All these courts have gone to subtle lengths to anticipate the problem of double liability. One method of solving the problem and still maintaining the rule of prior possession is to recognize the trespass or tort aspect of the action in trover and measure the damages which the plaintiff incurred rather than permitting him to sue for the value of the chattel. The greater the likelihood that the true owner would turn up in a litigious mood, the deeper the discount when otherwise the plaintiff in trover would obtain a judgment for the full market value of the converted chattel.

All of these cases have been analyzed in this Chapter in such a way as to protect the true owner's rights because she is the ultimate beneficiary of a rule of prior possession and the doctrine of relativity of title. There is, moreover, another reason to force your mind not just to dwell on the chattel involved in each case, but to ponder instead the range of persons who might have rights in it. Not to explore the diverse individual interests involved is to deny the law its full scope. Property law first and foremost serves people, not things.

CHAPTER IV

FINDERS

I. WHO IS A FINDER?

The popular maxim, "finders keepers, losers weepers," overstates what we learned in the last Chapter. The nineteenth century version—"losers seekers, finders keepers"—perhaps comes closer to the legal truth of the matter, and a much, much older Latin version of the maxim states, *habens ut nanctus*—translated as, he keeps that finds—is even more matter-of-fact.

As we saw in our discussion of *Clark* in the last chapter, a person finding a chattel acquires a qualified right of its possession. As an early English opinion states: "he which findes goods, is bound to answer him for them who hath the property." *Isaack v. Clark* (1615). To acquire this right the person must, as a threshold matter, qualify as a finder. The rules of law qualifying him may be paraphrased from Chapter I's discussion of wild animals. They have the two elements akin to the rule for both possession and abandonment: there must be an intent to control the chattel on the finder's part and there must be an act of control over it.

Recall the *Eads* case: plaintiff marked the location of a wreck of a Mississippi steamboat by attaching buoys to it. He intended to return the next day to raise the cargo, but was detained so that when he returned defendant was in the process of raising the cargo for himself. *Eads v. Brazelton* (1861). Attaching a buoy to the wreck gives no notice to others that the plaintiff intended to appropriate the cargo and its attachment to the wreck similarly is not the equivalent of actual control over that cargo. The court suggests that if the plaintiff had kept his boat over the wreck, he might have been able to show an intent to control the cargo, although he would still lack actual control. The intent to possess and the act of possession are distinct elements of both possessing and finding, although (to quote *Eads* again) "the action of possession need not have been manual."

The situation of the wrecked steamboat is but one instance of the judicial requirement that to qualify as a finder, a person must be very close to actual possession of the chattel at issue. A chattel located inside another object—such as a stocking, a safe, or a bureau—is not found until an actual discovery of the valuable item is made. The discoverer then becomes the finder. Moreover, a discovery can be made by more than one person. Where one of several boys picks up an old stocking and the boys play catch with it until it breaks open in the hands of one of them, revealing $800 in currency, the money belongs not to the boy who first treated the stocking as a plaything, but to all the boys scrambling as a group for the money in it. *Keron v. Cashman* (1896). Similarly, a person buying a safe or bureau and later leaving it with another for resale, without discovering, as the sales agent does, that it has a hidden drawer containing money, is not entitled to the money. *Durfee v. Jones* (1877). There must be an actual discovery by the person or persons who claim the chattel as a finder. No constructive finding of a chattel within a chattel is possible.

Similarly, there must be an intent to control the discovered chattel in order to qualify as a finder. If the boys who used the stocking as a plaything had sought parental advice, it could be argued that they *and* their families "found" the money because their intent to appropriate it was incomplete before their parents recognized their rights in it. *Edmonds v. Ronella* (1973).

Thus the act of possession must at minimum be sufficient to warn off subsequent possessors and put them on notice of the prior find. With a small, portable, chattel only actual possession is likely to accomplish this. *Lawrence v. Buck* (1874). The first finder with an intent to control and who actually seizes control, has the right of possession prior to all others in the process of finding the same chattel.

II. BARRING THE TRUE OWNER'S RIGHT

The taking of possession by the finder must be done openly. Were the law otherwise, finders would never be able to run the applicable Statute of Limitations for personal property against the right of the true owner to bring a replevin or trover action and no finders would acquire title by adverse possession. To run the Statute the finder must possess the found chattel as openly as its normal use would permit. Its later sale, rental, or use as collateral for a loan, may be evidence that it was so used; it is certainly evidence of a conversion of the chattel as against the true owner. The finder's becoming a convertor at the time of the find or later clearly starts to run the Statute.

III. THE FINDER'S RIGHT

As a prior possessor, the finder of a chattel has rights in the chattel superior to all subsequent finders or possessors but inferior to possessors prior to him and the rightful or true owner. So his rights are, for example, superior to someone with whom he leaves the goods for safekeeping, e.g., a bailee. *Armory v. Delamirie* (1722), discussed *supra*, Chapter III. His rights are also superior to those of a second finder and a subsequent converter of the chattel. *Anderson v. Gouldberg* (1892) (trespassing loggers had a better right to possession of logs than defendants who took possession at sawmill), discussed *supra*, Chapter III as well.

Exclusive possession of a chattel may be actual or constructive. Actual possession requires physical and manual control, whereas constructive possession requires only a showing of authority over or control of the chattel. When a finder or other claimant has not been in actual control of the chattel but asserts the same rights in it that would follow or be inferred from its actual control, those rights involve the concept of constructive possession on which may be based prior rights—prior, that is, to the finder's. The prime example of such a claimant might be the owner of the *locus in quo*—the Latin phrase for the land on which the chattel is found. So the *locus in quo* owner may also have rights prior to a finder's.

Defining who is the owner of the *locus in quo* is sometimes difficult. Where for example a landlord claims personal property from a finder who has found it on leased premises, the landlord must typically show that the tenant has abandoned or otherwise relinquished her right to it. *State v. Green* (1984). Thus the owner of the *locus in quo* is a person in possession or entitled to the present possession of the property on which the find is made. A landlord is only entitled to future possession of the property—after the tenant's lease expires—and so only qualifies in the absence of the tenant's right.

For the *locus in quo* owner to claim to be in constructive possession of a chattel of which, in most cases, he was unaware at the time of finding, is oft-times presumptuous and would probably strike most courts as just that. In this connection, it is all too easy to slip the adjective "lost" into a restatement of the *Armory* rule, so that it becomes, "a finder has a right in a lost chattel superior to all the world except the true owner." Lost? By whom? If the answer is the true owner and thereafter the owner of the *locus in quo* claims that awarding him possession of the chattel will best serve the true owner's recovery of it, he has outfitted his claim with a rationale that sounds less presumptuous and at the same time introduced an element of public policy into the court's consideration of the relative rights of the finder as against those of the owner of the *locus in quo*. (In this section, the finder will be designated as F and the *locus in quo* owner O).

O's claim, viewed as a matter of the law of "possession," is that he had prior, constructive possession at the time the finder claims his (the finder's) rights arose. But if this were acceptable to the courts, O would always win under a rule of prior possession. However, in *Armory,* a finder won. So the facts of that case must, so far as O is concerned, be distinguished. This is easily done. There is no discussion of the place of the find in the opinion in *Armory.* Therefore, O might argue, the court must have found it unimportant. So it was, when one considers that the litigation in *Armory* involved a finder and a subsequent convertor of the chattel. Here O is no such bad actor. Rather, O is a person who only wants to serve the interests of the true owner.

In some instances, and depending on the place of the finding, O is also a person who has expectations of his own and asks the law to protect them. A home owner may quite naturally expect that anything found in his house is his, regardless of whether he knows that the chattel is there beforehand. But see, *Hurley v. City of Niagara Falls* (1967). This expectation follows from his idea that his home is a private place from which he has the right to exclude whomever he chooses. The owner of a garden or cropland may have some similar expectations. The owner of unimproved woodland would not. Neither might the owner of an apartment house or hotel.

Although it helps, a person asserting the rights of the *locus in quo* owner need not be in present possession. A former owner of the real property may be in as good a position as the present owner to know who the true owner of the found chattel is. This is particularly true if the chattel is old fashioned, dusty, or otherwise bears indications that it has been on the premises since the former owner was in possession. However, a purchaser of the real property with an equitable title to the land under a contract of sale would not just by executing that contract acquire constructive possession of the find. *Willsmore v. Oceola Township* (1981).

A.   PUBLIC/PRIVATE PLACE OF THE FIND

When a chattel is found in a place to which the public is invited (e.g., a department store aisle), F has a right prior to O. In this situation, O would have no expectation of constructive possession, nor would he have any duty to safeguard the chattel for its true owner. Further, as the true owner is unlikely to leave the chattel in a public place, he is presumed to have lost it there. *Pyle v. Springfield*

Marine Bank (1946); *Paset v. Old Orchard Bank and Trust Co.* (1978).

If, however, the place of finding is private, O will have the prior right. This decision fulfills his expectations about private places and avoids rewarding a trespassing finder. Second, it recognizes the possibility that the true owner's leaving the chattel there established an implied bailment. Third, it rests on the assumption that if the true owner placed the chattel on private property, he did so intentionally, will be able to remember its location, and will return to reclaim it. In this instance, the goods are not merely lost but instead are mislaid.

B. LOST/ABANDONED/MISLAID CHATTEL

The distinction between lost and mislaid goods was early culled from F v. O cases and elaborated on, until it became an all or nothing proposition for both litigants. *Bridges v. Hawkesworth* (1851). A true owner has unintentionally parted with lost property. It is a chattel that its owner has, through neglect, carelessness, or inadvertence, parted with or suffered to pass from his control and possession so that he has no knowledge of its whereabouts. Its loss is always involuntary. If a chattel is lost, F wins because there was no sense allowing O to take custody to hold it for the true owner's return. The latter would be unlikely to retrace his steps and reclaim it because he does not know and cannot ascertain its whereabouts.

On the other hand, mislaid property is intentionally put in a place, but later forgotten by its true owner. If the chattel is mislaid, that owner is likely to retrace and reclaim it. The place of the find is an important factor is determining that a chattel is mislaid. *McAvoy v. Medina* (1866) (owner of a shop awarded property found there); *Terry v. Lock* (2001) (cash in cardboard box found above motel ceiling tiles held mislaid); *Ray v. Flower Hospital* (1981) (jewels found in eyeglass case on top of hospital information desk by receptionist F held mislaid and hospital awarded possession). The place and the circumstances of the find must support the inference that the chattel was intentionally placed where found for it to be deemed to have been mislaid. *Benjamin v. Lindner Aviation, Inc.* (1995) (owner of airplane has right prior to the plane's routine servicer finding "mislaid" money in wing panel), noted at 82 Iowa L.Rev. 717 (1997). The length of time the find appears to have been in the place where found, is irrelevant to the issue of whether the chattel is lost or mislaid.

However, in other cases, chattel may be abandoned. The circumstances of the find must here support the inference that the chattel has been thrown away or otherwise voluntarily forsaken by its true owner. Here that owner is thought to remember where it is, but to have given up his claim to it. This is not lightly presumed. For example, criminals know better than to assert claims to the spoils of their crimes, and so might be presumed to abandon such claims to avoid prosecution. Abandonment of a chattel works the same legal consequence as losing it: F obtains a judgment. Those who abandon lose title, and the first later finder becomes its owner. *Eads v. Brazelton* (1861); *Chappell v. United States* (2000); *Schley v. Couch* (1955).

Another category of presumably long-abandoned personalty consists of "treasure trove." It consists exclusively of gold, silver, plate, or bullion, or their paper representative. It has been secreted in (not on) the ground or, in some few recent cases, another private place. It must be an antiquity: it must support the inference that it has been concealed or hidden for a sufficiently long time that its owner is probably dead or unascertainable. It is treated as if it too were a lost or abandoned chattel. Because of its negotiable nature, the policy is to return it to circulation and the finder, being encouraged to do this, is awarded the prior right in it. This fourth category is discussed more fully later in this chapter.

In the lost/mislaid/abandoned chattel cases, there is some discussion of giving incentive to the finder to return the chattel to circulation and the societal value of doing this. It is doubtful, however, except perhaps in the case of professional treasure hunters in search of treasure trove, that this policy can be implemented because finding is by definition a fortuitous event. The overriding distinction between cases holding for F and those for O is a determination of which of the two is in best position to return the chattel to the true owner. Courts do this by hypothesizing the state of mind of the true owner when he lost, mislaid, or abandoned the chattel. John Orth, *What's Wrong with the Law of Finders & How to Fix It*, 4 Green Bag 2d 391 (2001); Edward Cohen, *The Finders Cases Revisited*, 48 Tex.L.Rev. 1001 (1970) (articles elaborating on these judicial assumptions).

In most situations, of course, the person in the better position will be O. If the true owner is going to retrace and reclaim, he will find himself once more on O's property. Harking back to an earlier chapter, *ratione soli* as a generalized application of the idea of constructive possession also supports O's claim. *South Staffordshire Water Co. v. Sharman* (1896).

Why then does O not always win? One reason might be that F, upon locating the chattel, has also made his own search for the true owner, or had given the chattel over to those in a position to do this (e.g., the police). If this search has been reasonably vigorous and has gone on for a reasonably long period of time, there is no reason to award the chattel to O, unless his expectations about its constructive possession are strong, as in instances in which F was a trespasser on O's land and O would not expect to find him on the *locus in quo*.

Unless F defeats his own claim to having an honest intent to locate the true owner by being a trespasser and violating O's expectations at one and the same time, there is another reason for holding for F after he had made his own reasonable search for the true owner. That is, the true owner will never be located unless F turns the object over to someone in a position to know who the true owner is or to locate him. The whole search process will not even get started unless the finder is honest in the first instance. When F identifies himself as a finder, thus admitting that his rights are subject to the true owner's, and later searches publicly for the true owner, he should be rewarded for his honesty. *Hannah v. Peel* (1945).

IV. OTHER CATEGORIES

A. CHATTEL EMBEDDED IN OR ON TOP OF THE SOIL

An owner in possession and control of land has a prior possessory right to chattel found embedded in the soil (other than treasure trove). The rationale is that the embedded object is considered part of the soil itself. It need not be totally buried to be considered embedded for these purposes, so long as it is firmly affixed to the land. *Chance v. Certain Artifacts Found and Salvaged from The Nashville* (1984) (steamboat embedded in river bottom). This distinction is similar to the lost/mislaid one. *Corliss v. Wenner* (2001) (rejecting the law of treasure trove, combining the rules for embedded and mislaid property for a find of gold coins, and awarding their possession to the *locus in quo* owner). In a case involving buried gold coins, it was said the embedding repels the idea that the coins were lost by the true owner. *Morgan v. Wiser* (1985); *Ritz v. Selma United Methodist Church* (1991). Other examples are a prehistoric boat or canoe of archeological value, mineral ore of various types, or a meteorite. A chattel unconnected to the soil is F's by prior right.

There are some exceptions to the rule that embedded chattels are the property of the landowner. They are typically created by statute for special types of chattel. First, artifacts associated with Native Americans, found in burial mounds or sites, may be subject either to statutory or treaty rights given the tribe. Their burial itself repels the assumption that the tribe abandoned the artifacts. In one case, tribal artifacts were taken secretly from the graves by a finder who did not own the *locus in quo*. The finder then sued the *locus in quo* owner and the tribe to gain title to the artifacts. The state bought the locus in quo and intervened. The court awarded the right to the artifacts' possession to the tribe. *Charrier v. Bell* (1986), discussed in Calvin Trillin, *U.S. Journal: Louisiana, The Tunica Treasure*, The New Yorker (July 27, 1981) at 41–51. Second, embedded chattels of archeological value may be subject to special state statutes. *Hunziker v. State* (1994). Third, statutes governing the preservation of burial grounds may also create an exceptional situation. *Hughes v. Cobb County* (1994). In this situation, the landowner typically takes title to the real property subject to the rights of the heirs of the deceased not to have the human remains and associated artifacts disturbed. These three exceptions aside, there is a strong presumption that embedded chattel not associated with Native Americans, archeological finds, or burial grounds, are the property of the landowner.

B. SMALL/BULKY CHATTEL

An O in possession and control of real property similarly has a prior possessory right in a bulky chattel found on his land. If it is bulky enough to be immovable, then even though it is on top of the soil, it has become affixed to the land. The best example is a house. In legal parlance, this chattel has become a fixture—a chattel annexed to the real property and so necessary to its present use or functioning as an economic unit. A small chattel is not so connected or necessary, and F may have the prior right in it.

C. LIMITED ENTRY CASES

Finally, some cases have ruled that, although F is not a trespasser and is properly on O's real property when finding a chattel, he will not be found to have the prior right when he entered upon the realty for a limited purpose. The leading case is *South Staffordshire Water Co. v. Sharman* (1896). F might be an employee of O's and so, at the time of the finding, his agent, with a duty to deliver the chattel over to his principal. *Morrison v. United States,* (1974) (involving a soldier finding money in Vietnam). A restaurant waiter finding a patron's pocketbook, a chamber maid cleaning a room in a hotel, a railroad conductor, a bank employee—if any of these people find a chattel on the premises of their employment, their duty is to turn it over to their employer. The place of finding is usually restricted with regard to access by the general public, so arguably qualifying as a private place. More than that, however, is the possibility of fraudulent finding if the rule were otherwise. What's to prevent an employee from relocating the chattel to the nearest public space and "finding" it there if they could improve their rights in the object? *Flax v. Monticello Realty Co.* (1946).

For purposes of this rule, employees can be distinguished from independent contractors; the latter are persons hired to produce a service or product, but not told how to go about it. Because their work methods are their own, their presence on the land is not attributable to O's direction and their finding is their own. *Erickson v. Sinykin* (1947) (involving an interior decorator). R.H. Helmholz, *Equitable Division and the Law of Finders*, 52 Ford.L.Rev. 313, 316–321 (1983) (providing a review of cases on the various distinctions).

D. THE PLACE OF FINDING, TYPE OF GOODS, AND LIMITED ENTRY CASES

Whether a chattel is lost or mislaid, abandoned or mislaid, embedded or atop the soil, or small or bulky, the courts in F v. O cases are using these labels to protect the interests of the true owner of the chattel. These labels should not be taken as ends in themselves; either they are aids to analysis or they should be discarded. For example, with the passage of time chattel lost in a riverbed can become embedded by the current, then uncovered, then embedded again. *Eads v. Brazelton* (1861). Similarly, over time, a lost or abandoned chattel can become embedded in the soil. If it is lost, it usually is F's, but if it is also embedded—O's, so the labeling is not going to help. *Favorite v. Miller* (1978) (concerning a Revolutionary War era statue of George III left by the colonists in a swamp).

Because winning or losing the law suit depends on the label attached to the chattel and because the rationale for the court's decision is the same (that the true owner's recovery of the chattel is furthered), the all or nothing outcome between F and O seems inappropriate. Letting O hold custody of the chattel for the period during which the true owner is reasonably likely to turn up and giving custody (and really ultimate control) to F thereafter, seems more logical. This outcome gives F incentive to report his find and start the search process. See *Paset, op. cit.*

Giving ultimate control of the chattel to the finder endorses his good luck. Who can tell how deep such a response goes into the American psyche? Good luck and good fortune have always been attributes of a finder, and when title to land or some larger question is not present (*Goddard,* discussed *supra,* Chapter II), American courts have made distinctions and found ways to favor him. When

Tom Sawyer and Huckleberry Finn discuss where next to dig for the buried gold, Tom says:

"I reckon maybe we'll tackle the old tree that's over yonder on Cardiff Hill back of the widow's."

"I reckon that'll be a good one. But won't the widow take it away from us, Tom? It's on her land."

"*She* take it away! Maybe she'd like to try it once. Whoever finds one of these hid treasures, it belongs to him. It don't make any difference whose land it's on."

Samuel Clemens, *The Adventures of Tom Sawyer*, Ch. 25, "Seeking the Buried Treasure" (1876). See also, Million, *Sawyer et al. v. Administrator of Injun Joe*, 16 Mo.L.Rev. 27 (1951) (a fictitious, annotated decision based on Tom Sawyer's finding the gold in the haunted house, the decision going for Tom and Huck who get to keep the gold).

Nowhere in American law is a bias in favor of the finder more evident than in matters involving treasure trove, a category of personal property to which this discussion now turns. American courts have here turned the rule inherited from the English on its head.

E. TREASURE TROVE AND BURIED TREASURE

Treasure trove is another—the fourth, after lost, mislaid, and abandoned—type of found personal property. It refers to gold or silver coin, plate, bullion, or money that has been concealed by the owner in a private place. *Morgan v. Wiser* (1985). It must have been concealed or hidden so long ago as to indicate that its owner is unknown or in all probability dead. If found buried in the earth, the rule in England was to award ownership to the Crown. *Attorney General of the Duchy of Lancaster v. G E Overton (Farms) Ltd.* (1980) (declaring the royal prerogative confined to gold and silver articles).

The early assertion of a regal prerogative in treasure trove was the impetus for the judicial development of the law of lost and mislaid personalty. Developing the latter categories was a method of limiting the Crown's claim. The governments of the United States, federal and state, have never asserted this sovereign prerogative, so the law relating to this type of found chattel has been merged with the law of finders generally. Some jurisdictions hold that there is no such merger, but many American courts' rules are at least as favorable toward the finder as toward the landowner of the real property on which the treasure is found. Absent a statute to the contrary, most American courts declare that treasure trove belongs to its finder. Thus treasure trove is treated as a lost chattel, this treatment overriding the fact that its concealment indicates that it was not lost.

Treasure trove is personal property that has been hidden or concealed by its now-unknown owner. The concealment implies an intent on his part to keep the property from the rest of the world and, like Bluebeard or Captain Kidd, to return for it. Where gold or silver chattels are buried in a grave as part of a religious ritual or for use by the deceased in the nether world, there is no intention on the part of those who buried them to reclaim them. So whether they can be considered treasure trove is in doubt.

1. Wreck of the Sea, Historic Shipwrecks, and Embeddedness Redux

Property of the type referred to as treasure trove is buried in the earth. Property lost at sea, but later washed ashore, is called "wreck of the sea." The English Crown claimed that too. This regal prerogative was codified in 1275 A.D. By the time of the American Revolution, whether this applied to sunken treasure was in dispute. This dispute was settled by litigation in the Crown's favor, but not until after the Revolution; so its resolution was not received as part of the English common law in the United States. The resolution is inchoate in our law. Treasure recovered from the seabed is not a wreck of the sea, in that it has not been washed ashore. Sunken treasure, moreover, is not treasure trove unless the ship was scuttled by the former owner of the treasure to conceal it.

Increasing amounts of sunken treasure and undersea artifacts, thought lost forever before recent technological advances in undersea exploration, are being brought to the surface. In 1987, Congress enacted the Abandoned Shipwreck Act (ASA). Pre–ASA, courts used the embedded/atop the land distinction and found that the state and federal government respectively, had title to a sunken vessel in submerged lands. *Klein v. Unidentified Wrecked and Abandoned Sailing Vessel* (1985); *Chance v. Certain Artifacts Found and Salvaged from The Nashville* (1984). The ASA asserts federal title to historic shipwrecks, then immediately cedes that title to the states when the wreck is abandoned and embedded in submerged state lands or coral. A state must show, by a preponderance of the evidence, that the wreck meets the ASA's requirements. Abandonment for ASA purposes may be shown by lapse of time or lack of salvage efforts. Originally the requirement of embeddedness was intended to conform the ASA to the common law and, in particular, the landowners' exception to finders' rights for chattel embedded in the *locus in quo*. Subsequent litigation has lowered this requirement as well: the wreck need only be partially buried in the bed of the state's coastal or inland waters, the need for heavy equipment to raise the wreck is evidence of its being embedded, and part of the wreck's submersion in easily stirred silt has been sufficient. *Fairport Internat'l Exploration, Inc. v. The Captain Lawrence* (2001). Moreover, embeddedness has been used as a surrogate for the wreck's historic value.

The policy basis for this broad interpretation of what is embedded for ASA purposes is found in (1) the changing hydrology of submerged lands, where shifting currents cover and then expose new levels of sea bed (after all, what is embedded this year, may be sitting on the bottom the next), (2) the large debris fields of many wooden wrecks (meaning that part of the wreck may have to be determinative of the status of the whole), and (3) the protection of investment in tools needed by professional salvors and divers.

Under the ASA, states have established permit systems for raising and regulating the recovery of historic wrecks. Absent an assertion of state regulatory power under the ASA, persons who take possession of sunken ships or cargo are entitled either to the rights of finders or salvors—the latter being persons who take possession under federal admiralty law. *Adams v. Unione Mediterranea Di Sicurta* (2000). Which body of law applies (finders' or salvors') is a muddle. Finders' law has been applied when the vessel's hull or cargo has been abandoned. An abandonment must, however, be shown by clear and convincing evidence. Because of this high evidentiary standard, most cases have found salvors' law applicable, although salvage law has been applied to a vessel's hull and finders' law to part of its cargo. *Bemis v. The RMS Lusitania* (1996).

a. Finders at Sea

The law of finders applies when the ship or its cargo has been abandoned. *Fairport Internat'l Exploration, Inc. v. The Shipwrecked Vessel* (1999). Thereafter, the first finder to possess the vessel or its cargo after abandonment gains title to it, with two exceptions, for its being first embedded in the seabed, and second subject to the constructive possession of another.

However, an express abandonment is needed. Lack of technology may be considered in determining whether lapse of time and a failure to undertake salvage constituted an abandonment. If no abandonment is found, an explorer representing the owner has rights superior to competitors, and may have an injunction granting exclusive recovery rights. *Yukon Recovery, L.L.C. v. Certain Abandoned Property* (2000). Competing explorers are entitled to enter and search the area where the abandoned property is located and are also entitled to an injunction freeing them of unreasonable interference from each of their number. *Eads v. Brazelton* (1861). The first explorer to take possession of the property acquires title to it and the court releases the property to the finder. *Eads, op. cit.*; *Adams v. Unione Mediterranea Di Sicurta* (2000). *Treasure Salvors, Inc. v. Unidentified Wrecked and Abandoned Sailing Vessel, "Nuestra Senora de Atocha"* (1981).

b. *Salvage*

In admiralty law, a salvor is a person who acts (1) voluntarily and (2) successfully in (3) rescuing a vessel or its cargo from some maritime danger or peril. These three elements defining a salvor present courts with questions of fact for adjudication, although underwater wrecks are presumed to be in peril because of the risk of loss. When salvors foresee competition, the would-be salvors can subject themselves to the personal jurisdiction of our federal courts and adjudicate their claims, even when the vessel or cargo lies in international waters. Otherwise, a would-be salvor first typically invokes federal admiralty *in rem* jurisdiction and "arrests" the vessel or cargo. Arrest is the process by which a court obtains exclusive control over the vessel or cargo. Either actual or constructive control may be used as a prerequisite for jurisdiction, so something less than actual possession of the *res* is sufficient. The typical alternative to actual control is the actual delivery to the court of artifacts, components of the cargo, or other chattel from the vessel. Photographs or video tapes may do as well. *R.M.S. Titanic, Inc. v. Haver*. The arrest must be sufficient to provide notice to competitors of a claim for salvage. It provides either an exclusive right to proceed with salvage or security for the satisfaction of any judgment or award that might be awarded the salvor. Personal service on known competitors or, if that is not possible, posting the arrest warrant in the courthouse atrium, gives the court jurisdiction. *Ehorn v. Sunken Vessel Known as the Roscino* (2002).

The typical act of salvage is raising a wreck, saving it from being stranded, or, more typically still, towing a ship in danger of floundering at sea into port. When a salvor comes upon a vessel in distress, he can presume the owner wants assistance. This presumption is particularly strong if the vessel has been deserted by its crew. A successful salvor's rights cannot be contested after the fact; salvage may only be rejected in a timely manner. A salvor takes possession of, but not title to, the distressed vessel and its cargo, and may then claim an award for the successful completion of his task. *Columbus–America Discovery Group v. Atlantic Mutual Ins. Co.* (1992). This award itself is called salvage. It is not a claim of title or possession to the vessel or cargo saved, but is rather like a lien on the proceeds of the sale of the cargo or the profits of the voyage.

This compensation is court-awarded. It is intended to be generous enough to encourage heroism and discourage embezzlement in the course of a rescue of life and property. The greater the labor, skill, energy, quickness, risk, danger, and value of the saved chattel, the greater the award. Where the risks are high and investments required by the salvor expensive, the award is based on making a return on a comparable, highly speculative investment, with the result that 70% of the value of the salvaged vessel or its cargo is not atypical. *Columbus-America Discovery Group v. Atlantic Mutual Ins. Co.* (1995). As with a vessel like the Titanic, where the decision may be to leave it on the seabed, the award may be the exclusive right to photograph or view it. See generally, Robert Peltz, *Salvaging Historic Wrecks*, 25 Mar. L. 1 (2000). Similarly, when the cargo consists of coins or art objects that might flood and disrupt the market for them, the inventory on which the award is based may be sealed.

c. *Comparing Finders' and Salvage Law*

Some comparisons between these two bodies of law reveal important differences. Finders' law only applies when the property has been abandoned and it has, as one of its purposes, the retitling of the property so that it can be put back into use and service. Salvage law assumes that the title to the property remains with its prior holder, although property cannot be salvaged until subjected to a maritime peril or distress. Thus if finders' law is applied, the property's title goes to the finder; if salvage law is used, the successful salvor acquires a right of possession, not title, to the property—the salvor's possession being only to the extent necessary to save it and return it to the stream of commerce. The successful salvor gains an inchoate lien on the vessel or its cargo.

An intent to save the property, and actually saving it, are two elements necessary to justify a salvage award and are akin to the elements necessary to a successful finder. Salvaged property is subjected to federal court jurisdiction; once the court has passed on any disputed claims on the property, it is returned to its true, prior owner and the court then determines an appropriate salvage fee for the salvor.

The finder is a solo operator and his search has an all-or-nothing quality about it: he either is awarded the title, or not. He must possess a higher degree of control to win a judgment. The salvor can act alone and receive an award, but he can also act in tandem with others and share an award with them in proportion to his efforts and accomplishments. *Hernandez v. Roberts* (1988) (pleasure boat-er entitled to $500 salvage award for staying with sinking vessel until the arrival of Coast Guard).

The finder taking possession at sea as well as the successful salvor both take their rights subject to governmental claims. Several states have enacted statutes akin to the ASA. Some like California's, are broader, protecting archeological sites too. While all these are limited statutory assertions of jurisdiction, treaties and international conventions apply when foreign nationals are involved in disputes over sunken and wrecked vessels. The Law of the Sea Convention, for example, contains both finders' and salvage law provisions. Under it, finders' rights are qualified in that consent to them must be obtained from the country of origin of the find.

State statutes protecting sunken antiquities are common in coastal states, particularly in the Southeast and along the Gulf Coast. Searchers for treasure under these statutes apply for permits for specific search areas. Such permits look like leases for the search area, are issued only to archaeologists, and are executed in exchange for a percentage of the treasure and subject to giving state experts an opportunity to study and evaluate the artifacts recovered—even the seizure of artifacts connected to the state's history and culture. Subject to such controls, a treasure hunter's best hope is to find fungibles in the cargo.

When such legislation is passed, the easiest cases are those where treasure seekers trespass on state-run excavations already underway. Harder are cases in which the state seizes artifacts of which the government has no knowledge, but which are found by private citizens who are not even compensated for their time and effort. Such a decision has however been taken. *State of North Carolina v. Armistead* (1973). It can be justified by a recognition that the legislative assertion of title to historical artifacts has as its objective the regulation and control of the methods used to gather them, in an attempt to make sure that those methods represent sound archaeological practice. With so much litigation about finders' and salvors' rights reported to date, it may be time to reconsider the applicability of both finders' and salvage law, and to consider shipwreck sites of a certain age—say, 100 years old—an archeological site and impose appropriate regulation on it.

V. FINDERS' STATUTES

If a thief buries a stolen chattel on O's land and F finds it, the thief may have the better right to possess the chattel than the finder. This result is consistent with the rule in *Armory*. The thief may get caught and may want to lead the authorities to his cache in the hope of plea-bargaining or in just plain remorse for his misdeeds. Moreover, he knows of the true owner, of whose identity the finder usually hasn't a clue. Nonetheless, the result seems strange, favoring as it does a bad guy over a finder, so that if the finder can be encouraged to live the law's oft-repeated justification for protecting finders' rights in order to protect the true owner's, then the finder should be preferred. Legislation has therefore attempted to encourage the finder to report his find. *Willsmore v. Oceola Township* (1981).

In 20 states[1] and the District of Columbia, there exist statutes which provide that a finder must, under penalty of the criminal code, report his find to local authorities and deposit it with them. After the publication of notice of the find, or sometimes just after the police have retained custody for a stated period of time (sometimes the period varies with the value of the chattel), the chattel is returned to the finder if unclaimed and the right of the finder becomes absolute. The right of a prior possessor or the true owner to claim it thereafter is cut off.

When, through the use of these statutory procedures, the chattel is returned to the true owner, these statutes typically make provision for the finder to receive a reward. It is either fixed at a percentage of the value of the chattel, or at a reasonable amount, otherwise undefined, but related to the level of effort required of the finder, the promptness in reporting the find, and the expenses required to preserve it. See, e.g., McKinney's—N.Y.Pers.Prop.L. §§ 251–258 (2002). However, in New York, there are exceptions for negotiable instruments found by a state employee undertaking official duties (they

1. Alabama, California, Connecticut, Florida, Illinois, Iowa, Maine, Massachusetts, Michigan, Missouri, Montana, New Hampshire, New York, North Dakota, Oklahoma, Oregon, South Dakota, Vermont, Washington, and Wisconsin, have such statutes.

escheat to the state), chattel found on bank safety deposit box premises (the bank takes them), and a chattel found by an employee under a duty to deliver it to his employer. See *Paset v. Old Orchard Bank and Trust Co.* (1978).

Many states provide for a statutory duty to compensate the finder for his expenses; others provide only for a statutory reward for the finder. Such provisions have generally been upheld against the argument that they deprived the true owner of property without due process of law.

Finally, some of these statutes have been held to abrogate the common law of treasure trove, although not all courts considering the issue have reached this conclusion.

A. THE EFFECT OF STATUTES ON THE COMMON LAW OF FINDERS

Many finder's statutes apply to "lost" personalty. Such statutes raise a definitional question whether "lost" refers to (1) the popular meaning of the word—as in "lost and found"; (2) the legal meaning of the word, as in a description of one of the four common law categories of personal property—lost, mislaid, abandoned, or treasure trove property. Because these statutes give expression to a legislative policy of encouraging finders to report their finds to public officials or others in a position to locate the true owner, the word "lost" might reasonably be given a meaning broad enough to permit use of the statute in a wide variety of circumstances. Lay rather than legal definitions might thus be used by the courts. This makes sure that the policy behind these statutes is implemented, and avoids putting the lay finder in the difficult position of being forced to classify the find as one of several types of personal property in order to determine whether the statute applies. Avoiding putting the finder in this difficult position will be particularly important if the statute carries criminal penalties.

However, most of the cases decide otherwise. *Benjamin v. Linder Aviation, Inc.* (1995) (collecting the cases maintaining common law distinctions in the face of finders' statutes). This is particularly true when the statute interpreted was enacted in the 19th century and the legislature has long had the opportunity to amend the statute to make it clearly applicable to all types of found personalty: legislative acquiescence in the narrow judicial interpretation is then presumed.

Delaware has a statute with a narrower scope. It requires that the state police make reasonable efforts to locate the true owner of "personal property of any kind" and any money turned over to the police. Such property shall, after a year, be disposed of at public sale. The sale proceeds shall become the property of the police retirement fund if stolen and of its finder if "lost or abandoned." 11 Del.C. § 8307(a)-(c) (2001) (also designating any money turned over to go to the retirement fund after a year). The reference to "lost or abandoned property" has been held to encompass all of the common law categories of lost, mislaid, abandoned, or treasure trove property. This statute does not require turning over such money to the police. When turned in, however, the finder of non-stolen money acquired absolute title to it after a year. (If the common law were to apply, he would get only the right to possession.)

In one Delaware case, the police had argued that the plaintiff in a replevin suit did not turn over money in good faith because he first avoided them and when he found the money, was working undercover in return for immunity from criminal prosecution. This statute contains no requirement that there be a good faith turnover of money. So long as the property came into police "custody," the court held that the statute applied. Moreover, under it, there is no presumption that money turned over was stolen. Such a presumption would defeat the legislative policy in the statute to encourage people to turn in money that they find. However, money found on thieves' property, amid other stolen property, in a safe previously stolen, in a large amount, in bundles of small denominations—from all these circumstances, its being stolen might be reasonably inferred. But such an inference is not compelled. When only one of the bills was traced to a specific theft, but police inquiries failed to link the rest of the money with another theft, such a failure could reasonably justify the inference that the money was not stolen. *Campbell v. Cochran* (1980) (cross motions for summary judgment denied in a finder's replevin action for money turned over to state police).

B. FINDERS' REWARDS

Sometimes a finder is held to have a lien on a chattel for the payment of a reward publicly advertised by the true owner who later refuses to pay it. Such a lien is often unnecessary because, in this situation, the finder arguably also has a claim to have fulfilled an owner's unilateral contract regarding the promise of a reward for the finder's act in returning the lost chattel. Such a contract provides a separate cause of action against the owner. Providing that finder with a lien on the chattel, encourages litigation because this lien arises only by returning the chattel to the true owner and thereafter can only be perfected or foreclosed in court. A contract claim will serve the finder just as well as a lien will.

Nor is the contract to pay a finder's reward void for an unlawful consideration under criminal statutes requiring finders to report their finds and give them over to the true owner. Only if the finder knows the true owner's identity at the time of finding do these statutes impose an immediate duty to turn over the find to its owner. Otherwise the finder must deposit the find with a public official and then search for the owner. Reward contracts are intended to encourage such searches and so implement and supplement such statutes, rather than supplant a finder's statutory duty. An owner will take into account the legal duty imposed by such statutes, calibrating the amount of the reward accordingly. However, the statute should not be read as nullifying such contracts, particularly because owners might use them to encourage finders to return a chattel and comply with the law.

One state's finder's statute entitles the finder to a reasonable reward for the return of the chattel to the true owner, without further defining what amount is reasonable. In one case, the court found thirty percent of the value of the coins returned to be unreasonably large. It considered relevant to the amount of the reward the fact that the finder had spent a little more than $1,000 of the more than $8,000 found. It also permitted recovery of the finder's expenses in preserving, storing, and safe-keeping the find. *In re Unknown Silver Coins* (1988).

Other states provide by statute that a finder will receive a fixed percentage (say 10%) of the value of the lost and found chattel, but again such statutes should be taken to provide a standard that can either be supplanted by private agreement or construed to set a statutory minimum on the amount of the reward.

However, before the finder can claim a reward the chattel "found" must indeed have been "lost." For example, supermarket carts scattered around the neighborhood of the market cannot be deemed lost where they had been left by shoppers. When a defendant systematically appropriated carts where they had been left, held them a few days, and then demanded a finder's fee from the market before returning them, he is guilty of larceny and it is no defense that the carts were legally lost. Under these circumstances, they were not lost. *People v. Stay* (1971); *Michael v. First Chicago Corporation* (1985) (involving certificates of deposit "found" by purchaser of bank's cast-off office furniture).

The *Stay* case brings us back to the beginning of this discussion. Where the true owner of a "found" chattel is readily ascertainable from the circumstances, it is not "lost" and not subject to the law of finders. A stock certificate or savings bond with the holder's name and address, travelers checks with the payor's signature on them, or shopping carts in the locale of the market—all are examples of a rule that says, only the truly lost chattel, may be found. The taxicab driver keeping a wallet with identification found on the back seat of the cab is more likely to be guilty of larceny than found to be a finder.

A final rule suggested by examining these statutes is that what is of no value to a finder, cannot be lost within the meaning of these statutes. Registered or non-negotiable stock certificates and bonds fall into this category.

C. ESCHEAT

Escheat is a legal procedure, known to the common law as early as the twelfth century, whereby the sovereign acquires title to a deceased's property when after a number of years, no heir owner appears and claims it. Its early applications were limited to real property, but in this country it has usually been applied to both real and personal property. This power exists in the state because it either has jurisdiction over the property or over its last holder. It is a matter of statute in all states, but the dormancy period varies greatly from state to state, ranging from as little as two to as many as 20 years.

D. UNCLAIMED, INTANGIBLE, PERSONAL PROPERTY ACTS

About 40 states have enacted statutes promulgated by the Commissioners for Uniform State Laws in 1954, 1966, 1981, and 1995 concerning the disposition of unclaimed, intangible, personal property. To see the need for such statutes, one has only to think of the number of dividend checks issued each year by large, publicly-held corporations, and then to imagine the (remote) possibility that all of those checks will reach the owners of the corporate shares represented, and that all those checks will thereafter be cashed.

What should be done with the funds deposited to pay the uncashed checks? One resolution is to give them to the state. All the states have escheat laws under which property, including intangible personal property, reverts to the state because no one is available or competent to inherit it. However, it is difficult to make the assumption that because one object of personalty has not been claimed, its holder has no heirs. Some states have special statutes dealing with unclaimed bank deposits within their jurisdiction. These laws presume that such property has been abandoned after a statutory period of time, and possession of unclaimed deposits is transferred to the enacting state.

But which state's escheat law should apply? Conflicting claims among the states meant that the holders of unclaimed personal property might be subject to multiple liability if they disposed of the property. In the case of a corporate dividend check, four states might claim the property: (1) the state of incorporation of the corporation, (2) the state in which that corporation has its principal place of business, (3) the state having the most contacts with the payment of the dividend, or (4) the state of the shareholder's last known address. Unclaimed Property Acts have adopted the fourth alternative because this will distribute this property among the states in proportion to the commercial activities of their residents and because it provides a simple, easily-administered rule.

Unlike the escheat laws, the Uniform Acts do not give title to the state; instead the state of the last known address of the lost owner of unclaimed, intangible personal property acts in a custodial manner: it holds the property in perpetuity for its owner. The Acts create a "presumption of abandonment" for unclaimed personalty after the lapse of a statutory period of time. After that time, the property is turned over to the state of the last known address of the lost owner. Because the law abhors a forfeiture, the Act is preferred over the escheat laws. The presumption is rebuttable whether the property is in the hands of a private holder or the state. These Acts have generally been found constitutional.

Unclaimed, intangible personal property is broadly defined by the Acts. Any monies held on account, or reserved for payment to another, are included. Examples include money orders, traveler's checks, unclaimed dividends, unpaid wages, unused airline tickets; monies deposited to redeem stocks or bonds, monies payable under insurance policies, monies distributable to pay fringe benefits to wage-earners; as well as tangible personalty in any unclaimed safe deposit box. Property covered by the Act must be held by a banking or financial organization, business association, insurance company, public utility, state court, public agency, trustee, or a debtor in possession of another's property.

The holder of unclaimed, intangible personal property is required by the Act to notify the owner and then to file a report with the state administrator (a public official named in the Act). This report lists property unclaimed in its possession and the lost owners' last addresses. The administrator is authorized to take possession of this property, sell any property not money, and deposit all money and the proceeds of sales in a custodial account maintained by the state for lost owners. The lost owner's rights to a *pro rata* portion of this account are never forfeited; rather, the state acts as a conservator of the funds representing the property. However, the property itself may be sold free and clear of its owner's claim. The Acts also detail procedures for an owner to use in making a claim against the administrator.

The period of time during which the property must be unused by the owner varies with the type of personalty. The default dormancy period is five years in the 1995 version of the Act, down from 7 in the 1966 Act. Various periods are provided for different types of property, ranging from one to 15 years. Various states, in adopting the Uniform Act, have substituted general dormancy periods of between 10 and 20 years. The trend has been to shorten the dormancy periods in the recent adoptions of the Uniform Act. This both increases the chance that the last owner will be located and, more importantly, raises the amount of revenue that these Acts produce for their adopting states.

The earliest two versions of the Act tied the enacting state's claim to abandoned personalty to its ability to assert personal jurisdiction over the holder. In 1965, in an escheat case, the United States Supreme Court untied this connection. *Texas v. New Jersey* (1965). To make the Act consistent with the holding in this case, the 1981 version of the Act provides that unclaimed intangible property is payable to the state of the last known address of the owner or, if that information is unavailable, to the state of the holder's domicile. The state of a corporation's domicile has a first claim on unclaimed securities distributions, but if a shareholder's last known domicile is in another state, that latter state may claim escheat. The latter state may make its claim in a transaction-by-transaction basis or by some other "proper mechanism" such as a computer code. *Delaware v. New York* (1993).

Litigation concerning these Acts has involved three types of problems. The first is their retroactive effect when a type of property is newly covered by an Act. Many states specifically enact some retroactivity period. Second is the issue of whether the reporting requirement included property for which the relevant statute of limitations has expired. Most courts hold that, notwithstanding the fact that the statute has run, the property must be reported and then turned over to the state. Third is the issue of when the dormancy period starts to run. What if an offer to settle an insurance company claim is made, to be payable for six months thereafter? Does the dormancy period run from the date of this offer to settle, or has it already started to run based on the date the claim is made? The latter date has been preferred. What if the owner is undetermined? Must such determination be made before the period starts to run? Two courts have held not. See 8C Uniform Laws Ann. 87 *et seq.*(2001).

In sum, these Acts protect (1) the holders of unclaimed intangibles against the risk of multiple liability on the same property and (2) the rights of the lost owners. They also (3) encourage interstate agreements over the disposition of unclaimed property, (4) allow unclaimed tangible personalty to be put back into circulation, and (5) provide revenue for the states.

CHAPTER V

BAILMENTS

I. THEIR NATURE AND DEFINITION

A bailment is rightful possession of a chattel by one who is not the holder of the title to it. This is a minimal definition, avoiding a long-standing controversy of whether a bailment is governed by the law of property or of contract.[1] If the law of property governs, then a bailment is the delivery of possession of a chattel to another who intends to possess it and takes possession, agreeing that his possessory right in it will cease upon a demand by the transferor for redelivery. There must be a delivery and acceptance of the chattel, with an actual transfer of the chattel itself. This definition is akin to a common law conveyance of land by livery of seisin.

If contract law governs, a bailment is a transfer by mutual consent of the possession of a chattel for some specific purpose under an express or implied contract to carry out the purpose of the transfer and to return the chattel to the holder of its title

1. Historically, bailments were contracts. This was clear in the first half of the 19th century when contracts were identified not as the product of a bargain and consideration, but by the status of the parties to it. Contract rights were then, by the same token, a subset of property rights.

once that purpose is accomplished. *B.A. Ballou and Co., Inc. v. Citytrust* (1991).

Does it make a difference whether the contract, the property, or the minimal definition of a bailment is used? Indeed it does. A bailment arises under the law of property, upon delivery of the chattel, regardless of whether any consideration passes between bailor and bailee. *K-B Corporation t/a Central Motor Company v. Gallagher* (1997). Contract law, on the other hand, requires consideration. Further, if the contract definition is used, there will be cases that will be hard to classify as bailments, but that the law has traditionally regarded as such. What if a car, parked in an attended parking lot, is stolen from the lot with valuables inside the trunk? Even if the car was the subject of a bailment, were the valuables in its trunk also subject to bailment? Were the valuables bailed when the car was left in the lot, even though the attendant had no knowledge of their presence? Or how about a purse left in a restaurant by a patron? If it contains valuable jewelry, is the jewelry the subject of a bailment? There is authority in each instance for holding that there was a bailment of the valuables and that the bailee—the owner of the parking lot, restaurant, or shop—assumes the risk that the car or the purse will contain chattel more valuable than he knows.

In the parked car and restaurant patron cases, the contractual definition of a bailment requires that there be some notice by the bailor of the chattel delivered to the bailee. That definition will be stretched nearly to the breaking point by these "closed receptacle—or bailment within a bailment" cases. The notion of a constructive bailment will either have to be introduced into the law, or the test for whether or not a bailment arises will have to be generalized into a test of whether, considering the attendant circumstances, the bailee could have reasonably expected that the receptacle would contain the valuables that it did. Thus a hotelkeeper might be expected to know that some of his guests will arrive with purses and suitcases containing valuables, or a parking lot owner might reasonably be expected to know that some cars left in his possession will have valuables in their trunks. Similar and stronger expectations can be imputed to the bank which accepts valuables for storage in safe deposit boxes, even where the bank cannot gain access to the box without a key in the depositor's possession.

In these cases, the law would probably be better served if, instead of engaging in the fiction of a constructive bailment, the courts adopted either the property or the minimal definition of a bailment. Then the bailee's risk of increased value arises when the delivery and acceptance of the receptacle takes place (under the property definition) or when the bailee assumes possession of the chattel (under the minimal definition). Under either definition, a bailment arises when the alleged bailee assumes possession or takes control of the chattel, with an intent to exercise control.

Under either, as well as in a jurisdiction in which the courts strictly maintain a contract definition, a threshold question is whether the bailment or the contract was not set in motion because there was no delivery to, or assumption of possession by, the bailee. This approach has negated a bailment in cases in which the chattel is allegedly bailed in an area (say a cloakroom) set physically and visually apart from the primary place of business (say a sales floor or the dining room of a restaurant). This factual context of the alleged bailment speaks to the question of whether the shopkeeper, as an alleged bailee, knew of the presence of the chattel on his premises. If the bailee has no knowledge, there can be no intent to possess the chattel on his part, and hence no bailment.

However, it may also be important whether the deposit of the chattel left behind by the customer facilitated the transaction in the shop, as where a customer removes his coat in order to try on a new one in a clothing shop. This aspect of the alleged bailment indirectly addresses the question of whether the shopkeeper, as an alleged bailee, should have known of the chattel's presence, whether it was in his sight or not.

Considering both the closed receptacle cases as well as cases in which the knowledge of the alleged bailee is at issue, it becomes obvious that a bailment does not require and does not result only from a separate or express contract, but may also arise when the parties to it deliver and accept possession of a chattel. Yet even this latter definition of a bailment may be too detailed, and it might be better to say that for a bailment to arise all that is needed is the consent of the parties to the transfer of possession.

A. FINDERS AS BAILEES

If a minimal definition of bailment is a consensual transfer of possession of a chattel, it must then be asked whether the consent of the parties can in any circumstances be implied, and if so, what those circumstances might be. One circumstance that arises out of the discussion in the last chapter pertains to the law of finders. If F finds O's watch, what obligations does F owe to O? Ralph Aigler, Allen Smith, & Sheldon Tefft, 1 *Property* 47 (1960) suggests the following problems:

a. What if F tires of keeping the watch and throws it in the trash? F had no duty to take possession of the watch in the first instance, but once he decided to keep it, he should realize that he has only the right to possess it and not the title to it. In consequence, he should keep it safe. Treating it as trash when it clearly has great value, would be gross negligence. *Isaack v. Clark* (1615) ("[F]or at the first, it is in his election, whether he will take them or not into his custody, but when he hath them, . . . he ought to keep them safely.").

How will this liability arise? There is no consensual arrangement between F and O to support a contract-based bailment. Today a bailment on such a basis would founder either on the bargain (or offer and acceptance) principle of contract law or on the doctrine of consideration.

Neither is this a tort duty imposed on F. The duties imposed by the law on tortfeasors are duties owed to all the world, and F knows that the watch he found probably had but one owner. To that person, F might reasonably expect to have some duty to preserve the watch, but his duty is not owed to the public in general. F's duty is more particular. It is to search for the true owner and hold the watch until there is no reasonable expectation of the true owner's being found. Until that time comes and goes, F should not throw the watch away. His duty to search becomes the purpose of a bailment implied by law.

Whether F's period of search for the owner is shorter or longer will depend to some degree on some assumptions which F can reasonably make about the duration of O's interest in the watch. If it is an inexpensive time-piece then it may quickly reach the point at which the cost of repair exceeds the cost of replacement; then F might reasonably assume that O's interest in the watch will the more quickly wain, and F will be able to throw it away sooner. The more expensive the watch, the longer the period of O's interest in it can be assumed to be and the longer will be the time before F can throw it away. These are rules of reason and of reasonable expectations. Absent circumstances on which reason can work, no definitive answers can emerge.

b. What if F wears O's watch while swimming, has it cleaned, or lends it to a drunken man? It is often said that the degree of care required of a finder is slight. This rule of slight duty is inferred from the slight benefit (that's benefit, not consideration) that the finder received from any implied bailment between himself and the true owner of the chattel. A finder is a gratuitous bailee, liable only for gross negligence. The idea of a slight benefit was engrafted onto the law as a method for inferring that some consideration was given to the finder in order to sustain the finder/owner relationship as a contract of bailment, but if it is a contract, it is an implied contract. An implied contract has those terms that can be reasonably expected by the parties to it and so imposed by the law. These expectations and terms are modified by circumstances, and if the finder's degree of care is modified by the benefit conferred on him, then it is an overstatement to say that a finder *always* has a slight duty of care. If the find involved a watch set with diamonds, the courts may increase the duty of care for the finder accordingly.

If F were to wear O's watch while swimming and it turns out not to be waterproof and the works were damaged, the question is whether he treated the found watch as a reasonably prudent person would treat his own watch. If so, no liability is likely to attach. It is unlikely that a person would not know whether his own watch is waterproof, so that if a cleaning was necessary because of the dunking that F gave it, F's responsibility is to restore it to its former condition. However, if the watch was in need of a cleaning beforehand and F had it cleaned, the question arises whether the costs of the cleaning, when O turns up shortly thereafter and is benefitted thereby, can be charged to O. O will be in a poor position to deny liability for routine maintenance of the watch, and if that is what this cleaning was, he will be liable for the charges. F can undertake reasonable expenses to preserve the watch and charge them to the owner who later claims it.

If F lends the watch to a drunken man who smashes the watch's crystal while falling down dead drunk, F will be liable for the decrease in value because F might reasonably expect that if he gave his own watch away in this manner it would be damaged.

After F's swim he will be able to recover the maintenance and repair charges from a reclaiming O. After the drunken man smashed the crystal, however, because F's negligence made the charges necessary, no recovery by F will be possible against O. That O might be held liable for routine maintenance or maintenance to preserve the watch from harm, is a matter of a promise which the law will imply.

The blend of property and contract law in the law of bailments may be seen in instances where the bailee seeks to recover these repair costs. It is unlikely that F could withhold the watch from O until the repair charges are paid; rather, he has a separate suit based on a contract theory of bailment for the amount of those charges. Where the repairs are necessary to preserve the watch or chattel itself, however, the courts are more willing to entertain the possibility that F can retain possession until such charges are paid by O. Even for the recovery of such repairs, when O continues to refuse to pay, it is doubtful that F could sell the chattel to satisfy his claim. Rather, he can sue O, have his judgment satisfied, and then surrender the possession of the chattel to O. There is, however, some authority for the proposition that F need not turn the watch over to O before O pays the reasonable expenses which F has incurred in holding the watch. Courts sometimes speak of F's having a lien on the watch for the payment of these expenses. Such a lien, being a creature of the common law of property, is one that permits F to withhold delivery of possession, but probably would not permit F to sell the watch to a third party to satisfy his claim.

c. If F found a diamond-encrusted watch and when O claims it, it is damaged, what result? If the diamonds are nicked when O claims it and O proves that F, while in possession presented the watch to a jeweler for appraisal in an undamaged condition, then O has at least shifted the burden of proof to F to show that F did not damage the watch. Absent such evidence, the damage may have been done before F found it, and O will have no claim in trespass or conversion for the damage.

d. If, when O claims the watch, F cannot find it, and O cannot show that F treated the watch negligently, what result? A court might still impose liability on F to deter finders from "losing" their finds when they are claimed, but if O cannot show that F treated the watch other than in a non-negligent manner, F would have no liability. Absent a showing by O that F misdelivered the watch to an unknown or absconding third party, many courts would not indulge in a presumption of misdelivery.

e. Finally, what procedure should F use to ascertain that O is indeed the true owner if O shows up to claim the watch? F need not give up the watch on demand. He also need not give in to a demand that the claimant inspect it because that would preclude his satisfying his own duty to ask reasonable questions as to the nature and identity of the watch in order to meet his duty to safeguard it for the true owner. If the questions are answered wrongly and the trier of fact can conclude that the finder has a reasonable basis for refusing to give over the watch, then no action of replevin or trover will thereafter lie against him because he has not yet converted the watch—his questions indicate no act of conversion; they instead show a desire to hold the watch for its true owner, not for himself.

1. The Right to Sue and the Causes of Action

For centuries, common law judges debated whether or not a bailor could maintain an action against a person who wrongfully took a bailed chattel from a bailee. So long as the essence of the action against the trespasser was criminal in nature, or sounded in tort, the crime or the tort was committed against the bailee and on this basis the courts held that he alone had the remedy. Likewise, the bailee had the present right to possession, and his duty to deliver the chattel out of the bailment constitutes an interest in the chattel on which to ground his suit. Finally, however, the common law rule came to be that both bailor and bailee could maintain trespass.

Often the bailee is said to have a cause of action against convertors of the property because he is liable over to the bailor. This notion was given the lie in the case of *The Winkfield* (1901), where the bailee was the English postal system and was not liable to its bailors, the persons posting letters. Nonetheless, the court decided that the bailee could maintain suit against a ship, The Winkfield, which negligently collided with another ship that carried the mail and sent the mail-boat to the bottom of the sea. So the bailee was suing a third-party tortfeasor that negligently interfered with the bailment. The court held that the bailee's possession is good as against a wrongdoer, and that the latter would not have the defense of *jus tertii*.

The history of bailments shows two things: that the bailee has a right to sue where he is liable over, and that he is liable over because he has the right to sue. Which one of these rules has priority in the law, is now difficult to say. Where the bailee is strictly liable, he arguably should be the one with the right to control the suit against the tortfeasor, trespasser, or convertor of the chattel. When as today he is liable only if negligent, and even then has often limited his liability by contract, this right should be shared—and today both bailor and bailee have the right to sue on the theory that the one to do so will be the more diligent pursuer of the remedy. Today, in an age in which strict liability has fallen away from the bailee and a bailor's suit against a bailee depends upon the proof of facts and the circumstances of the case, the bailor might as easily run the risks of litigation against the third-party wrongdoer. At the same time, to deny the bailee a right to sue would deny this right to a party who often will have the best access to the facts of the case. The careful conclusion is that today both bailor and bailee should have the right to sue, together or separately, but that only one judgment per incident can be obtained between them.

The cause of action for the recovery of the value of a bailed chattel is trover. The bailor may bring a trover action even though he does not have the right to possess the chattel at the time he brings the action. He has a "general property" in the chattel; this consists of his title to the property and a future right to possess it. At the same time, the bailee bringing the same action is said to have a "special property" in the bailed chattel—the right to present possession of it. Both thus have a possessory interest in the chattel sufficient to maintain an action in trover, although if one of them pursues this action to a judgment, the other is precluded from doing the same. *Associates Discount Corp. v. Gillineau* (1948).

Permitting the bailee to sue in trover may at times work a hardship on the bailor, who in the usual case has a greater interest than the bailee in the chattel. The bailee's right to recover damages rests on the hypothesis that he is the bailor's agent and is charged to protect the property entrusted to him. Permitting the agent to sue in trover is in effect a decision to permit the title to the chattel to pass to a convertor once the judgment is satisfied. To have the bailor's rights in the chattel concluded by a bailee who may not have adequate incentive to litigate vigorously, without giving the bailor notice of the suit or any settlement of it, is a situation that begs for some procedural reform. This is particularly true in a jurisdiction in which the bailee has only a limited liability—say for gross negligence only, as would a finder have sued as a gratuitous bailee. On the other hand, if the bailor has put his trust in the agent-bailee, he should look to him for redress; if the bailor has damages uncompensated by the trover judgment secured by his bailee, he still may have a separate action in trespass for any uncompensated interference with his rights in the chattel and, in any event, the bailee is usually liable over to him for the value of the chattel. If the bailee's attorney is negligent in prosecuting the litigation, or if the bailee fails to obtain a full recovery, the bailee is also liable as a fiduciary in an equitable action for an accounting.

Likewise, both bailor and bailee have a sufficient interest in the possession of a bailed chattel to bring an action in replevin.

B.   BAILMENTS, LEASES, LICENSES
AND SALES

1.   Safe Deposit Box Cases

When a bank customer "rents" a safety deposit box, the weight of authority holds that the relationship between the customer and the bank is that of bailor and bailee. Some courts have held that this relationship is not a lease—the transfer of the exclusive possession of premises for a definite amount of time. When access to the box is obtained by the customer's presentation of identification and the use of one (of two, the latter being in the possession of the bank) key to unlock the vault in which the box is stored, the transfer of an exclusive possession of the vault and box necessary for a lease is not present. When the contents of the box are lost or stolen, most courts hold that the contents of the box have been the subject of a bailment. This result obtains even when the bank knew neither the exact contents or value of the chattels in the box; instead, courts infer that the bank knew their general nature. And even though the bank may not have exclusive control of the contents, its possession is sufficient for most courts to find a bailment. So many courts regard this as the best characterization of the legal relationship between the bank and its customer. As one might expect, its "possession" is a relative term: a bank need not disclose or deliver property in a debtor-bailor's box to a creditor, even one asserting a state statutory right to the disclosure or delivery, although authority on this question is split. Lord, *The Legal Relationship Between the Bank and Its Safe Deposit Customer*, 5 Camp. L. Rev. 263 (1983).

2. Parking Lot Cases

The same type of definitional problem arises in the case of a car left in a parking lot. Where the lot operator does not provide attendants or guards, the car stolen from such a lot is not the subject of a bailment. The car owner has left his car in a specific parking space and expects to find it there upon his return. In this situation, there is a transfer of the exclusive possession of a definite space necessary for a lease, or at minimum a license—a right to use the space without liability for trespass. Both a lease and a license last for a limited or definite period of time. The operator's lack of physical control, exercised independently of the owner, over the car indicates no bailment. Thus unattended, open air, "park and lock" lots around sports stadiums provide little grounds for concluding that a bailment is present. On the other hand, the owner's surrender of the car and the keys to it is, by the same weight of authorities, indicative of a bailment of at least the car. *Allright, Inc. v. Strawder* (1984). Surrendering the keys is a delivery giving the operator a possessory right sufficient for a bailment. The operator is thus responsible to take due care of the car if damaged or stolen from the lot. *Allen v. Hyatt Regency–Nashville Hotel* (1984). This is so particularly when the lot is enclosed, attended, and contained in a specially constructed structure.

Conflicting results occur when the parking structure is specially designed, but is unattended upon entry, when the owner obtains a time-stamped, automatically dispensed ticket (usually with an exculpatory notice) to be presented at the exit. It is there, at the exit, where a car owner first makes contact with an attendant in the collection booth and where the car's exit is barred until the attendant is paid the fee. Often these cases arise in downtown or airport locations, where alternative parking is unavailable. When the car is parked and its keys retained by the owner, delivery to the bailee operator and possession by the operator, are arguably not present; thus no bailment, only a license, is present. *Sparrow v. Airport Parking Co. of America* (1972), discussed in *Kostin v. Mehlbaum* (1995). On the other hand, with exit barred until the fee is paid, it can hardly be said that the owner's control of the car is unfettered; so the operator's placing limitations on the movement of the car and the owner's acceptance of those limits, has more often than not, been sufficient for a bailment. *Richard v. Massachusetts Port Authority* (1974).

"Bailment within a bailment" liability is often at issue in parking lot cases. If the car is not bailed, neither are its contents. However, assuming a bailment of the car, the operator is responsible for valuable chattel that he might reasonably expect to be in its glove compartment or trunk. The customary components of a car (including essentials like the engine and tires, but also hubcaps and dash-board radios, tape and CD players) are typically bailed when the car itself is. So are objects in plain view, unless they reasonably might be expected (by their owner) to encourage thievery—e.g., a wallet left on a car's seat.

One court, although using negligence terms rather than the law of bailment, found the equivalent of a bailment in an enclosed, park and lock, unattended lot for the purpose of making the lot operator liable for the theft of a car tape deck and cassettes. *McGlynn v. Parking Authority of City of Newark* (1981). *McGlynn* analyzed the indicia of possession and control over the car left in the lot as part of its discussion of whether the lot operator owed its customers a duty of due care. It discarded what it said were the outmoded distinctions between bailment, license, and lease used in most parking lot cases. It then distinguished the two issues of the case—the extent of the duty, and whether to apply a presumption of negligence. It found that there was a duty and, on the second issue, held that the operator has the burden of coming forward with evidence showing that it was not negligent when a parked car leaves the lot damaged. On both issues, then, the court's conclusions are consistent with the law of bailment. Its treatment of the case as one involving negligence leads to the rule that the more apparent the possibility of a theft, loss, or damage is, the most likely the operator will not be liable— with the caveat that minimal protections must be provided as a matter of public policy, otherwise the operator is only offering customers "a space in 'hell' " (*McGlynn's* phrase).

Sometimes the lot operator will attempt to exculpate himself from liability for loss or theft of the car by language on the claim check given the car owner upon his arrival at the lot. Typically the check is hurriedly given, received, and shoved into the owner's pocket without a reading. In such cases, the owner would not have notice of the limitation of liability, and most courts hold that the bailor is not restricted to the amounts or conditions printed on the ticket. Such a rule works a result preferable to holding otherwise. As Professor Brown notes, however, it places a "disturbing premium" on not reading the claim check. Where a portion of the check is placed on the car, some courts may conclude that its primary purpose may be to identify the car rather than to state the terms of a bailment contract.

When the check is read, most courts construe it strictly against the lot operator or other party standing to benefit from its enforcement. It may not, moreover, excuse the operator's gross negligence. Broadly speaking, it is hard to see why a person whose business is being a bailee should be permitted to exculpate himself from even ordinary negligence for damage or loss that can be reasonably expected to arise in the course of his business.

Where the attempted exculpation is not total, but limited, and the parties can be found to have agreed to it, the issue becomes whether the restriction of liability is out of reasonable proportion to the loss. A reasonable limitation will then protect the operator from loss or damage due to the actions of third parties but not from his intentional conversions of the bailed chattel; it may also set an upper limit on a bailee's liability by an agreement as to the value of the chattel bailed.

A majority of courts hold that a contractual provision that would protect a bailee against liability for his own negligence is void because it is against public policy. Some courts have sustained such exculpatory clauses in situations where the bailee's business does not involve being a bailee for the public; with a public bailee such as a parking lot operator, however, this contractual exculpation is invalid.

Thus in parking lot cases, the presence of a bailment of the car and its contents holds the key to the lot operator's liability. A failed bailment has the characteristics of a lease or license. Courts, taking the surroundings and the circumstances into account, examine the amount of control exercised by the operator to determine whether there is a bailment shifting to the operator the risk of theft, loss, or damage. Finding a bailment in effect permits courts to determine what minimum amounts of protection must be provided owners' cars and their contents. See generally, William Vetter, *The Parking Lot Cases Revisited: Confusion At or About the Gate*, 40 Santa Clara L. Rev. 27 (1999).

3. Photography Cases

The purpose of a bailment is often the performance of a service. When a person brings exposed film to be processed by a photo lab, the relationship between the photographer and the processor is one of bailment. The photographer has title to the film, and transfers its possession to the processor for developing. The bailee does not have the use of the film and must return the negatives and the prints made from them to the photographer, even though the negatives are worth more than the exposed film initially transferred. Whatever profit arises from the use of the images, is the photographer's. See *Carr v. Hoosier Photo Supplies, Inc.* (1981), noted, 16 Ind.L.Rev. 83, 90; 283, 288–290 (1983).

But not all photographers have complete use of the image on the film they use. A commercial photographer, asked to make a photographic portrait of a person, may hold either the title to or have the right to permanent possession of the negative produced, but the person hiring him and sitting for the portrait has the right to control the use of the negative. *Corliss v. E.W. Walker Co.* (1894); *Pollard v. Photographic Co.* (1888); *Hochstadter v. H. Tarr, Inc.* (1947). Next time you sit for a photographic portrait and want the negative, or do not want your black and white portrait colorized, make the arrangements before the shutter clicks.

4. The Bailee's Personal Injuries in the Bailment for Hire

Often courts and writers use the terms lease and bailment for hire interchangeably in situations in which temporary possession of a chattel is exchanged for a consideration, as when a person "rents" a car. Older authorities considered a bailment for hire to be an entrusting of a chattel for safe-keeping with a bailee and the lease as a transfer of a right to use the chattel. This distinction is important in situations in which the chattel supposedly bailed is misdelivered and the bailee seeks to avoid the strict liability that applied to a conversion, but may also be too technical to be useful in tort litigation involving personal injuries to the "bailee" of a car.

In tort litigation, for example, the locus of the title as between bailor and bailee will not likely prove dispositive of the suit. When the chattel proves defective and the bailee suffers personal injuries, the bailor's liability will be based on and calculated according to the doctrines of negligence or, in a minority of jurisdictions, strict liability. In such a lawsuit, the locus of title is unimportant. Moreover, a personal injury suit may be conducted by first finding an implied warranty in the transaction between bailor and bailee, and in this event, the implied warranty may be part of an implied contract between the parties which has consequences for the burden of proof. In tort, the burden is on the plaintiff-bailee, but if the implied warranty arises in an implied contract, the burden of proof will shift, and once the plaintiff invokes the warranty, it is the bailor who must show due care.

5. Negligent Entrustment

In a situation similar to a bailment for hire, but in a non-commercial context, some states recognize that when a person supplies, directly or through a third party, a chattel for the use of another whom the supplier actually knows or has reason to know, is incompetent to use or operate it, that person is liable to those injured through its use or operation. The incompetence may be due to youth, inexperience, or feebleness of mind or body. Scienter on the supplier's part is a necessary element of the proof of this tort. Supplying an automobile to an incompetent driver is the most litigated context for it. Restatement (Second) of Torts, § 390 (1965). This tort is not one of imputed negligence—in that the negligence of the user is not imputed to the supplier; instead, the supplier's negligence is in supplying the chattel to a person incompetent to use it.

6.　Sales Distinguished From Bailments

A bailment is a transfer of possession. It is not a transfer of a consideration given in exchange for possession and title—that would be a sale. If a transferee acquires possession "for approval" or "on trial," no title is yet transferred and a bailment results, although the bailee has an option to purchase the chattel at the end of the approval period. If the option is not exercised, the identical goods must be returned.

On the other hand, if the chattel's possession and title change hands at the same time, a sale results and the law of sales in the Uniform Commercial Code (UCC) applies. The UCC's § 2–509 rejects the location of title as the test for which party—vendor or purchaser—bears the risk of loss, but the location of the title is still applicable to decide whether a transfer is a bailment or a sale. In a bailment, where the title has not been transferred from bailor to bailee, the risk of loss remains on the bailor if the chattel is destroyed without the fault of the bailee. Under UCC §§ 2–401 and 2–509, once the property is identified, title to it and the risk of its loss pass from a vendor to a purchaser "in any manner and under any conditions explicitly agreed on by the parties." If the parties have no agreement, the title passes if its transfer "completes the vendor's performance with reference to the physical delivery of the goods." UCC § 2–401(1) and (2).

Under the UCC, title is still an important concept, but less so. Under it, the title might pass between the parties for some purposes, but not for others. An agreement between the parties may assign the title and so allocate the risk of loss for the purpose of (say) suing a third-party wrongdoer, but not for the purpose of filing an insurance claim for the loss of the chattel.

C. RETURNING THE CHATTEL

The eventual objective of a bailment is the delivery of the chattel's possession to its true owner or prior possessor, the bailor, or to a third party at the bailor's direction. When the time of the bailment for the bailor's sole benefit is indefinite, the law implies a reasonable time within which the bailor may request return of the chattel. Typically the outer limits of reasonableness is set by the applicable statute of limitations for personal property actions. The bailee who refuses to deliver the chattel, or who does not deliver it because he has lost it, has committed a conversion of the chattel against the bailor. His duty is to return the chattel, and any other act of dominion over it is a conversion—for example, a bailee's using it as collateral for a loan for his own business. *Pagliai v. Del Re* (2001). The bailee who delivers the chattel to the bailor is not liable for a conversion, except that, when the bailee delivers the chattel to the bailor after a true owner has notified him of a claim on it, a conversion may result because the delivery in this instance is a denial of the true owner's rights. *Texas Diamond International, Inc. v. Tiffany and Co.* (2001). Viewing a finder as a gratuitous bailee is premised on the rule that a bailee who refuses to deliver the bailor or true owner's chattel is its convertor.

If the objective of the bailment is by definition the delivery of the chattel to its rightful owner or the bailor, misdelivery is then a risk inherent in a bailment. The courts assume that no bailee will undertake the relationship without realizing this and so a bailee is strictly liable for a misdelivery. So, too, it might be argued, is the risk of third party actions, like theft, or acts of God, or a fire started by lightning. Strict liability for a failure to deliver also discourages a bailee from engaging in fraudulent misdeliveries. This delivery must be of the identical chattel that was bailed initially. Without a duty to return the identical chattel, there is no bailment.

Many cases have arisen in agricultural settings. If, for example, a farmer delivers his wheat to a miller on the understanding that the latter will deliver back one barrel of flour for every four of wheat, the majority of courts hold that there is no bailment because the identical goods are not to be returned. If, in the meanwhile, the mill burns and the wheat is destroyed, the risk of loss falls on the farmer, not the miller. That the flour delivered back need not be milled from the wheat delivered to the miller, indicates a payment for a completed sale. However, this majority rule ignores the possibility that there was a bailment of wheat, followed by its sale at the time of its milling, so that if the miller had processed some grain and converted the rest, a finding of a bailment is not precluded.

In another group of cases raising a similar issue, there is some authority for the proposition that the provider of seed under an agricultural share-crop contract is a bailor of the crop eventually grown. Again, however, a contract to return some fraction of the crop need not give rise to a bailment of the whole of it. Moreover, there can be no bailment for a chattel not yet in existence, so if the seed and the crop are regarded as different chattel, this rule will preclude a bailment in this instance. Nonetheless, the person who provides the seed needs to have his interest protected: when the farmer sells that portion of the crop promised to the seed purveyor to third parties, that may be a conversion—an unauthorized exercise of control over another's property—but for this an adequate remedy lies in damages, instead of the return of the share-crop portion.

On the other hand, if the issue is the allocation of the risk of seeds' loss due to drought or another naturally occurring event destroying the crop, the issue of whether identical goods need be returned is again raised. Then a court can allocate this risk, presumably with the same result as in the milled wheat cases—i.e., that there was no bailment and the risk that there would be no crop was on the provider of the seed.

1. Fungible Goods

Some chattel are fungible, that is, of such a nature that another object may easily replace it and perform the same function. Money is an example. A bank depositor would not reasonably expect, upon a withdrawal, to get back the same identical dollar bills which he presented for deposit. Grain—that currency of the Midwest—when deposited in an elevator, presents another instance in which the identical kernels will not be returned; instead, the depositor will receive an amount of grain of like quality and quantity. If the grain elevator is destroyed before the return, the risk of its loss falls (under the majority view) on the operator of the elevator because a bailment exists in this situation. Similarly, because of the bailment, the operator does not have a mortgageable interest in the grain. It is there for him to return to the depositor or the latter's designee. Thus a bailment can exist in fungible chattel where it normally would not if non-fungible goods were involved.

On the other hand, if chattel are delivered into the hands of another, on the understanding that (as with a herd of sheep) animals of like species, age, and condition are to be returned, this may look like a bailment of fungible goods, but the bailor's creditors will not be able to levy on the herd unless they can show that the identical sheep are to be returned. Otherwise the shepherd's ability to manage and increase his flock would be hindered. Similarly, the risk of loss of the flock falls on the shepherd. Where the alleged bailee is given the power to use the chattel as his own, no bailment results, even if the chattel are fungible.

D. STANDARD OF CARE

The care required of the bailee generally varies according to the totality of circumstances surrounding the bailment. In particular, courts emphasize the extent of the benefit received by the bailee through the bailment to determine the standard of care. *United Farm Family Ins. Co. v. Riverside Auto Sales* (2001). If the benefit of the bailment accrues to the bailor solely, the care required of the bailee is slight. He will be liable only for gross negligence. A finder is such a bailee, and so is liable for only gross negligence because the benefit of the bailment is the bailor's or the true owner's. If the bailment is mutually beneficial to both bailor and bailee, the bailee is required to exercise due care and is liable only if negligent. *Price v. Brown* (1996). When a hotel desk clerk receives a valuable chattel to hold for a guest, a bailment of mutual benefit to both the hotel and the guest is created. *Peet v. Roth Hotel Co.* (1934). If the bailment is solely beneficial to the bailee, and absent contract language to the contrary, even the slightest neglect resulting in the loss, injury or destruction of the bailed chattel is actionable. Any borrower of a chattel is such a bailee.

This three-tiered classification is one that most courts, in Professor Brown's words, "pay lip service to." It requires an initial characterization of the bailment which may go a long way to deciding the whole case. Moreover, since two of the three classifications require a finding of *sole* benefit to either the bailor or the bailee, such findings will be rare and the bulk of a jurisdiction's case law will probably fall into the "mutual benefit" type of bailment, requiring due care from the bailee. After all, if I borrow my neighbor's hedge clippers today, he can borrow my saw—and much more easily borrow a cup of sugar—tomorrow, so such neighborliness becomes of mutual benefit to both parties.

On the other hand, the classifications involving a sole benefit interpose rules that prevent the courts from reaching unexpected decisions. An art museum borrowing a painting for an exhibition, is commonly thought to establish a bailment for the bailee's sole benefit because great care of the painting in its possession is reasonably expected, although the painting is likely to increase in value by being exhibited. In the case of a bailment of sole benefit to the bailor, the classification allows a court to prevent exposing a finder to unexpected liability and, in fact, encourages finders to hold onto chattel they come across. However, even here it is difficult to conceive of a find that is not of some benefit to the finder, who will get to keep the chattel if its true owner does not claim it.

Conceptual difficulties, then, with the three-tiered classification of bailments has led some courts to conclude that one standard of care—due care under the circumstances—should be the test. Ease of administration and flexibility commend this uniform standard to the courts adopting it. *Peet v. Roth Hotel Co.* (1934). In determining the due care required of the bailee, the purpose of the bailment is only one of many factors considered by the courts. They will also consider the method of transfer of possession, the terms of any contract of bailment, the type of goods bailed, and whether any consideration was given for it. Some courts have used a standard of care requiring a bailee to safeguard the chattel as if it was *his* own property. Most of the authorities require that the bailee act like a reasonable person. The difference is more than anything else a matter of proof, for evidence that the bailee did not treat the chattel as he would his own requires a showing of his own subjective state of mind, while a "reasonable person" standard puts more objective and wide-ranging types of evidence before the court. The more objective "reasonable person" standard is fairer to the bailor; the types of proof which will show a lack of due care encompass the subjective type, but are not limited to such matters that are, after all, within the bailee's knowledge and control.

E. THE BURDEN OF PROOF

1. The Majority Rule

Separate from the issue of what standard of care should be applied to the bailee is the issue of which party should prove the required negligence. Most states require that the bailor must prove that there was a bailment, that the bailee has failed to deliver, and that the bailee was negligent in carrying the bailment out when the chattel was lost, injured, or destroyed. This makes the party alleging the wrong-doing prove it and will deter spurious claims. *Knight v. H & H Chevrolet* (1983) (discussing cases reviewing this traditional rule and other rules presented *infra*, this section).

2. A Second View

Other states hold that if a bailed chattel is lost, injured, or destroyed, a rebuttable presumption of negligence on the bailee's part arises once the bailor shows that there was a bailment. *Tannenbaum v. New York Dry Cleaning, Inc.* (2001). In defense of this rule, it is said that the bailee will be the person in possession of the facts or at least be in the best position to acquire them. *Nissho Iwai American Corp. v. New England Warehousing & Distribution, Inc.* (1986). Its critics charge that the bailee is here forced to prove a negative—always a difficult matter—but in practice the proof is likely to consist of evidence showing that the chattel was subjected to a prudent regimen or was treated prudently and no differently than the bailee's own property. If successful in this, then sometimes the burden is met and shifts back to the bailor to present further evidence of lack of due care.

The operation of this presumption, however, raises the question of how much evidence the bailee must produce to rebut it. Merely proving that there was a theft or a fire is clearly insufficient. A few states permit him to rebut it by showing that loss or damage was by a fire of an unknown origin or that the loss and failure to deliver was due to the theft of the chattel by someone not under the bailee's control. A majority of states using a presumption of negligence go further and require that the bailee show his due care of the chattel with probative evidence sufficient to win before the trier of fact. *Classified Parking Systems v. Dansereau* (1976).

Imposing the heavier burden on the bailee seems to be the wiser course. First, the policy underlying the presumption is to encourage bailees to take care and the "due care" rule best implements this policy. Second, this rule places the burden on the party with the likeliest access to the facts, while the minority rule tempts the dishonest bailee to conceal facts relevant to the litigation. Third, the other rule is inconsistent with the presumption of negligence; it permits the trier of fact to draw an inference of non-negligence from the fact of, e.g., a fire, theft or act of God when through the presumption, the law has already settled the legal consequences of the facts the other way. *Knowles v. Gilchrist Co.* (1972). Fourth, the other rule often penalizes a plaintiff's honesty in formulating his pleadings. Often a theft or a "mysterious stranger" defense arises through a fact alleged in the plaintiff's pleading, as where the complaint states that plaintiff saw his watch on the arm of some unknown party leaving the repair shop as he entered it, or saw his car being driven out of a parking lot as he approached to reclaim it. The inference in both cases is that a theft has taken place. This plaintiff, who knows a little about the loss, is in a worse position than the plaintiff who knows nothing or does not plead what he knows. Finally, the "due care" rule simplifies the recovery by bailors for loss or damage to the bailed chattel.

3. A Third Rule

A third group of states requires that when a bailor sues in tort, he has the burden of proof that the bailee was negligent, but if the bailor sued in contract, the burden is on the bailee to show his own due care in carrying out the bailment contract. *Thummel v. Krewson* (1989). Here the burden of proof is allocated with regard to whether the plaintiff has pled his case in tort or contract. Such a reliance on the pleadings gives a legal advantage to the plaintiff wise enough to hire skillful counsel rather than to a plaintiff with a good case on the merits. *Knowles v. Gilchrist Co.,* op. cit. Moreover, the hybrid nature of a bailment makes such facile pleading possible in many, perhaps most, bailment situations.

F. THE MEASURE OF DAMAGES

The usual measure of damages for the complete loss of a bailed chattel is its market value at the time of the loss.[2] For damages to the chattel, the bailee receives the difference between the fair market value of the chattel before and after its injury. *Dado v. Jeeninga* (2001). Where the lost or damaged chattel has no ready fair market value, courts permit the plaintiff bailor to show its actual value to the bailor. If, for example, my bailee loses the incomplete manuscript for this book, I am entitled to the value of my time and labor in replacing it. If I complete the manuscript and the publisher loses it while in the process of publishing it, I will receive its market value. Where a bailor entrusts family papers, portraits of loved ones, or photographs of deceased relatives, the fair market value may not be great or even be provable. If the papers can be reconstructed, the cost of doing so becomes their actual value to the bailor. If the portrait is unique, the only one of the bailor's deceased father, that fact may be considered in assessing its actual value. If the photographic negatives of deceased relatives

2. For example, if I take my $200 dress shirt for laundering, and the laundry that would charge me $2 to clean it loses it, the laundry is risking $200 in liability so I can buy another $200 shirt for its $2 charge. In most cases, the market value of the lost chattel will be its purchase price. Is it any wonder that the ticket for my laundry is likely to have a disclaimer and limitation of liability on it?

are destroyed, that fact may be considered as well. Courts have split on the issue of whether actual value may include a chattel's sentimental value; on the one hand, sentimental value is speculative and prone to exaggeration after the fact, but on the other, the plaintiff's special feelings for a chattel is one factor in any assessment of their actual value because they indicate the lengths to which a bailor will go to repair or replace it.

Similarly interesting issues have arisen in cases discussing rights in photographic negatives. When a person returns from a trip with several roles of exposed film and delivers them to a bailee for processing, the measure of damages for breach of the bailment for services is not merely the replacement value of the film in its unexposed state. The subject of the bailment being the exposed film with images on it, the damages are measured by the value of the images to the photographer. *Carr v. Hoosier Photo Supplies, Inc.* (1981) (also enforcing a written limitation of liability). When the bailor has just returned from a world tour and presented films of his travels for processing, he is unlikely to recover the cost of retaking the trip and the photos; the measure of damages is more precisely the value of remembering the trip through the photos, not the cost of the trip itself. Cf. *Hoffman v. Eastman Kodak Co.* (1929) (involving travel pictures, interpreting state statute, and limiting liability to replacement cost of film).

If the bailee has previously recovered an amount more than the bailor proves in damages, the former is not bound to account to the bailor for the difference. A bailment is not a fiduciary relationship and no such accounting as would be imposed on a trustee is necessary because, in contrast to a bailment situation, a trustee would have title to the chattel subject to a trust. *City of Waltham v. Tukay Furs Service Company, Inc.* (1978). Generally, the burden of proof with regard to damages is on the bailor, as the party with the knowledge and expertise to present this type of evidence.

G. THE BAILEE'S LIABILITY FOR MISDELIVERY

An ordinary, voluntary bailee is absolutely liable for loss of the chattel if a redelivery is made to some person without a rightful claim to it. In misdelivering the chattel, the bailee has committed an act of conversion, interfering by definition with the rights of the bailor as a prior possessor or true owner.

This liability is not extended to involuntary bailees like finders. Neither is it imposed on a person to whom a chattel is delivered by mistake. *Cowen v. Pressprich* (1922). The involuntary bailee who in good faith is trying to return the chattel should not be held liable for making the same mistake—misdelivery—made by the initial deliverer. Indeed, if the attempt to return is promptly undertaken, the actions of the involuntary bailee defeat the notion that he ever agreed to the bailment. Certainly there was no contractual bailment, and no acceptance of delivery to complete the bailment under the law of property. Only the loosest use of the term will sustain the presence of any bailment here.

So the involuntary bailee is not liable unless he is found to have acted negligently in attempting to return the misdelivered chattel. The possibility of a fraudulent misdelivery, as where the bailee claims to have misdelivered a chattel of which he really still has concealed possession, has not persuaded the courts to adopt a different rule. Neither has another con-game: when a chattel was ordered by a swindler from a plaintiff for delivery to the eventual defendant who then becomes an involuntary bailee, and at whose premises the swindler then picks up the goods while claiming to be the plaintiff's agent, the rule is the same and there is no liability for misdelivery to the swindler. *Krumsky v. Loeser* (1902).

H. BAILEE'S FAILURE TO RETURN CHATTEL

In situations in which the bailee has not misdelivered the chattel, but without excuse fails to return or retransfer it to the bailor at the appointed time, the bailor has an election to make. A demand can be made for the return of the chattel and an action brought for breach of the bailment in contract or tort or, at the bailor's option, the latter can treat the chattel's retention as a continuation of the original bailment. Electing the second course of action would entitle the bailor to recover rent at the rate specified in the original bailment agreement.

Some courts however have expressed concern that, when the original agreement is extended to its full term, payment of the rent for the full term may work a hardship on the bailee intending to retain the chattel for a shorter time. *Bibby's Refrigeration v. Salisbury* (1992) (collecting the cases).

II. COMMERCIAL BAILMENTS

The outcome of negligence litigation involving bailees' liability is often hard to predict. Because bailments are commonplace, this uncertainty was long seen as a hindrance to commerce. So the Uniform Commercial Code (UCC), Article 7, was drafted for commercial transactions involving bailments to warehousers. A "warehouseman" is defined by the UCC as "a person engaged in the business of storing goods for hire." The business need not be conducted for profit, so state-run and co-operative warehousers are covered by the Code. The warehouser cannot avoid the reach of the Code's provisions by pleading non-compliance with a governmental regulation because his own misconduct does not diminish his responsibility. Still, the warehouser must be "engaged for hire." Storing one's own personal property will not subject one to Code liability.

The other type of commercial bailee for whom the uncertainty of the common law standards of care was unsuitable was a common carrier. Along with inn-keepers, common carriers were subject to strict liability for a failure to deliver bailed goods. They were in effect insurers of the personal property entrusted to them. The receipt issued by a common carrier is called a bill of lading. Under the UCC, § 7–102(1)(a), a bailee subjected to the UCC is "the person who by a warehouse receipt, bill of lading, or other document of title acknowledges possession of goods and contracts to deliver them."

For these commercial bailees, then, the law makes their bailments the subject of state statutes, rather than the common law or any contract. These control the relationship of bailor to bailee and produce in commercial situations a standardized bailment.

A. STANDARD OF CARE

1. Warehousers

UCC § 7–204(1) is declaratory of the common law and appears to change nothing of substance in it.

A warehouseman is liable for damages for loss of or injury to the goods caused by his failure to exercise such care in regard to them as a reasonably careful man would exercise under like circumstances but unless otherwise agreed he is not liable for damages which could not have been avoided by the exercise of such care.

The primary emphasis on "damages" in the phrase "damages for loss of or injury to the goods" incorporates a rule *de minimis* into this section of the Code. Further, the "reasonably careful man" standard is not that of a prudent owner. The rejection of the latter, more subjective standard involving an owner's state of mind for a more universal and objective standard of a reasonable man permits introduction of a wider variety of proof on negligence issues. So the warehouser must take the care that a reasonably careful man would use under like circumstances. The warehouser is not an insurer of the chattel bailed with him. He must exercise that degree of skill and care which a reasonable man would exercise operating the business in which he engages.

2. Common Carriers

In many states, a common carrier, such as a railroad or a trucking company, is an insurer of the safe delivery of personal property in its charge. Except for acts of God, inherent defects in the goods, the fault of the owner, and absent an express contract to the contrary, the carrier has a strict liability for non-negligent loss and misdelivery of the goods. UCC § 7–309(1) provides that the UCC "does not repeal or change any law or rule of law which imposes liability on a common carrier for damages not caused by its negligence" and otherwise imposes on a carrier who issues a bill of lading the same reasonably careful man standard that warehousers owe the public.

B. A BAILEE'S BURDEN OF PROOF AND PERSUASION FOR DAMAGE TO BAILED GOODS

The warehouser or common carrier under the UCC has, in most states and by the weight of authorities, both the burden of proof and the burden of persuasion as to any of seven defenses listed in § 7–403(1). Two of these defenses pertain to matters previously discussed in this chapter. These two lawful excuses which the warehouser can use to defend against a failure to deliver to the bailor "entitled to delivery" under the warehouse receipt are (a) "delivery of the goods to a person whose receipt was rightful as against the claimant" and (b) "damage to or delay, loss or destruction of the goods for which the bailee is not liable." The second defense will be discussed first.

Under UCC § 7–403(1), the bailee is not strictly liable (as he would have been at common law) for the bailed chattels.[3] Strict liability is not the rule in UCC bailments in part because the bailor's cause of action lies partly in tort and partly in contract law—in either trespass on the case or assumpsit. The plaintiff bailor pleads a relationship with the bailee, but whether his cause of action is premised simply on the relationship itself, on any express or

3. In some instances, the practical difference between holding the warehouser and the common carrier liable for negligence or strictly liable, as at common law, is not that great. This is due both to the propensities of juries and to procedural problems involved in a suit against either a warehouser or a common carrier.

implied contract springing from it, or on the bailee's tortious interference with the bailor's right to a redelivery of the bailed chattel is unclear. Thus courts can have flexibility to decide cases based on the theory of each case. Bailment is (again) a relationship that is a hybrid of tort, contract, and property law. This hybrid nature of a bailment is still important under the Code, because even though many aspects of the law have been codified in the UCC, it does not provide the bailor who cannot recover chattels with a remedy. For that, he must look to the forms of action in conversion, trover, or replevin—all continue to exist independently of the UCC.

Under the UCC, the bailee, whether a common carrier or a warehouser, has a duty to "deliver the goods to a person entitled under the document." UCC § 7–403(1). This is the person who pays the bailee's shipping or storage charges, and surrenders the bill of lading or warehouse receipt for cancellation. UCC § 7–403(2) and (3). It is also the document's holder if it is negotiable, or the person to whom delivery is to be made under its terms if it is non-negotiable. This permits the document to control the bailee's liability for misdelivery, so long as the bailee acts in good faith, i.e., behaves honestly in fact. UCC § 7–404. The adept forgery of a warehouse receipt or bill of lading will not place the risk of a misdelivery on the bailee.

Under the UCC § 7–403(1)(b),

The bailee must deliver the goods to a person entitled under the document . . . unless and to the extent that the bailee establishes any of the following: . . . (b) damage to or delay, loss or destruction of the goods for which the bailee is not liable. . . .

This says it that it is the bailee who has the burden of establishing his non-liability for the bailed goods' loss or damage and that he has the burden of proving that he acted like a reasonable, careful person with regard to the goods. The bailee must, in other words, show himself free of negligence.

An optional clause, which the Code drafters advise can be added just after the last quoted language, underscores this point: " . . . the burden of establishing negligence in such cases is on the person entitled under the document." The "burden of establishing" negligence is in § 1–201(8) defined as "the burden of persuading the triers of fact that the existence of the fact is more probable than its non-existence." This phrase is the Code's term for what the law of evidence calls the burden of persuasion, to distinguish it from the burden of proof.

The burden of proof usually refers to the necessity of adducing evidence to avoid an adverse ruling or judgment, and generally this burden is satisfied if a trier of fact could draw an inference from the fact or facts presented that (say) the bailee was not negligent. By presenting this evidence, the bailee avoids an adverse judgment at an early stage of the litigation. The inference drawn is not the only one possible and, indeed, the trier of fact need not draw it.

Later, after the bailee has produced evidence that a trier of fact could use to infer his non-negligence or due care, what if no more evidence is presented by either bailee or bailor? Four outcomes are possible. First, the case could be decided at that point. However, no jurisdiction does this. Second, the judge could rule that the burden now shifts back to the bailor to present conflicting evidence of at least equal weight. This outcome is illogical. Wouldn't you think it illogical to assign the same burden of proof twice? Third, the judge could rule that the burden never shifts—and that the bailee has to present facts from which the trier of fact could infer due care, as well as facts from which the trier of fact could not help but infer due care. Finally, and fourth, the judge could rule that the burden shifts back to the bailor, who then has the burden of adducing not only evidence of equal weight, but also of adducing facts from which no other inference but the lack of due care is reasonable. In the third and fourth options, the judge has assigned the bailee and bailor respectively the so-called burden of persuasion—of coming forward with facts from which the trier of fact not only could infer but also could not help but infer, the controverted proposition. Allocating this burden carries with it an allocation of the risk of non-persuasion.

The fourth alternative—assigning the burden of persuasion to the bailor—is what the optional language of § 7–403(1)(b) proposes. Unless this optional language is used, the majority of jurisdictions have concluded that the third alternative is preferable and the burden of proof is on the bailee to adduce a fact or facts from which non-liability can be inferred. This burden thereafter never shifts, and encompasses both the burden of proof (in the sense of presenting facts from which non-liability could be inferred) and the burden of persuasion (presenting facts from which no other or only one inference could be drawn); both are assigned to the bailee. Some courts have also held that the allocation of this burden applies in both negligence and contract causes of action.

The negative phrasing of UCC § 7–403(1)(b) reenforces the majority of jurisdictions in their conclusion: the "damage ... or loss ... for which the bailee is not liable" indicates that the drafters intended to incorporate the common law of torts pertaining to the bailment controversies. They did not state what liability is because the standards for finding it vary from state to state, and not wanting to change state law, they put the bailee's burden in the negative. Since §§ (1)(b) speaks of a bailee's defense, the fourth alternative is not open to a court deciding a UCC § 7–403(1)(b) case, and the third becomes the better view.

Thus an action for loss or damage of bailed goods is premised on an undertaking to deliver the goods up out of the bailment upon its fulfillment or upon demand. The UCC recognizes this undertaking ("the bailee must deliver the goods ..."). A showing by the bailor that 1) the goods were delivered to a bailee in good condition, and 2) that upon demand, the bailee could not deliver, or delivered the goods in a damaged condition, is sufficient to throw the burdens of proof and persuasion on the bailee.

This procedural discussion has a substantive result. If the bailor shows that goods were delivered to the bailee and either not delivered back or delivered in a defective condition, this leaves a factual vacuum between these two events. The bailee must fill this void. The Code's requiring him to show non-liability amounts to a presumption that whatever happened to the goods in between these two events was caused by the bailee's negligence. This presumption authorizes factual omissions from the bailor's compliant. Out of § 7–403(1)(b)'s assignment of the burden of proof, then, comes a presumption that the bailee was negligent until he proves otherwise. The earlier a presumption can be applied in judicial proceedings, the more powerful it is, because a presumption allows a court to single out a particular fact or set of facts and draw a legal conclusion from it alone. When a bailor shows a bailment and non-delivery or loss, he has made a *prima facie* showing that he is entitled to recover in replevin or trover against the bailee. This result follows pre-Code cases, the Code itself, and most cases decided under it.

Afterwards, when a bailee then comes forward with facts that show that he has no record of a delivery of them, or shows that their loss or damage was due to a fire of unknown origin, has he made a *prima facie* case for his own non-liability? No, because, as we have seen, even though a presumption of either negligence or non-negligence might now be permissible, UCC § 7–403(1)(b) requires more. The failure to produce any record of their delivery or a failure to find an origin of the fire causing the loss or damage all have this in common: in each instance, the bailee has shown no more than "loss" or "damage." However, § 7–403(1)(b) requires a showing of non-liability. The warehouser's ignorance is not an excuse and itself suggests fault. A bailee has to "establish" his non-liability. "Establish" is the same verb used to define the burden of persuasion. The type of legal presumption involved here is one that skips from the bailor's *prima facie* case to a finding of lack of due care on the part of the bailee. If this telescoping of the legal analysis of the case were to be put into a substantive rule of law, the rule would be, "non-delivery or delivery in a defective condition is *prima facie* evidence of a bailee's lack of due care." This is a mandatory presumption unless the bailee rebuts it with further proof.

1. Theft From a Warehouse

A bailee, including a warehouser, is excused from his duty to deliver when § 7–403(1)(b) applies, but that section covers "damage to or delay, loss or destruction" and does not expressly cover theft. Of course "loss" may include loss by theft. If theft is included within this term the warehouser will be liable if the theft is caused by the warehouser's lack of due care, and the warehouser must plead and prove his due care, carrying both the burden of proof and the burden of persuasion. If the thief is in the employ of the warehouser, the negligence of the warehouse may include a failure to screen or supervise the thieving employee. However, the common law rule was that the warehouser is not liable for the employee's theft because it was beyond the scope of his employment and so was (obviously) unauthorized by the warehouser.

In this instance, this last common rule is probably overruled by the UCC and "loss" should include loss by an employee's theft. First, consider that if the employee were negligent and as a result a stranger stole goods from the warehouse, the warehouser would at least have the burden of showing his due care in supervising the employee entrusted with the chattel and would probably be liable because the negligence of the employee would be imputed to his employer. If an employee's negligence is within the scope of his employment, why should not the more heinous act of stealing be within the scope of the employment as well? Second, the common law rule thwarts the rule of § 7–204(2) of permitting only reasonable limitations on liability by allowing the warehouser to escape theft liability altogether. Third, the common law rule runs counter to the general rule of due care imposed on the warehouser in § 7–204(1). Finally, consider a textual argument: the defenses listed in § 7–403 are an illustrative, non-exclusive list of excuses for a warehouser's failing to deliver; reading "loss" broadly implements the policy of construing the section liberally. See Murray, *The Ware-houseman's and Carrier's Liability for Theft by Their Employees in England and the United States*, 39 U.Pitt.L.Rev. 707 (1978).

C. MISDELIVERY

UCC § 7–403(1) provides that a bailee, including a warehouser, must deliver the bailed chattels to the person entitled under the document. His is a strict liability for a misdelivery unless he can establish one of the defenses outlined in sub-sections (a) through (g) of § 7–403(1).

The first defense, listed in § 7–403(1)(a), is that "the delivery of the goods to a person whose receipt was rightful as against the claimant." Under this language, the warehouser who delivers goods to the true owner after their deposit by a thief incurs no liability. Similarly, delivery to a person with a claim of prior possession, never abandoned, would be excused. Thus the Code restricts the rule that "the bailor's right to a delivery is good against all the world, except those with a better right."

Suppose, however, that the true owner is not the first to claim the goods. In any later action by the true owner, the warehouser must show, according to § 7–404, that he made any prior delivery of the chattel "according to the terms of the document" and also that he acted in good faith and according to reasonable commercial standards. A bailee who has delivered chattel to a prior possessor, whose "claim was rightful" as to the bailor, would when sued by the true owner, lose his excuse for a failure to deliver under § 7–403(1)(a). The same result would obtain even if the prior possessor had obtained a court order, although compliance with that order is strong evidence of the bailee's good faith and adherence to reasonable commercial standards. See UCC § 7–404, discussed *infra*.

Two reasons support these results. Certainly the warehouser has a remedy in a replevin or trover action against the person to whom he misdelivers, except in the instance of a good faith purchase of a voidable title. So he has some remedy available to him. And in the second situation in the last paragraph, were he not to comply with the court order, his good faith and adherence to reasonable commercial standards would be doubtful, particularly when he knows of and seeks to judge conflicting claims.

Under the Code, then, the warehouser acts at his peril if he does not ascertain that the claimant of the goods is entitled under the document. This should be ascertained even when the warehouser does not know of the existence of any competing claims.

D. LIMITATIONS ON WAREHOUSER LIABILITY

UCC § 7–204(2) provides for a limitation of damages in situations in which the warehouser is liable. It does not authorize this type of bailee to immunize himself from, or contract out of, liability for his own negligence; and indeed, under UCC § 7–202(3), any attempt to contract away his liability for negligence is ineffective. Instead, it permits him to set forth a specific liability per article or item, or value per unit of weight, beyond which he shall not be liable. *Griffin v. Nationwide Moving and Storage Company, Inc.* (1982).

The warehouser cannot limit his liability on a warehouse receipt as a whole. He cannot stipulate that he is liable only up to a certain amount on any one deposit receipted by him. *Gonzalez v. A–1 Self Storage, Inc.* (2000). What he can stipulate is that his liability on (say) a deposit of 5000 pounds of fish is limited to 50 cents a pound. The bailor of fungible chattels can thus easily calculate the financial risks involved in the bailment. The bailor of non-fungible chattels is by the same token encouraged to itemize his chattels carefully for the warehouse receipt in order to minimize the impact of the bailee's limitation on his liability. If any items of special or unique value are itemized separately, this type of limitation of liability will avoid the common law's problems with bailments of closed receptacles discussed previously.

The limitation's effectiveness is subject to three qualifications. The first one sets up a procedure by which the bailor may increase the bailee's liability by a written request to him. This request must be made within a reasonable time of the bailee's delivery of the warehouse receipt to the bailor. The bailee can charge increased rates for storage based on the bailor's increased valuation of the bailed goods, but a further ceiling on both valuations and charges may be imposed by a lawful limitation of liability contained in the warehouser's tariff, the schedule of charges imposed by governmental regulations. If within the tariff, the bailor's timely request is binding on the warehouser.

The purpose of authorizing such requests for an increased valuation is to prevent the bailee from imposing a valuation below that requested by the bailor, so long as the increase keeps the valuation within any limits imposed by the warehouser's tariff. Such requests are probably limited to instances in which the warehouser is under a duty, enforced by governmental regulation, to accept the offered bailment.

Other governmental regulations may also have an effect on the validity of a limitation on liability. When a warehouse is not fireproof and governmental regulations call for fireproofing, a tariff limitation on fire losses may be invalid, having been authorized only for warehousers who conform to the regulations. Indeed, where such regulations are proven to embody the standards of "reasonable care under the circumstances," any limitation on liability authorized under UCC § 7–204(2) may arguably be invalid as well.

The second qualification on the warehouser's ability to limit his liability is stated in the last sentence of § 7–204(2): "no such limitation is effective with respect to the warehouseman's liability for conversion to his own use." This is a restatement of pre-Code case law and emphasizes the fact that these sections of the Code define the warehouser's duties without providing specific remedies or affecting pre-existing forms of action. Because a common law conversion is a convertor's exercise of dominion over the chattel, the phrase "to his own use" is superfluous and, if so, any misdelivery of bailed goods would lift the limitation on the warehouser's liability; he would then be strictly liable for his misdelivery. The common law rationale was that misdelivery was an inherent risk of any bailment. The need for the common law rule must be weighed against the canon of statutory interpretation that presumes against the superfluity of a word or a phrase.

A third qualification is the most sweeping. It is contained in UCC § 7–404 which provides:

A bailee who in good faith including observance of reasonable commercial standards has received goods and delivered or otherwise disposed of them according to the terms of the document of title . . . is not liable therefor.

This section applies to both warehousers and common carriers. The bailee who stores or transports chattel when he has knowledge that there is a serious question about the property rights of the person bailing the article with him is liable for its conversion but not otherwise.

E. A FINAL WORD ON INNKEEPERS

At common law, inn-keepers had strict liability for the chattels of their guests; they were an insurer against loss, theft, or damage to these chattels while on their premises. Today that rule of strict liability is eroded by many state statutes which limit the liability of inn-keepers to maximum dollar amounts and require that a guest notify the inn-keeper of the presence on the premises of chattels which might produce liability over the dollar limit; some statutes also require that when the guest notifies the inn-keeper of this extra liability, the guest must deposit the extraordinarily valuable chattel with the inn-keeper for safekeeping in order to make a claim for its later loss.

Such statutes limiting an inn-keepers liability are enacted in all fifty states and the District of Columbia. Besides statutory provisions of the type just described, some states expressly permit an innkeeper to limit its liability regardless of its negligence. *Associated Mills, Inc. v. Drake Hotel, Inc.* (1975). And regardless of its receipt for safekeeping of chattel worth more than the maximum dollar amount. *Nicholaides v. University Hotel Associates* (1990). In contrast, other state statutes establish a maximum dollar amount, but further provide that this maximum is inapplicable when the guest proves that the inn-keeper was negligent. In the latter states, then, having proven negligence, the guest can recover the fair market value of the lost chattel or all damages to it. *Shamrock Hilton Hotel v. Caranas* (1972) (holding hotel liable for purse and jewels contained in it).

A final type of inn-keepers' statute is silent on the relationship between the stated maximum amount of liability and the law of negligence. Such a silence is taken by the courts to mean that the issue is left to them to decide, and as might be expected, courts have both enforced the limitation in the face of an inn-keeper's negligence, and refused to do so.

Another common provision is to the effect that notices informing guests of the dollar limitation and other provisions of the applicable statute be conspicuously posted. *Terry v. Lincscott Hotel Corp.* (1980) [Sandra Day O'Connor, J. (now Justice O'Connor)]. This conspicuous posting is typically done on the back of the door to every guest room. *Skyways Motor Lodge Corp. v. General Foods Corp.* (1979). Often legally effective in this position, this location for the posting has also probably acquired the status of a custom or usage of the hotel industry, giving the location extra effectiveness. Care must be taken by the inn-keeper writing this notice to inform the guest of the procedures offered for the safe-keeping of chattels of extraordinary value.

CHAPTER VI

SALES AND GOOD FAITH PURCHASERS

A sale of personal property is defined as transfer for money or other legal consideration. It is completed by a delivery, accompanied typically by the delivery of a deed transferring the title to, or a bill of sale for, the chattel. The deed or bill of sale states the purchase price and the terms of the sale.

With regard to a sale of personal property, as against everyone but the vendor, the delivery of possession of the chattel is necessary for the completion of the transaction and the transfer of their title or ownership. Thus when O sells the same goods to A and then to B in equally valid transactions, the first to take possession of them prevails against the other. *Lanfear v. Sumner* (1821). This rule was necessary because the law could not conceive of title and possession being separated when the title was in dispute. A corollary rule (taken from the phrase, "as against everyone but the vendor") was that, as between O and A or B, delivery was unnecessary to the transfer of title to the purchaser: as between those parties, the contract of sale controlled. *Slayton v. Davis* (1926).

How might O come to sell something twice, you ask? The answer is that O might retain possession after his sale to A. Today, a sale "consists in the passing of title" from the vendor to the purchaser "for a price." Uniform Commercial Code § 2–106(1) (hereafter UCC). In a sale the "obligation of the seller is to transfer and deliver and that of buyer is to accept and pay in accordance with the contract"—UCC § 2–301—and (if applicable) the Code. Today, if O did retain possession the outcome of litigation between A and B would not depend on the transfer of possession and title. If O were a merchant, B could retain the goods against A if B was a good faith purchaser of them. UCC § 2–403. If O was not a merchant, then UCC § 2–401 would require that B prove O had ostensible authority to sell them. The modern focus has shifted from an examination of the vendor's title to the status of the purchaser—and explaining this shift is the subject of this chapter.

This shift has occurred not only because of a need to sort out disputes between persons like A and B, but also because vendors such as O might have claims made and judgments docketed against their goods, and that brings on disputes between those claimants or creditors and persons like A or B. The purchaser of a chattel who gives a valuable consideration (1) paid in the belief that the vendor had a right to sell and (2) parted with in circumstances which would not make him inquire into the vendor's title and right to sell, is said to be a good faith or bona fide purchaser. In short, such a person is an "innocent purchaser for value."

The initial common law position was not favorable to the good faith purchaser, but the latter has increasingly sought and won the law's protection, not because his innocence was to be rewarded, but because he served a commercial function that was growing in importance. He represented the needs of increasingly regional and national markets for sales made without an elaborate investigation of the chattel's title and made in reliance on the putative vendor's possession of the goods.

I. THE PROBLEM

The rise in the legal fortunes of the good faith purchaser has been rapid over the last century. He is part of a legal triad including a chattel's true owner, a rogue, and himself. In skeletal form, the facts producing the litigation in which he has had to engage can be reduced to the following: the rogue acquires a chattel from the true owner and transfers it to a good faith purchaser. The rogue either is judgment-proof or disappears. Later the true owner discovers that the good faith purchaser has the goods and seeks to replevy them or recover their value in trover from the purchaser.

With the rogue gone, a legal problem of some difficulty remains: which of the two innocent parties left is going to suffer the loss occasioned by the rogue's crookedness?

Other names for a bona fide purchaser are "the law student's 'sad sack'" and a "bona fide dummy." Although this may sometimes be the case, the problem, in its pure form, requires more analysis than any such *ad hominem* provides. If it is impractical to expect a vendor to inquire into the honesty of the purchasers with whom he deals, is it any more impractical than expecting a good faith purchaser to investigate the title of a vendor? Investigating honesty is an inquiry everyone can undertake, but an investigation of title is a more specialized undertaking. If these tasks are conceded to be of equal difficulty, the law may be correct in choosing to favor the party representing the societal interests of trade and commerce; individual equities being relatively equal, a judge is free to choose an expedient solution. Finally, where both the true owner and the purchaser have been equally diligent in protecting themselves against theft and acquisition of a defective title, the law will need to resolve conflicts among its doctrines in such a way as to give it the discretion to decide sometimes for the true owner and sometimes for the purchaser as the facts of the case tip the equities in the balance now to one side and then to the other. These conflicts are explained in the ensuing discussion.

The primary justification for protecting a purchaser involves an inquiry into his good faith. With good faith present, the law needs to carve out an exception to the general rule to the effect that, if a true owner does not intend to transfer title to a

chattel to another who nonetheless obtains possession of it, that person acquires no title to it and
cannot pass good title to it to yet another transferee
to whom its later transfer is made. This is called the
"void title rule." If a title was void in the hands of a
transferor, its quality does not improve in the hands
of the next transferee.

The idea that "one can't give what one doesn't
have," in Latin, *nemo dat quod non habet*, underlies
the general rule. It implies the commonly-held notion that along with the transfer of the chattel
comes a transfer of title. Title here is intended to
refer to a basic unit of ownership.

A requirement that possession and title be transferred together is evident in the common law attitude toward the requirement of a delivery in the
law of sales and gifts. Moreover, it made sense in
local markets in which vendors and purchasers of
goods met face to face and transferred the goods in
exchange for cash. Besides, in some situations, it is
impractical to have the title to personalty pass
independent of possession. The rule that no title is
passed by a person without title cannot control in
the case of money, negotiable commercial paper,
promissory notes or bank checks. Even a thief can
pass good title to money or negotiable instruments.
The needs of capital markets and trade overwhelm
the void title rule here.

In England, certain marketplaces on certain days
and all of London's shops every business day were
designated by charter to be "markets overt,"

wherein a good faith purchaser could take good title to chattels to which his vendor had no title. The doctrine of a market overt has never been accepted or applied in the United States. Even in a sheriff's sale of a debtor's property to satisfy a judgment, the doctrine has been rejected. The majority rule is that the successful bidder at such sales acquires no better title than the debtor had going into the sale.

The void title rule is intended to instill an attitude of wariness in purchasers: *caveat emptor*—let the buyer beware. It worked well in local face to face markets, but became increasingly questioned in markets which were broader in scope. Indeed, in regional or national markets, the good faith necessary to protect the purchaser tended to be proven, not by a showing of subjective good faith, but by the fact that the transaction conformed to customary commercial practices. When a purchaser's business practices conform to the norm, the court looks less into his individual good faith.

The void title rule has never been overruled. Courts have instead looked at the type of title transferred and have added a new issue, phrased to protect the good faith purchaser. Under common law (and now under the Uniform Commercial Code § 2–403), judges asked themselves two questions: (1) did the true owner of the chattel intend to transfer it to the rogue?; and (2) if the rogue received a "voidable" title, did the rogue transfer the title to a good faith purchaser in whose hands the voidable title becomes absolute?

These questions are addressed seriatim, in the order previously listed. This order is mandatory. If the true owner did not intend to transfer title to the rogue, then the title which the latter receives is void, and a court never inquires into the status of the purchaser. These two questions will now be discussed in turn.

A. VOID AND VOIDABLE TITLE

To protect a purchaser, then, the law first had to inquire into the concept of title. Its unitary nature had to be made divisible. The unit-splitting method of legal analysis was the concept of the true owner's intent to transfer title to a person who, under the general rule, would not be able to pass on any title.

The judge's motivation in litigation over a chattel between a true owner and a good faith purchaser is easily seen. Both of the litigants are to some degree innocent parties, but the judge may regard this innocence as a relative matter and think one more innocent than the other. First, after all, the owner's innocence can be seen as naive, simple-minded, or artless, and as the cause of the good faith purchaser's troubles.

Second, the judge is caught between conflicting principles of law. On the one hand, he probably believes, along with his common law brethren, that no owner should be deprived of his property without his consent (e.g., by a thief). This belief will be strongest in cases where the chattel concerned are his private possessions—items taken out of the stream of commerce and devoted to his personal use. On the other hand, the judge also probably believes that purchasers need a secure title to the goods they purchase, particularly if the transaction takes place in a commercial setting where the purchaser may want to resell the goods rather than use them himself. As Grant Gilmore has argued, she needs a way of maintaining the void title rule in non-commercial settings while relaxing it in commercial settings where there is substantial deviation from customary commercial practice in the true owner's parting with the goods, but no such deviation in the subsequent purchaser's acquisition of the same goods.

The concept of "voidable title" is an intermediate position for the judge. It allows him to maintain both of his beliefs. It works as described in the next several paragraphs.

The early common law did not distinguish between a transfer of title to and possession of a chattel. However, widespread use of the executory contract changed all that.

Once a transfer of title depends on more than a delivery of a chattel, but instead takes place when the parties to the contract intend it to be transferred, courts are given discretion to distinguish between various types of transactions in which the true owner surrenders possession of the goods. If for example the chattel is stolen from the true owner, he can have no intention to transfer it to the thief, and the void title rule applies even where the thief later sells the chattel to a good faith purchaser. The same is true when the parties make a mutual mistake when contracting with each other. The title in the hands of the transferee is void.

Likewise, a transfer by a bailee confers a void title on the bailee's transferee. Why? Because the bailor did not intend, when the bailment was created, that there be a delivery by the bailee to any person other than himself; this by definition is what a bailment involves, and unless there has been an entrustment (see *infra*, this Chapter), a void title results.

However, when the true owner is induced to part with the goods through some fraud or misrepresentation by the transferee, one can say that the owner did intend to part with title. The true owner intended to transfer the chattel, even though fraud was used to induce that intent. In such situations, the true owner of the chattel can replevy them upon finding out that the original transaction was fraudulent. In this sense the title of the subsequent purchaser is voidable—liable to being revoked by the true owner or an assignee of his rights. However, this ability to void the title ends when the chattel comes into the hands of a good faith purchaser. At that point, the voidable title becomes absolute.

A voidable title is created voluntarily. It can only be created voluntarily. It occurs when an owner voluntarily delivers the possession of a chattel to a purchaser, even though the delivery is procured by fraud or larceny. *Kenyon v. Abel* (2001). The purchaser likewise conforms the transaction to the appearance of a voluntary one; he never pulls a gun on the owner, or obtains delivery by stealth. After the owner makes a voluntary delivery, the owner is properly allocated the risk that the purchaser acted fraudulently, and thus the subsequent good faith purchaser does not run this risk. This allocation of risk not only promotes trade and commerce, but it also allocates the risk to the person best able to bear it by care and investigation.

Thus there are two types of title which can be passed on to subsequent purchasers—void and voidable. Which type of title was transferred is a matter of ascertaining the intent of the transferor. The vocabulary of common law estates can assist in this classification. Where there is no title to give, the courts can regard the transfer document as neither a contract for, nor a conveyance of, the chattel. It is void *ab initio*. When the title is voidable, the title might be regarded as having been conveyed subject to a condition subsequent; here the transferee acquires an absolute title, subject to the right of the true owner to rescind the transfer, demand the chattel back, and replevy it while it remains in the hands of the fraudulent transferee. From any later transferee's viewpoint, a voidable title gives an innocent purchaser *not* paying value, who has after all performed no known wrong against the owner, an opportunity to return the chattel before being rendered liable for a judgment in conversion. *State of New York v. The Seventh Regiment Fund, Inc.* (2002).

A voidable title is a defective title, but it is not wholly defective. It is a title that has been transferred by a deed or contract that one party to the document (the true owner or his agent) has the power to rescind. The title is then voidable by the person with the right of rescission, but it is not voidable by the other party. The right to rescind is often called the equity of rescission.

Asking a court to exercise this equity is like asking a court to compel the surrender of some right, title, or advantage by the defendant. Equity will compel such a surrender only when it is unconscionable for the defendant to retain it. If the defendant acquired title with notice of the plaintiff's equity, or if he did not pay value (but was without notice), he will have to surrender it.

Before these rules became incorporated into the substantive law of personal property, all this was a matter of equity pleading. This highlights an interesting feature of a voidable title. It has a procedural origin. Defining any substantive concept in terms of its procedural origins is to leave a good deal of imprecision in the concept. Grant Gilmore has called a voidable title the courts' "happiest discovery" and "a vague idea, never defined and perhaps incapable of definition." Grant Gilmore, *The Commercial Doctrine of Good Faith Purchase*, 63 Yale L.J. 1057, 1059 (1954). Its greatest virtue was its capacity for growth.

B. THE GOOD FAITH PURCHASER

When a court reaches the question of whether a transferee qualifies as a good faith purchaser the answer depends on whether (1) he gave a fair or reasonable value for a chattel, (2) in an honestly held belief that he was (3) acquiring its title, or whatever legal rights he bargained for, and (4) under circumstances which would not lead him to question his vendor's title or right. Thus he must, (1) for value and (2) in good faith, (3) purchase property (4) without notice. Therefore a donee would not qualify.

A good faith purchaser must advance some new consideration, surrender some security, or do some act which will cause him to be in a worse position if the transfer is rescinded. All these things must be done in advance of any notice to him of the true owner's adverse claim. Likewise, a person who acquires a chattel with either actual or constructive notice that his vendor used any fraud or deceit to acquire possession of it, does not qualify. Thus someone in collusion with a rogue can never become a good faith purchaser.

Many aspects of the definition of a good faith purchaser are today found in cases controlled by the provisions of the Uniform Commercial Code. See *infra*, this Chapter, for a discussion of the UCC.

C.   INSURABLE INTERESTS
IN STOLEN CHATTEL

In disputes involving the true owner, a rogue, and a purchaser, the issue as between the true owner and the purchaser is one of priority of title. When either of these parties loses, they can still pursue the rogue for fraud. In addition, the purchaser will in some situations, as with (say) the purchase of a stolen automobile, have insured the chattel, and there is no reason to deny that he has an insurable interest in the vehicle even though it turns out he has no title to it. The insurance policy will be governed by contract law rather than the law of personal property. Even if the law of personal property is held to control the determination of whether the insured held an "insurable interest," the void title rule can, for stolen goods, be restated to the purchaser's advantage using the relativity of title doctrine; that is, a good faith purchaser of a stolen chattel had a right to that chattel good against everyone save the true owner.

One reason the insurance company might be interested in the state of the title to the insured object is that the insurer, having paid the claim made under the policy, will want to pursue its insured's right to replevy or sue for damages for the theft. In the case of a theft, however, this right (of subrogation) will often be a hollow one because the rogue will many times have disappeared. If the true owner rather than the purchaser had taken out the insurance policy, the insurer's subrogation right would not be any the less hollow.

Moreover, the doctrine of relativity of title means that there is some right in the purchaser to be subrogated to the insurer. It is not the absolute or "sole and unconditional" (the phrase is from many insurance contracts) interest in the chattel insured. However, if only such interests could be insured, the insurer could ignore many claims in which the insured's right of possession gave rise to his expectation of an interest in the insured personal property. To protect this expectation, the sole and unconditional ownership clause in the insurance policy functions only as a warranty of an insured's good faith belief that the title is in the insured. It has not been interpreted as a warranty of facts of which the insured has no knowledge, such as the fact that the chattel was stolen.

Could not the finder of a jewel insure his interest in it? If the courts will allow the chimney sweep in the *Armory* case to recover in an action of trover, it does not make a lot of sense to say that he cannot at the same time have an insurable interest in the jewel. If a watch is left for repair, cannot the bailee repairman insure against its being stolen? Insurance companies will lose a lot of business if an insurer can require an absolute title of its insureds.

Another reason that the insurer wants to be subrogated to the rights of its insured is that it does not want to have to engage any insured who wants thereafter to recover twice, in a race to find the rogue and sue him. The settlement of the claim between the insurer and insured is in effect the insured's foreswearing any further legal action against the rogue; in the manner of a forced sale in trover, any rights he has are transferred to the insurer. So the purpose of the sole and unconditional ownership clause is fulfilled when the insured settles his claim.

There is authority to the effect that a purchaser of a stolen automobile (the main litigation-breeder on this question) does not have an insurable interest in it. *Hessen v. Iowa Automobile Mutual Insurance Co.* (1922). Recent authorities, however, hold that the purchaser of a stolen automobile has an insurable interest in it, although there continues to be a split in the cases in this area. Dispositive for some courts deciding that there is no insurable interest is the fact that state statutes requiring the public registration of title to automobiles provide also that a transfer of title be accomplished by a transfer of the certificate of title to the vehicle and that transfers not so accomplished are void. Where certificates of title are routinely used, the purchaser who does not require one from his transferor is less deserving of protection, but unless the purchaser did not take in good faith, knew of the true owner's identity or had the means to find it out, the doctrine of relativity of title should be enough to give the good faith purchaser an insurable interest in the chattel.

D. EXTINGUISHING THE TRUE OWNER'S TITLE IN FAVOR OF A GOOD FAITH PURCHASER

If a legislature is going to cut off the right and title of a true owner in favor of a good faith purchaser, it must do so clearly. For example, if statutes on sheriffs sales for payment and satisfaction of a debt are intended to cut off the true owner's rights, they must clearly state that this is their effect. Most state statutes do not so state and so their effect is to provide that the purchaser at the sheriffs sale acquires no more title than the debtor had going into the sale. *Griffith v. Fowler* (1846).

In the field of international law, if a foreign government, in a declaration of war or expropriation, cuts off a true owner's rights, such an action normally would be recognized by our courts or would place the owner's rights beyond their jurisdiction. Thereafter, Congress must be clear that it intends to reverse this action in our courts; otherwise any Congressional resolution condemning the action will not reinstate the jurisdiction of our courts. *Williams v. Armroyd* (1813).

The first clear legislative reversal of the void title rule in the United States came with the so-called Factors Acts. A factor is an agent employed to sell goods consigned to him in his own name for a commission. Never uniform among the states, the Acts were nonetheless similar in approach. They shifted the loss caused by the fraudulent factor from the good faith purchaser to the true owner who, after all, selected the broker, transferred the goods to him, and enabled him to accomplish the fraud.

Later legislation, first the Uniform Sales Act, § 25, and now in all states except Louisiana, the Uniform Commercial Code, codified both the void title rule and the void/voidable distinction. The UCC also added one further qualification to the void title rule—the so-called entrustment doctrine. Because of the near omnipresence of the UCC, some extended discussion of its relevant provisions is in order.

II. THE UNIFORM COMMERCIAL CODE (UCC)

The UCC has now codified the general rule and the doctrine of good faith purchaser of personalty in its § 2–403(1), using the following language, first to restate the void title rule:

A purchaser of goods acquires all title which his transferor had or has power to transfer except that a purchaser of a limited interest acquires rights only to the extent of the interest purchased.

Under this language, a transferor with a void title confers nothing on his transferee. However, once a transferor has acquired title through this section (or by later portions of § 2–403 as well), his subsequent transferees take his rights under the Code.

This is the "shelter" principle of this section. (It is also found in later portions of § 2–403.) A second aspect of this general rule is found in the language "or had power to transfer." This means that the law of agency, apparent agency, and estoppel applies to implement the general rule to the effect that "what title the vendor appears to have, the purchaser gets." The pre-UCC common law was moving in this direction. See e.g., *O'Connor's Administratrix v. Clark* (1895) (replevin of a horse-drawn wagon).

This section then goes on to state the exception to the general rule:

> ... A person with voidable title has power to *transfer* a good title to a *good faith* purchaser for *value*. When goods have been delivered under a *transaction of purchase* the purchaser has such power even though
>
> (a) the transferor was deceived as to the identity of the purchaser, or
>
> (b) the delivery was in exchange for a check which is later dishonored, or
>
> (c) it was agreed that the transaction was to be a "cash sale," or
>
> (d) the delivery was procured through fraud punishable as larcenous under the criminal law.

The italicized words are discussed below.

The second sentence provides in (a) through (d) some examples of situations that have often been litigated. Under these subparagraphs, a true owner's transferring of a chattel to a rogue in an "all cash" sale, in exchange for a check that bounces or in circumstances punishable as a violation of the criminal code—a forged check—does not deny a subsequent purchaser the status of a good faith purchaser.

A. TRANSFER

The drafters of the Code do not use the word "delivery." Therefore, a question arises as to whether or not a person must first take delivery of the chattel before claiming to be a good faith purchaser of it. The examples which follow in subparagraphs (a) through (d) make plain that delivery will usually be present, but paying value for a document of title is sufficient to "transfer a good title" too. Examples of a document of title are a deed, a warehouse receipt, or a bill of lading which a purchaser can thereafter present to a bailee.

The expanded phrase "transfer a good title" suggests that a good faith purchaser acquires title. After all, that was what the true owner is about to lose. For example, a person who is only a party to an executory contract for a chattel cannot become a good faith purchaser. Such a purchaser's title is equitable, not legal, and so must yield to the equity of the owner. A good faith purchaser must hold the legal right or title to the chattel in dispute before asserting good faith purchaser status. Similarly, a licensee or lessee may not become a good faith purchaser. The underlying rationale here is that the contract purchaser, the licensee, and the lessee of a chattel have rights and remedies in the contract, license, or lease that should suffice.

B. GOOD FAITH

The common law and the Code protect only subsequent purchasers whose transferor has a voidable title to a chattel and who take title in good faith. A transaction is undertaken in good faith when it is in fact done honestly, whether or not the transaction is performed negligently.

When the transferee is a merchant, however, a higher standard applies. A merchant must observe reasonable commercial practices for the same or similar transactions. If reasonable commercial practice demanded more care than the merchant observed, he will be denied good faith purchaser status by the courts. For example, when a person purchases a car with a rubber check and resells it to a dealer in another city, that second dealer should require a title certificate or other customary proof of title to the vehicle, and failing to do so will deny that dealer good faith purchaser status. Similarly, a transaction between two dealers is judged by higher standards than would prevail in a sale by a dealer to a consumer; unless required by statute, no certificate of title would be required when a consumer claims good faith purchaser status. Moreover, as we shall see in the next section, that a purchaser is offered a chattel at well below its fair market value is not enough to put him on notice that his transferor's title is defective or impose on him any duty to inquire into the state of its title. Again, however, more leeway in this regard may be given the non-commercial purchaser than is given his commercial counterpart.

In particular markets for personal property, new registries for lost or stolen goods will render easier a purchaser's investigation of a vendor's title. Checking trade association registries for art works are well along to becoming customary practice for interested purchasers, so that in the future not checking such a registry will deny a purchaser good faith status.

C. VALUE

A purchaser for value need not have a suitcase full of cash to exchange for a chattel. To use the example in the last paragraph again, when the thief who buys a car with a rubber check resells it for one half of its fair market value, a purchasing dealer may be denied the protection of § 2–403(1) because he has not given value. A non-dealer purchaser can, however, pay far less than the fair market value and not be denied the status of a protected good faith purchaser. The reason for this is that courts are reluctant to undo a bargain struck by agreement. Inadequacy of price alone will not deny a person a protected status, unless the price is so inadequate as to "shock the conscience of the court." Moreover, not only can a contract price be paid in installments, but the contract itself can be given in consideration of a preexisting debt of the transferor. Generally under the Code value is any consideration sufficient to support a simple, executory contract or a purchaser's pre-existing claim— that is, any contractual consideration, present or past, is sufficient to support the claim that a purchaser paid "value" under the Code. See § 1–201(44) (b), (d). Donees are excluded from protection by the phrase.

D.   TRANSACTION OF PURCHASE

This phrase is broader than any fraudulent action enumerated in the subparagraphs which follow it. So it includes any transaction which results in the purchaser therein obtaining a voidable title. Courts have applied a functional analysis to this phrase: if the transaction, no matter that it is denominated a lease, is in reality a conditional sales agreement, the courts will treat it as a "transaction of purchase." They will look to the substance of the transaction rather than to its form.

E.   ENTRUSTING CHATTEL

If you leave your watch for repair, should you look around the jeweler's shop to find out if he also sells watches, particularly second-hand ones? The answer today is yes, but at common law, you need not have been so careful. At common law, leaving the watch created a bailment. The true owner intended to pass no title to it to the repairman but instead only wanted to give him its possession for the (limited) purpose of fixing it. If the bailee resells it, his title being void, he transfers nothing to a purchaser, even one with good faith. *Baehr v. Clark* (1891).

Indeed, the purchaser in many jurisdictions committed a conversion of the watch by the very act of purchasing it as his own. Some jurisdictions mitigate the harshness of this doctrine by requiring that the conversion is complete only when the true owner makes a demand for the watch's return and the demand is refused, but this only delays the liability of the purchaser for the conversion.

Today the true owner's cause of action for the bailee's conversion of the watch survives; the UCC does not affect it. What the UCC does affect is the true owner's action against the purchaser of the watch—no such action survives the passage of the UCC. Why? Because even though purchasers from bailees are denied the protection of § 2–403(1), § 2–403(2) creates an additional class of purchasers entitled to special protection. This class consists of those who buy "in the ordinary course of business" from one to whom a chattel has been entrusted. In the somewhat cryptic language of the UCC,

> Any entrusting of possession of goods to a merchant who deals in goods of that kind gives him power to transfer all rights of the entruster to a buyer in ordinary course of business.

The next sub-paragraph (3) of this section defines entrusting as including "any delivery and any acquiescence in retention of possession," regardless of any condition placed on the transfer between the parties and no matter that the possessor's disposition of the chattel constituted the crime of larceny.

Delivery is a precondition of an entrustment. So delivery of your watch for repair to the jeweler who also sells second-hand watches may be a statutory entrusting, no matter that you only intended a common law bailment. In this sense, an entrustment includes any retention of possession after delivery, regardless of any condition placed on the delivery by the parties to it. Because it is designed to enhance the reliability of commercial sales, the particular purpose of the entrustment is irrelevant so long as it is made to "a merchant who deals in goods of that kind." § 2–402(2). Similarly irrelevant is whether the entrustor was acting in the course of his own business, or just dealing occasionally and for his own purposes: all commercial and quasi-commercial entrustments are treated alike. *DeWeldon, Ltd. v. McKean* (1997). Likewise, the delivery of a chattel on consignment by a wholesaler to a retailer of such chattel means that a purchaser in the ordinary course of business with the retailer will take free of the wholesaler's rights, even if the wholesaler and retailer agreed that the former would retain title to them. Finally, the entrusting is sufficient to entitle a purchaser to Code protection: the latter need not take delivery of the chattel; a transfer of title to him is enough to cut off the entrustor's rights.

An entrustor's clothing the possessor with the power to transfer is, insofar as the term "power" is concerned, a repeat of a phrase used in § 2–403(1). It also serves as an incorporation by reference of § 2–403(1) into the terms of § 2–403(2) and (3). The principle involved in the phrase is one of estoppel. The entrustor is estopped to deny the possessor's transfer because he set up the situation in which the buyer in the ordinary course of business relied on the title of the possessor.

The facts of a famous pre-Code case are illustrative. In *Zendman v. Harry Winston, Inc.* (1953), the plaintiff went into an auction house on the Atlantic City, N.J. boardwalk and purchased a diamond ring at auction. The defendant had actually left the ring with the operator of the auction, as he often did, with a memorandum in which the defendant retained title. When the defendant learned of the sale, he demanded the ring back.

In its common law form, estoppel requires proof that the appearances at the auction reasonably induced the purchaser to rely on the title of the auctioneer. Reliance is shown by a subjective belief. The concept of a "buyer in the ordinary course" has the effect of permitting appearances, rather than the state of mind of the purchaser, to control the showing of reliance. It may now be shown by objective facts: if the public could reasonably have expected, from all the circumstances surrounding the auction, that the auctioneer had authority to transfer title to the chattel sold, then the entrustor is estopped.

Common law estoppel is usually a shield, not a sword; it does not give rise to a cause of action, but the positive wording of the Code's entrustment rule indicates that this is no longer true. Thus the true owner of goods who without protest allows another to treat them as his own so that a third person is induced to purchase them in good faith, cannot replevy them from that person, and the latter has an action to quiet title to the chattel that he was induced to purchase.

In deciding the *Zendman* case, the court concluded that Harry Winston had created an implied authority in the auctioneer to deal with the ring as his own. It also cited the fact that Harry Winston had previously and several times approved sales unauthorized by the title-retention memo which Winston left with the auctioneer. This past practice between the entrustor and the possessor will have no significance to the purchaser unless he knew about it; and of course if he knew of this practice, the purchaser could not have acted in good faith at the auction. The past practice does, however, go to show that the goods were entrusted to "a merchant who deals in goods of that kind." To negate this effect, the defendant would have had to make some effort to notify the public at the auction that the ring entrusted to the auctioneer did not belong to the latter.

The *Zendman* case is pre-Code evidence that the common law was coming to accept something like the concept of the "buyer in the ordinary course of business." The "course of business" referred to is the vendor's, so that a buyer purchasing out of a vendor's inventory of like goods and chattels is most likely to achieve this protected purchaser status. The Code, however, makes no reference to a purchase from inventory. (There is discussion of such purchases in the commentary to § 2–403.) However, although the vendor to the protected purchaser need not necessarily have an inventory of goods similar to those sold, vendors who normally do not own the chattels in their possession will have a hard time sheltering their purchasers under the Code's aegis. Brokers in commodities or other types of personalty are examples. They themselves, when acquiring possession, are not "buyers in the ordinary course," although they may be purchasers with a voidable title under § 2–403(1). Neither will a purchaser acquiring the chattel from them be a buyer in the ordinary course. However, in the instance of the pawnbroker, a purchaser might reasonably expect that the period of pawn has expired before he purchased and so he become a protected purchaser of a frequently pawned item of personal property.

Finally, any rights acquired by a "buyer in the ordinary course" are incorporated into the general rule of § 2–403(1) and provide shelter for his subsequent transferees.

The entrustment sections of the UCC favor and expand the role of some purchasers and commerce at the expense of true owners, so remember that the entrustment doctrine does not exclude the possibility of a larcenous merchant conveying a voidable title to a purchaser. Grant Gilmore, *The Good Faith Purchase Idea and the Uniform Commercial Code: Confessions of a Repentant Draftsman*, 15 Ga.L.Rev. 605, 618–619 (1981). The voidable title/good faith purchaser rule and the entrustment doctrine are exceptions to the void title rule and continuing rights of true owners. Although the choice between two equally innocent parties is seldom tension-free, the true owner deserves protection when these exceptions do not apply.

F. RESALE BY A VENDOR IN POSSESSION

The Code treats the vendor-in-possession as a sub-category of entrustment. § 2–403(3). In the instance where a purchaser out of a merchant's inventory leaves a chattel in his vendor's possession and the latter resells it to a good faith purchaser, the UCC provides that the vendor's possession was an "acquiescence in retention" under § 2–403(2) and thus an entrusting of the chattel to a "merchant who deals in goods of that kind."

If, in the situation in the last paragraph, the vendor was not a merchant, the second purchaser must fall back on an argument from § 2–403(1) that the vendor's title was voidable in his hands and absolute in the second purchaser's. Even though no merchant is involved, there is still an "acquiescence in retention" and so a partial fulfillment of the policies underlying § 2–403(2) would dictate judgment for the second purchaser. Since,

however, the drafters do not tell us how crucial it is
that a merchant be involved, the outcome of this
litigation is hard to predict. If the underlying rationale is the encouragement of trade and commerce,
via lay-away plans, the first purchaser may win. If
the rationale is the encouragement of negotiability
of goods, then the second bids fair to win.

III. THE IDENTITY OF THE FRAUDULENT PURCHASER

Whether a transferor, either the true owner or a
subsequent possessor, has been deceived as to the
identity of a purchaser, is normally a question of
proof. This issue has also led some courts to engage
in some very subtle and maybe not so sensible
distinctions between various types of fraud. It arose
in pre-Code cases and continues to be a problem
under the UCC.

The distinction between a thief who obtains a
void title and a fraudulent purchaser who obtains a
voidable title has been difficult to maintain. First, if
the fraudulent purchaser tells the true owner of the
chattel that he is the purchasing agent for a corporation that in fact he has nothing to do with and
the owner-vendor intended to transfer the chattel to
the corporation, the transfer did not pass any title
to the purchaser who, in consequence, has a void
title. He could convey nothing to a subsequent good
faith purchaser.

What if, second, the fraudulent purchaser is
named Poore Byer, a pauper, but presents himself

face-to-face to the owner and represents himself to be a person named Rich Byer, a person of wealth? When the owner delivered chattel to Byer, who in turn sold it to a good faith purchaser, Byer here acquired a voidable title: the owner intended to pass title to the person appearing in front of him and that imposter could pass good title to a good faith purchaser. *Phelps v. McQuade* (1917).

Section 2–403(1) provides: "A person with voidable title has power to transfer a good title to a good faith purchaser for value." This language maintains the void/voidable distinction and continues to require that courts draw the line between the two types of title. Such line drawing has produced conflicting results in different states starting from this same statute and has been criticized by several treatise writers. Moreover, the last sentence contained in both the main paragraph and sub-paragraph (a) of § 2–403(1) provides that as to purchased and delivered goods a purchaser with a voidable title can transfer a good title "even though the transferor was deceived as to the identity of the purchaser." This language suggests that the "face-to-face doctrine," in the second hypothetical in the previous paragraph, should at least be extended to impersonations, whether by letter, telephone call, or telegraph. The Code provision is no more than a suggestion, however, since the language of subparagraph (a) requires that the transferor—the true owner or subsequent possessor—be "deceived as to the identity" of the impersonator. "Deceiving" is broader than impersonating and would seem to cover a broader range of frauds. The breadth of the idea of a deception will be tested soon with e-signatures and the many types of identity theft. Ways of authenticating purchasers' identities will change as well.

The focus for judicial analysis of purchaser-identity problems is the intent of the vendor. On this account, it makes no difference to the result in these cases that the convertor at the time of the impersonation had no intent to deceive but rather developed his bad intent when he saw the effects his appearance had. His fraudulent intent at the time of the sale is, however, evidence that the true owner meant to sell to him and parted with a title voidable in him and absolute in a later good faith purchaser.

The UCC language, moreover, suggests again that if there is a tendency in the law, it is to decide for the good faith purchaser. Such a result enhances the negotiability of goods and promotes trade and commerce. Arguments that § 2–403(1) represents this trend are particularly strong when the vendor with an otherwise voidable title is a merchant who regularly deals in goods of the type purchased by the good faith purchaser.

More generally, however, the very notion of a voidable title suggests that the trend in the case law will favor the good faith purchaser. Consider, for instance, what the true owner can do to recover the chattel while title to it is still voidable. He can replevy it from the rogue to whom he transferred it, but it is unlikely that someone so cagey will stay around to receive service of process in this action. If there is a device for doing so, he can notify potential good faith purchasers, but since he is not likely to know the whereabouts of the rogue, he is even less likely to be able to interdict the later sale to the good faith purchaser. To protect the true owner from the transfer which renders the voidable title absolute, a court is going to have to hold that a notice in the legal advertisements of a newspaper was sufficient to deprive the subsequent purchaser of his "good faith" status. Unless there is something routine about giving and searching out such notices, this result is unlikely.

IV. LIENS

If the owner of a watch leaves it for repair, the common law gave the repairman who improves its value a lien for the reasonable value of his services on the chattel or work so improved. The lien holder could not foreclose this lien and sell the watch; he merely has no duty to turn it over to the owner until his charges are paid. In other words, the lien merely suspended his duty. Common carriers and innkeepers, because they had to accept all comers to their carriers and inns, were also possessed of common law liens.

Pre–UCC law recognized several types of security interests in chattels. The simplest was the *pledge*. It is a bailment of a chattel for the purpose of securing payment of its sale price, a debt, or the performance of a duty. The fundamental idea is that the creditor (pledgee) retains possession of the chattel. If the primary purpose of the possession is for security, the possessor has a pledge.

Another security device was the *chattel mortgage.* This did not involve a transfer of the possession of the chattel but was regarded as a transfer of either a lien or title to it. The debtor-transferor transferred the title subject to a defeasance or condition subsequent, giving title back to the debtor when the debt was paid or, in the case of a mortgage lien, terminating the right to foreclose it when the debt was paid. The mortgage was generally given in conjunction with the personal note of the debtor, and both the note and the mortgage had to be recorded in a local public office in the county seat to render the mortgage valid against other creditors and subsequent purchasers. The constructive notice which such a recording gave denied good faith status to a subsequent purchaser or creditor extending funds to the debtor in reliance on the latter's ownership of the chattel.

If the vendor wants to retain title of a chattel being sold because the purchaser of it wants to pay for it in installments, a *conditional sales contract* provides that the title to the chattel will pass to the purchaser when the last installment is paid. Often the installment will include finance charges and the purchase price will be higher than if the sale were for cash. A close kin to this contract is a lease with an option to buy. When the purchaser defaults in the payments, the contract declares a forfeiture in the purchaser's right to possess the chattel. The vendor then repossesses his chattel. However, he cannot always retain all of the payments made under a conditional sales contract. Only so much of the payments which represent either his lost possession, the lost opportunity to resell, or a reasonable rental value of the chattel, can be retained.

All of these pre-UCC security devices and terms have been abolished and subsumed by the scheme embodied in the Code. Article 9 provides that a *debtor* may give a *security agreement* of whatever type in various types of personal property used as *collateral* to secure a loan. When the loan is made, a *security interest* attaches to the collateral and is effective between the debtor and the *secured party*. The latter can perfect the security interest by *filing* a *financing statement* effective against third parties. This security interest is an "interest in personal property which secures payment or performance of an obligation" [§ 1–201(37)] and is established in place of all the pre-Code devices as a single, unitary interest held by the only type of security interest holder recognized in the Code—the secured party. The filing is on the public records, usually maintained at the county level—and soon, under recent amendments to Article 9, filings may be in electronic form, authenticated electronically, and securing "electronic chattel paper." A single notice system for perfecting security interests was established. (Recall that a property system depends on being able to find out simply and cheaply who owns what, whether through possession or other informational devices.) The italicized terms are meticulously defined, in great detail, in the Code.

Article 9 of the UCC applies to all transactions involving personal property that are intended to create a security interest in that property or in personal property which has been attached to real property and become a fixture. For example, although a transaction is labeled a lease and although (again) a lease with an option to purchase the goods at the end of the leasehold does not make the lease a security agreement, a right in the transferee under the lease to exercise the option for a nominal consideration will render Article 9 applicable. Likewise, where a baker stocks a supermarket shelf with his goods under a consignment (i.e., a bailment for sale), the consignment agreement will be subject to Article 9. The bailor's reservation of title alone is sufficient to create a security interest. When Article 9 applies, the security agreement must be filed in order to be perfected.

This filing system operates on a first-in-time, first-in-right rule of priority. Behind it lies the assumption that the secured party is going to check to see (1) that the person in possession of the collateral is its true owner, (2) that no prior filings have been made or, (3) when there are prior filings on the same collateral, that it is in fact valuable enough to satisfy the claims of all filers, including his own. This third check can only be made by an inspection and physical evaluation of the chattel. Thus possession is the ultimate source of information about the validity and value of the security interest. If the secured party finds, from the information that possession and the filing system reveal, that he has adequate collateral to secure his debt, he need not take possession. He thus relies on the filing system to provide him with rights sufficient to secure his claim later on; he need not take possession now, but must file his security interest instead before he can shift the risk of insufficient security to others—that is, to persons who check the records later and find or should find his interest filed there. Not checking the records will sometimes deny him the status of a good faith purchaser: under the recently revised Article 9, good faith not only means honesty in fact, but also "observance of reasonable commercial standards and fair dealing." See UCC, § 9–102(a)(43) (2000). Honesty in defiance of an industry's custom is insufficient good faith.

Thus the secured party who either takes possession of collateral or perfects an interest in it by filing attains priority of title over persons interested in it, but not taking possession nor filing. Conversely, a second lien holder or creditor who does not find the filing of a previous one in the records, knows that he can rely on his taking possession or filing to attain rights superior to the previous one.

The concepts of an Article 9 *security agreement*, *collateral*, and *secured party* are ever expanding and flexible. The recently revised Article 9 has amended them to accommodate the advent of e-commerce and electronic documents and filings. Similar expansion can occur with the Code's recognition of statutory rights. For example, when a purchaser of personal property pays the purchase price and takes possession, but later claims statutory rights to rescind the purchase, he can claim to be a secured party in possession. *Ford Motor Credit Company v. Caiazzo* (1989) (collecting the cases for a counterclaim in the vendor's replevin action).

CHAPTER VII

GIFTS OF PERSONAL PROPERTY

A gift is a gratuitous transfer made voluntarily by one person to another and made without consideration or payment of any type. It is presently effective and does not take effect at some future time. It is not a promise to give a chattel sometime in the future (the law would treat that like an executory contract), and it is not testamentary in character (the law would treat that like a will, requiring that the transfer comply with the state's Statute of Wills).

There are two types of gifts. Gifts *inter vivos* (accomplished between living persons) and gifts *causa mortis* (made by a person contemplating his own impending death). The former are unconditional and irrevocable. The latter are revoked by the donor in fact living through the experience which he previously thought would kill him. Both types of gifts are accomplished by donor's *delivery* of the chattel or a deed to it, made or executed with the *present intent* to complete the gift, and the donee's *acceptance* of the chattel or the deed.

273

I. DELIVERY

Delivery is a transfer of possession, and so is essential to a gift of personal property. The opinion in the case of *Irons v. Smallpiece* (1819), opined that " ... by the law of England, in order to transfer property by gift there must either be a deed or instrument of gift, or there must be an actual delivery of the thing to the donee." In *Irons,* a son claimed that his father made a verbal gift of two colts some twelve months before his death. The possession of the colts stayed with the father until his death; the latter, however, agreeing (the son said) to purchase hay for them at a certain price which the father would advance and the son would ultimately pay. This agreement was not acted on until over five months later—some three to four days after the father's death. The son brought trover against the administrator of the father's estate, and lost. The court held that there was no transfer of possession and so the plaintiff acquired no rights on which to base his action. He was non-suited. Also rejected was the plaintiff's argument that the agreement to furnish hay was a recognition of the son's rights. And even so, said the court, that agreement was never executed, and was not otherwise confirmed, except by facts taking place too long afterward to refer back to an agreement "made so many months before."

The holding in *Irons* was reaffirmed in *Cochrane v. Moore* (1890). There the court declined to follow the lead of intervening cases suggesting that delivery was not an absolute requirement for a gift. (And there were like cases in the United States.) Delivery was not merely evidence of an intent to make the gift. The *Cochrane* opinion provides a long historical inquiry into whether the authorities permitted title and possession to move separately to a donee in a parol gift. The court concluded not.

The facts in *Cochrane* also involved a horse: Benson gave Moore an undivided quarter of a race horse and several days later informed the stable owner on whose premises the horse was kept of the gift. Benson later sold Cochrane the horse, and when Cochrane was told of Moore's interest, he said it was "alright." When Cochrane wanted to sell the horse again, an interpleader was filed in equity to determine the disposition of the one-quarter interest in the horse. It was held that Cochrane took his title in the horse subject to a constructive trust of which Moore was the beneficiary. That is, the gift of the interest in the horse to Moore was completed at the time Cochrane took the horse. The letter from Benson to the stable owner is not in form a deed of gift, but appeared to acknowledge that Benson held onto the horse subject to a constructive trust which could also be imposed on later purchasers of the horse.

"The doctrine of *Irons v. Smallpiece* was doubted in several later English cases, but it was reaffirmed in *Cochrane v. Moore*...." *Molenda v. Simonson* (1943). In *Cochrane*, both donor and donee relied on the third party purchaser of the horse and a fractional interest in the horse was incapable of actual delivery. If this reliance were justified and the defendant knew of it, then equity will act to carry out the reasonable expectations of the donor and donee. And if equity will do that routinely, then *Cochrane* has settled the legal requirements for a gift. "It is a settled principal of the common law that title to personal property having physical existence cannot pass by parol gift unless there is such delivery of possession to the donee as the nature of the property permits. That principle was declared applicable to a chattel upon great deliberation in *Cochrane v. Moore....*" *Millett v. Temple* (1932).

Thus delivery was not an early requirement of our law. The dates of both *Irons* (1819) and *Cochrane* (1890) being after 1776, neither was part of our common law as received from England. Why then were they such influential cases? The answer is that, by definition, a gift is without consideration, but it was throughout most of the 19th century regarded as a contract. Thus when consideration became the touchstone of contract law during that century's last decades, gratuitous transfers like gifts were left without a rationale. Delivery supplied that rationale. So delivery became, by the weight of both English and American cases and authorities, an indispensable element of a valid gift. See Roy Kreitner, *The Gift Beyond The Grave: Revisiting the Question of Consideration*, 101 Colum. L. Rev. 1876, 1905–1908 (2001).

Later, American courts worked out doctrines to liberalize the harshness of the common law requirement of delivery in cases in which there was evidence indicating that the donor really, really, intended to make a gift. These are the doctrines of constructive and symbolic delivery with which a later section of this Chapter will deal.

A.   A DEED OF GIFT

At the time the *Irons* case was decided in 1819, there was some question whether a gift could be accomplished by a deed of gift alone. With *Cochrane,* in 1890, a gift might be effected by deed, and in many states today a gift can be accomplished either by a deed or a delivery of the chattel. In most states, a deed of gift is effective to accomplish a gift only when delivery is impractical.

At the time of *Cochrane,* a deed was an instrument written under seal. Like the delivery requirement, the seal ensured the donor's deliberation upon the soundness of making the gift while he drafted the writing, heated and applied the wax, and impressed his sign upon the hot wax. Most state legislatures have since enacted statutes which eliminate the difference between sealed and unsealed writings, or otherwise abolished the need for a seal. (Caveat: one-third of our states have taken no action on this matter.) Many courts have by now decided that a gift may be accomplished by an unsealed deed or other instrument.

A "deed of gift" has a formal sound to it. It harks back to a time when deeds were used for many types of chattel transactions besides gifts. Sales, for example. Judicial interpretation of deeds of gift differed from those used for the sale of goods. In sales, deeds are construed, in cases of ambiguity, in favor of the transferee. But the transferee there gives a consideration that a donee does not. So deeds of gift were construed in favor of the donor. Why is this so? One reason is that people are not expected to, and do not naturally, give away their possessions. A second reason is that while a donor knows what the intended use of the gift is, the donee does not; the donor is really making a prediction about the donee's use, and some predictions turn out to be wrong. Then the gift goes unused, or underutilized. Think about all the clothes you been given that you don't wear, and all the gift books that remain unread. Unless the donee does not know his preferences, or the donor can afford gifts the donee cannot afford himself, the danger that the donor will value the gift more than the donee will, makes courts reluctance to validate gifts that are proven by anything less than clear and convincing evidence—a high, but prevalent, standard of proof. *Jamison v. Estate of Goodlett* (1997). A third reason for narrowing the class of gifts validated when contested, is that the best gifts are the product of altruism and our better natures. That is, the gift that is likely to be equally valued by both donor and donee has sentimental value—a family heirloom, a photograph of donor and donee, or bronzed baby shoes. Here it is good to give as well as to receive, and courts are on the lookout for gifts that fall into this category.

Today, a valid deed of gift has three components. It (1) must use language indicating a present intent to give ("I hereby grant," etc.), (2) must identify the donee and the subject of the gift, and (3) must be signed or otherwise authenticated by the donor, as well as comply with other formalities imposed by applicable state law.

The formality that the term "deed" implies has bothered some state legislators. At least eight states have statutes providing that a "writing" may be used in a gift of personalty as a substitute for the actual delivery requirement. It must be signed by the donor. Generally, these statutes are taken to mean that the document effectuating the gift may be more informal than a deed, and/or not under seal. Comment, *Statutory Treatment of the Requirement of Delivery in Gifts of Personal Property*, 7 Wayne L.Rev. 571, 572–79 (1961).

As to the first component of a deed of gift, judicial analysis of the language used in deeds of gift analyzes the words of the grant for their equivalence with words such as, "The donor by means of this deed does now grant and give...." The court may decide that a present interest was transferred by the deed or that a future interest was presently transferred, but this analysis of the "interest" transferred can get sloppy around the edges and is sometimes, when lay-drafted deeds are involved, no more than a cover for evaluating the intent of the donor. In one case the words,

"I wish to pay [for the comfort and care of my retirement home] ... the sum of $10,000 on demand. This may, however, be collectible against my estate if not demanded sooner, or paid by me,"

were held sufficient for a valid deed of gift. Holding that "I wish to pay" was the same as "I hereby grant," the Montana Supreme Court held that these words indicated a sufficient present donative intent on the donor's part. *Faith Lutheran Retirement Home v. Veis* (1970), noted at 35 Mont.L.Rev. 132 (1974). The delivery of the deed of gift performs the same functions as the delivery requirement does for parol gifts. Let us turn to an elaboration of those functions in American case law.

B. AMERICAN CASES

Some 19th century American judges were inclined, like their English counterparts, to balance the evidence indicating a present intent to complete a gift against the need for an actual delivery of the chattel, or of a deed to it, to the donee. This inclination made delivery not an absolute requirement of an oral gift, but rather of evidentiary value only. See *Whatley v. Mitchell* (1919). See Harlan Fiske (later Chief Justice) Stone, *Delivery in Gifts of Personal Property*, 20 Colum.L.Rev. 197, 200 (1920) (interpreting *Whatley* as consistent with *Irons'* holding of the essentiality of delivery and its facts as identical with *Irons*). At the same time, American judges have been less inclined to permit a gift to be accomplished by use of a deed alone when physical delivery of the chattel was possible. For them, the deed is evidence of donative intent, but the gift must be completed by a delivery.

The delivery requirement (first) echoes the time, long ago, when the handing over of possession of a thing was the only method of transfer—when, as Professor Mechem wrote, "things were things"; title and possession were then inseparable and went hand in hand. Philip Mechem, *The Requirement of Delivery in Gifts of Chattels and of Choses in Action Evidenced by Commercial Instruments*, 21 Ill.Law Rev. 341, 345 (1926). The requirement is (second) related to the idea that a delivery is regarded as integral to the idea of a gift—so integral as to be a definitional and functional component of a gift.[1] In this regard, (a) it serves to show that the donor formed his intention to give into a resolve to make the transfer; (b) the "wrench of delivery" (again, Mechem's phrase) serves to protect the donor from acting hastily and to impress upon him the finality of his act; and (c) it provides evidence of the gift. If these functions can be served without actual delivery of the chattel, American courts have shown a tendency to validate the gift by finding that some other type of delivery is present.

Its persistence is especially attributable to the last, evidentiary, function—and more particularly to a judicial reluctance to validate a gift when the only

1. That is, a donor cannot make a gift unless she gives it to the donee, and once she's given it to him, then he's got it, and if he has it, then she must have delivered it.

evidence of it is an intention of the donor to make it. Informal and gratuitous gifts are too easy for a donee to fake before a jury. Litigation often occurs after the donor's death. People are not to be presumed to have given away their property. Courts are thus wary of the fraudulent donee, except perhaps in intra-family cases in which the donee is a natural object of the donor's generosity.

A New York case illustrates this tendency. In it, a donor signed a document stating "I give this day to my wife, Sara, as a present on her 46th birthday, 500 shares of XYZ company common stock." *In re Cohn* (1919). In this deed of gift, the donor declared a present intention to give and identified the donee as well as the subject of the gift. Unlike a fraction of a horse, however, shares of stock are capable of delivery, so no matter how clear the writing is, the question arises whether the deed may be used as a substitute for actual delivery of the stock. The court held that it could. A prior New York case required that the donor of stock instruct the transfer agent of the corporation to change the owner's name on the corporate books in order to satisfy the delivery requirement. *Matter of Mills* (1916). See *infra*, this Chapter, for more on corporate stock transfers as gifts. The donor, Cohn, went (in the court's view) one step further by actually giving the donee a written declaration of a gift. However, Mr. Cohn continued to use the stock for his own purposes up to the time of his death six days after the alleged gift. He was, at the time of the gift, involved in establishing a new business partnership. He was using the gifted stock as his contribution to the partnership's assets. So, if he was not to lose the benefits of this partnership, the possession of the shares was temporarily beyond his grasp, until his death dissolved the partnership. Under these circumstances, the donor had done all he could reasonably be expected to do to deliver the stock and complete the gift. His writing manifested a present intention to deliver the shares in the future. It was a present delivery of a future interest in them.

C.   SYMBOLIC AND CONSTRUCTIVE DELIVERY

The default rule for the delivery of gifts requires an actual delivery. This rule is not inflexible. We have seen that a deed of gift may be substituted for actual delivery and, when actual delivery is impractical because of either the type of chattel given or the parties' relationship to it, a relinquishing of control over possession of the chattel may suffice. What is then required is "such delivery of possession to the donee as the nature of the property permits." *Millett v. Temple* (1932).

Thus too, delivery may be symbolic, as where the donor gives the donee a symbol that represents possession in situations where actual possession cannot be transferred. Mr. Cohn's writing was just such a symbolic delivery of the shares, particularly when as in *Cohn* there was no evidence indicating a revocation of the gift. Indeed, two days after giving his wife the gift, he urged his attorney to complete the establishment of the new partnership so that he might get his hands on the shares. *Cohn* thus involved an instance of *symbolic delivery*—giving a sheet of paper to stand for the shares.

In one other instance, that of a *constructive delivery*, American courts have permitted a donor to give access or the means of obtaining possession of the gifted chattel without delivery of the chattel itself. Constructive delivery is involved when the donor gives the keys to a lock box or a trunk. Because the donor has relinquished control over the contents of the box to the donee, the contents may be delivered in this manner when the donor is incapable of actual delivery of the contents or if the chattel is too big or heavy for the donor to lift and hand it over to his donee. In this last situation, the donor might deliver the keys to a bulky wardrobe intending that the delivery of the key be constructive delivery of the piece of furniture, but the key is not intended to stand for the chattel. It only gives access to it.

Although courts often use the terms "symbolic" and "constructive" delivery as if they were interchangeable, they are not. Constructive delivery is permitted when the donor relinquishes access to or control of a gifted chattel—which is what happens when there is an actual delivery so that the courts require that the end result in cases of both actual and constructive delivery be as close as the nature of the chattel permits.

Symbolic delivery cases, on the other hand, involve situations in which the gifted chattel may be small and capable of manumission but are unavailable for delivery. How unavailable must it be? Must the shares of stock, as in *Cohn,* be in a bank in a distant city from which the donor could order them sent to him? In the same city? The same building? The same room? These are Professor Brown's matters of degree, and no fixed rules apply. Courts inquire into the circumstances. The nearer to the donor, the less likely it is that a court will permit symbolic delivery. .

However, even if the shares are close-by, the health of the donor may not permit him to get to them. The donee who is given keys to the donor's bulky wardrobe may acquire that piece of furniture but will not become the beneficiary of a life insurance policy or shares of stock found in one of its drawers. The donee is likely to get only what cannot be actually delivered, i.e., the wardrobe.

What if an elderly invalid (now deceased) gave his nurse a bunch of house keys? Would the nurse become the donee of everything to which the keys gave access? Clearly not, unless it could be shown that the donor had a particular thing in mind when he delivered the keys. So the furniture in the sickroom might be transferred to the nurse, but not the furniture out of the donor's sight in other parts of the house. The key which unlocks the keyboard on the piano in the living room will only be deemed a symbolic delivery of the piano to a donee who can prove delivery. In this case, assigning the burden of proof is tantamount to saying that no delivery had occurred. (This paragraph is based on *Newman v. Bost* (1898).) The distinctions between things in the sick-room and those outside are purely practical ones involving compromises between the heirs of the invalid and the nurse whom the invalid intended in some way to benefit. They also represent the judicial tendency to construe gifts narrowly, in favor of the donor when the evidence is not clear.

A rancher can effectively give cattle on the open range to another rancher by changing his brand on the gifted cattle to that of the donee's. In this case, the fact that the cattle stay on the range means that the donee has access to them thereafter. In the case of an insurance policy or shares of stock of a corporation, just giving the policy to the donee will not make the latter its beneficiary or, in the case of stock, just changing the owner's name on the certificate will not suffice either. Access to the chattel itself is in each instance insufficient to transfer the benefits of the policy or the shares without a deed of gift on which the donee could get specific performance. In the one case, the rancher has given up control of the chattel, but in the other, more is required to give the donee access to it. The corporation's or the insurer's records must be changed. Unless a deed of gift is clear and capable of compelling a change in those records through judicial process, no delivery has occurred.

The same distinction is involved in gaining access to a safety deposit box in a bank. Delivering the key to someone will not provide unfettered access to the box since, if the usual procedure is followed, the alleged donor will have not only to give the donee a key, but also sign him into the vault area in which the box is located. Only with this second step complete can it be said that the donor has provided access to the contents of the box *and* relinquished control over them.

D.   GIFTS THROUGH THIRD PARTIES

American courts frequently hold that *inter vivos* gifts of personal property must be irrevocable and unconditional. If a chattel is given to a donee but is subject to a condition, oral or written, the condition is unenforceable. The rule is the same when the condition is written in a deed concerning the property and for the same reason: the delivery of the chattel takes precedence over any conflicting qualification on the title contained in the deed. This is just another way of reenforcing the requirement of a delivery.

This does not mean, however, that the delivery cannot be accomplished in two stages; first by delivery of the chattel or, where appropriate, a deed to it to a third party who, in turn, hands it to the donee in a second stage of the delivery. By this two-step procedure the donor gains the ability to impose conditions upon the person holding the chattel, the fulfillment of which permits the latter to transfer possession of it or a deed to it to the donee.

Frequently, however, the status of the third party holder becomes unclear, and the question arises whether he is the agent of the donor or the trustee of the donee. If the former, the donor still has the right to recall the gift, as it has not yet become irrevocable. If the latter, then the gift has become irrevocable pending only the donee's fulfilling the condition (if any) imposed by the donor: reaching his majority, graduating from college, marrying, etc.

Clear instructions to the third party can avoid these problems. Where the third party states that he is the donor's agent, this will normally be conclusive. *Innes v. Potter* (1915). The test, however, is the intent of the donor—of which the third party's perception of his status constitutes evidence but is not necessarily dispositive. For all practical purposes, if the donor has not communicated to the third party that the gift is irrevocable, he has a power to revoke it. Only where the donor can show that he did not know that he was possessed of this power should he be regarded as having made the gift irrevocable. For example, a donor might have posted a letter with instructions not to return the chattel to him, but unbeknownst to him, the letter was never received by the third party.

For some types of third parties, a classification as anything other than the agent of the donor will be difficult. Attorneys of the donor fall into this class because the attorney-client relationship creates a fiduciary duty for the attorney that precludes any representation of a party with an interest conflicting with his client. An attorney could not therefore receive the chattel as the attorney for the donor and at the same time hold it as a trustee for the donee.

For an attorney, then, any agency for a client donor arises as a matter of a presumption that the attorney was behaving as he should, i.e., with the limits imposed on his conduct by ethical canons governing the bar.[2]

Applying the agent of the donor/trustee of the donee distinction is usually not so clear-cut and depends rather on the circumstances of the case. A decision on the status of the third party should consider whether the donor or donee paid the third party, whether the donor or donee received any income from the chattel while he held it, whether the donor or donee instructed the third party and

2. What if the donor's attorney—or a trustee, or any person with a general power of attorney over the donor's goods—was the donee? When an inter vivos gift is challenged, and the person challenging it proves that a confidential relationship existed between the donor and donee, there is a presumption against the gift's validity. The gift will not stand unless fully explained and shown to be fair. This presumption is rebuttable, but will be difficult to rebut: the burden of proof shifts to the donee to establish, by clear and convincing evidence, that there was no abuse of the confidence. *Upman v. Clarke* (2000). This shift in the burden of proof is based on the twin assumptions that people normally wish to retain possession and use of their property while they are alive, and that any influence by a person in a formalized, confidential, relationship resulting in a personal benefit, is improper. On the other hand, a gift *causa mortis* (see infra, this Chapter) might be expected to go to a person such as a relative, close friend, or trusted employee, even though in some informal way the relationship might be deemed confidential. Such a relationship remains suspicious, but does not give rise to a presumption of invalidity; it is one suspicious circumstance to be considered, but the burden of proof remains with the one challenging the gift; it does not shift to the donee. *McAdoo v. Dickson* (1938).

whether or not such instructions were taken as binding on him by one or both parties to the gift.

E. CORPORATE STOCK

Shares of stock in a corporation are personal property even if the corporation owns only real property. Gifts of shares are a frequent source of litigation. In order for such a gift to be valid, courts require a delivery and donative intent, requirements no different from those for other types of gifts. There is, however, a unique aspect to these gifts: a transfer of ownership on the books of the corporation issuing the stock. This aspect of these transfers sometimes satisfies the delivery requirement and sometimes is an additional requirement.

Such a split in the case law arises because of confusion over what a share of stock is. If it is the certificate itself, that piece of paper must be delivered to the donee, and the transfer on the books is superfluous except as evidence of donative intent. If, however, the shares are a representation of an undivided fractional interest in the assets of the corporation or its operations, then the property is not capable of manual delivery. Thus the transfer of the certificate is a symbolic delivery, while a transfer on the books is a constructive delivery giving the donee access to the benefits of being a corporate shareholder; with only a symbolic or constructive delivery possible, the transfer on the books becomes a substitute for a actual delivery.

In either event, the transfer of the shares on the books of the corporation is "of great importance" but not dispositive in establishing donative intent.

The weight of the authority (although not a majority of American jurisdictions) holds that replacing the donor's name with the donee's on the corporate books as the owner of the shares is all that is required to complete the gift. An additional set of cases reach the same result by holding that the transfer agent is the trustee of the donee, and a third line of authority suggests that the transfer agent is in fact the donor's agent, thus making the gift incomplete without the donor's delivery of the new certificate to the donee.

The weight of authority carries with it the best reasoned rule. First of all, viewing the transfer of names on the corporate records as the completed gift gives rise to a rule that is certain of application, completes the gift at a time when the benefits of share ownership accrue to the donee (record status being necessary for receipt of dividends), and best protects the donee from the donor's temptation to retract the completed gift. Second, in jurisdictions which view the delivery of the certificate as either a symbolic delivery or transfer on the books as a constructive delivery of a share in the corporation, the transfer on the books provides the best evidence of a completed gift. Third, the instructions to the transfer agent will normally be in writing and may provide an instrument, writing, or deed of gift. Finally, this result conforms the law of gifts to statutes that in many states provide that the legal title to the shares passes to the donee when the name on the corporate register is changed. These statutes are intended to protect corporations from paying dividends to the wrong person, and this intent might arguably be defeated if the law of gifts did not conform to it.

In addition, the donee may acquire contract rights in the shares upon the name-change on the books because the donee is then the designated third party beneficiary of the contract in the instructions from the donor to the transfer agent.

Quite often litigation results when the donor regains possession of the certificate, now naming the donee as the owner of the shares, and that certificate is never forwarded to the donee. This happens when the donor has given possession of the certificate to a third party who is not the transfer agent to pass along to the transfer agent. In such situations the courts can inquire into the status of that third party as well as the transfer agent, and the donor has two opportunities to show that *his* agent remained in control of the certificate and thus that it never left his control. *Owens v. Sun Oil Co.* (1973).

In most of the cases in which a transfer on the corporate books has been held not to complete the gift, the donor regained possession of the certificate, and persons executing the transfer have been found to be *his* agents. Where the donor regains possession of the certificate, his long-continued retention of it serves as proof of a failure of donative intent.

Then a court has no reason to see the transfer on the books as a delivery. Some courts reverse this logic and state that unless a showing of donative intent can be made at the time of the transfer, the gift is incomplete without a later delivery of the certificate.

A middle ground is held by cases holding that the transfer is a burden-shifting event. After the transfer, the presumption is that a valid gift was intended and that a transfer on the books is a *prima facie* showing that such was the case. Thereafter the donor must establish by clear and convincing evidence that no gift was intended. *Young v. Young* (1990).

II. DONATIVE INTENT

To be valid, a gift must be made with donative intent on the donor's part. At minimum, this requires that the delivery be voluntary. *Kenyon v. Abel* (2001) (holding that the unintentional inclusion of a valuable painting in boxes taken to goodwill shop when cleaning out deceased relative's house negates a donative intent and invalidates the gift).

Judicial analysis of facts adducing that intent is often a matter of reducing the available evidence to one of several verbal expressions. This is often a dry exercise, taking all of the seeming humanity out of the facts of a case and reducing them to a skeletal form. First, a court may decide that a donor meant: "I give you this thing, but I am keeping the income or the use of it until my death." The gift is a present one, and the retention of the income or the use is consistent with keeping a life estate in the donor, followed by a remainder in the donee. Both interests in the chattel are simultaneously established at the time of the gift. As to the remainder, the donor has a present intent to establish a future interest.

Second, if the court can reduce the evidence of intent to a statement like: "You shall have this thing when you reach 21," then the gift is invalid as one taking effect in the future. The condition precedent to making the gift is a future event. The donor lacks a present intent to make the gift, and it falls afoul of the rule that an *inter vivos* gift must be unconditional.

Third, if the court can reduce the evidence of intent to a statement that: "You shall have this thing when I die," there is similarly no present intent, but the gift fails for an additional reason; i.e., the gift is, in effect, a testamentary one and should be contained in a validly executed will. Its failure to comply with the applicable Statute of Wills or Probate Code thus constitutes an additional reason for invalidating it.

Finally, the court might reduce the evidence of intent to the donor's stating that: "I give you this thing, but if I do X, I want it back." In this instance, there is a present intent to give the chattel, and the gift is valid but subject to a condition subsequent. *Lewis v. Poduska* (1992) ("I give you this thing, but if Mother wants it, give it to her.")

These distinctions, particularly the one between a condition precedent and subsequent, are formulaic, but the attorney's task is to fit the facts into one pattern or another. Courts will also be looking to the broader web of facts in which the gift was made. Whether it is witnessed by others, whether the donee is someone to whom the donor might be expected to make a gift (a parent, a spouse, an offspring, etc.), and whether the transfer looks like a *bona fide* gift or a tax avoidance scheme could all be important contextual facts; though each is not dispositive by itself, cumulatively they may have great weight.

Establishing the donor's intent is a question of fact. In the case of *Gruen v. Gruen* (1986), the court held that evidence established that a father intended to transfer ownership of a valuable painting to his son, reserving a life estate in it for himself and that letters from father to son were sufficient to establish a delivery by deed of gift. Written for the son's twenty first birthday, the letter said, "I wish to give you as a present the oil painting by [a named artist] which now hangs in the New York living room. Happy Birthday." In an accompanying cover letter, the father said that the son should destroy a prior letter mentioning that the father "want[ed] to use the painting as long as I live." For tax reasons, the father continued: "[t]hough I still want to use it," this should not appear in the letter, and the accompanying letter "will serve the purpose of making it possible for you, once I die, to get this picture...."

These two letters taken together, were sufficient to transfer title to the painting without the right to its present possession. A physical delivery, and redelivery would not serve to provide any better evidence of a delivery, the court said, than the two letters do.

As to the father's donative intent, the court found that while it must be a present intent, it need not involve the transfer of present possession, but only a present transfer of a future interest, such as the remainder interest created here in the donee. Once the gift is made, the donor's status is that of a holder of a life estate. His possession, maintenance, loan, and repair of the painting thereafter is not inconsistent with this status. Title to the remainder vests immediately, with possession postponed to the donor's death. Moreover, if donative intent may be established by present delivery of a deed of gift or its equivalent, it makes little sense to deny the donor's intent when the gift involves a tangible chattel such as the painting in *Gruen*. The son was still living in a college dormitory when the gift was made. Say that the son, for example, was going off to law school. (As he was.) In this situation, it makes sense for the father to retain possession.

A. CONDITIONAL GIFTS: ENGAGEMENT PRESENTS

The objective of much of the "interest" analysis in the four distinctions discussed in the last section is to effectuate the common law's prohibition on conditional gifts. No pre-conditions may be attached to a parol gift. In one situation, however, courts agree that a condition may be imposed on a gift; that is, where an engagement gift is given in connection with an ensuing marriage, the donor can sue in replevin or trover for its value or return if the marriage does not take place. Contract theories have also been used to achieve this recovery—mutual recission, mistake of fact, unjust enrichment and restitution, and a failure of consideration among them. *Sloin v. Lavine* (1933). However, most used is the rule that this conditional gift is revoked by the failure of the donee to meet the donor's condition.

Thus an engagement gift is conditioned on the marriage between donor and donee taking place. *Lindh v. Surman* (1999), noted at 113 Harv. L. Rev. 1876 (2000). This condition need not be express, indeed is seldom expressed, but it is one implied by law. The gift is presumed to be made with it attached. The easiest application of this presumption comes when the gift, by its nature, relates to the engagement itself. An engagement ring is an example. It symbolizes a pledge to marry and is given on the implied condition that the marriage will take place. *Lowe v. Quinn* (1971); *Lipton v. Lipton* (1986)

("An engagement ring is a gift to which a condition subsequent, the fulfillment of the marriage agreement, is attached.")

There is a presumption that an engagement gift is conditional. It is, however, a rebuttable presumption. Where the donee can show that the occasion for the gift was not dependent on fulfillment of the condition, the donor's cause of action will fail. Thus, if the gift was made to celebrate the fiancee/donee's birthday or a holiday, a valid defense exists. Some courts also distinguish between engagement and courtship gifts. The former are made at the time the marriage is proposed and accepted or thereafter. The latter are made beforehand to introduce the donor to the donee and gain favor. Courtship gifts are not presumed to have been made upon a condition of marriage.

Although some courts look to the time at which the gift is made or the type of property, the intentions of the parties is the controlling test, and in addition to engagement rings, donors have recovered or sued for the value of money advanced, furs, furniture, and automobiles. The more extraordinary the gift, the more likely it is that it is an engagement gift.

Where the engagement is broken by the donor, the traditional and prevalent rule permits the donee to retain engagement gifts or to sue for their value, and likewise deny the donor a right to recover even their value. Conversely, if the donee breaks off the engagement without legal justification or the engagement is ended by mutual agreement, the donor may recover the gifts. The justification for this rule is that engagements should not be entered into lightly. An engagement is an agreement to prepare for marriage, and once recognized as such, there should not be a reward for calling a halt to that preparation. On the other hand, a donee would be justified in breaking an engagement where the donor has made some misrepresentation of his marital or financial status. *White v. Finch* (1964). Likewise, a donor may recover a gift induced by a donee's fraud. In the same vein, where one party to the engagement dies, engagement gifts need not be returned, neither party being at fault as to the termination of the engagement.

The idea that the concept of fault controls the disposition of engagement gift cases has recently been criticized. See *Aronow v. Silver* (1987) [calling the application of fault "silly and sexist" in *his* action suing *her* for return of the ring (he wins), transfer of title in a jointly owned condo (he wins there too), and for transfer of stock (the action is remanded for adjustments in their respective interests)]. Some states have eliminated suits based on a breach of a promise to marry by legislation—the so-called "heart balm" statutes.

> The purpose of the initial heart balm legislation was to rid the courts of these actions where the "wounded" party appears in court to unfold his or her sorrows before a sympathetic jury. To require a determination of fault in order to entitle one to recover engagement gifts

would simply condone this same type of action in yet another form. The result would be to encourage every disappointed donee to resist the return of engagement gifts by blaming the donor for the breakup of the contemplated marriage, thereby promoting dramatic courtroom accusations and counter-accusations of fault.

In truth, in most broken engagements there is no real fault as such—one or both of the parties merely changes their mind about the desirability of the other as a marriage partner. Since the major purpose of the engagement period is to allow a couple time to test the permanency of their feelings, it would seem highly ironic to penalize the donor for taking steps to prevent a possibly unhappy marriage. Indeed, in one sense the engagement period has been successful if the engagement is broken since one of the parties has wisely utilized this time so as to avoid a marriage that in all probability would fail.

Gaden v. Gaden (1971). Just as "no fault" divorce has become prevalent, so it should be after an engagement is broken. No fault should attach to either party. Heart-balm statutes have been enacted in about a dozen states. They have generally been construed to apply only to prohibit suits based on a breach of a promise to marry, not to prohibit engagement gift suits. *De Cicco v. Barker* (1959). The return of an engagement gift under "no fault" principles makes plain that the donor's condition was that a marriage take place, not his agreeing to marry the donee.

Similarly, an action by the parents of an engaged person to recover the expenses incurred in planning the wedding ceremony or the honeymoon, is barred. Such expenses are incurred with knowledge that there may be no wedding and no honeymoon if the engagement is broken on either side. *Aronow v. Silver, op. cit.*

Where the engagement gift is to a person already married, the gift is unconditional. Allowing recovery of such gifts would encourage the dissolution of a previous marriage. Where a prior marriage of the donee is already in the divorce courts, engagement gifts may be recovered. Such results underline the basis of these engagement gift holdings as matters of public policy and the status of the parties.

Minority status has also been an issue. When the donee is a minor and without the capacity to contract, there is no engagement contract—no exchange of the promise of marry for the gift—and no remedy for the donor to use to recover even the engagement ring. This mixture of contract and gift theory indicates that the result is based on a public policy having to do with discouraging the marriage of minors.

B. PRESUMING DONATIVE INTENT

In some situations, where the alleged gift arrangement is long continued with the knowledge of a donor who acquiesces in it, a presumption arises that the gift is valid. Where, for example, a donor deposits money in a bank account maintained in the names of both the donor and the donee as joint tenants with a right of survivorship, the transfer of the money into such an account creates a presumption that the donor intended a gift to the donee as the surviving joint tenant. Often such cases involve intra-family gifts and so the presumption operates in a context in which the donee is the natural object of the donor's beneficence. Such a presumption is rebuttable, however, and if clear and convincing evidence is available that no gift was intended, the presumption is overcome. Usually the evidence used to overcome the presumption concerns the use of and the authority over the joint account, whether the donee thought he had access to the account, whether the account was maintained for the convenience of the donor, and the percentage of the donor's assets held in the account.

Nor is a presumption of donative intent likely to be defeated when the donor obtains some benefit from the gift. In *Gruen v. Gruen,* op. cit., the donor had a tax benefit in mind in making the gift of the painting to his son. The gift was nonetheless valid. Nor is a failure to establish the intent likely to be affected. In *McCune v. Brown* (1983), noted at 38 Ark.L.Rev. 446 (1984), a parent made a gift of a quarter million dollars worth of gold pieces to his child, in order to avoid subjecting them to his spouse's claims in an up-coming divorce proceeding. After the divorce was final, the parent brought a replevin action to revoke the gift and enjoin the child's removal of the coins from a safe deposit box. The court held that the lack of the donor's clean hands in making the gift in the first place was irrelevant to the issue of the presence or absence of donative intent and that the gift was invalid for lack of such intent. The child, the court found as a matter of fact, knew she was to re-deliver the gold after the divorce.

C. SOME PROBLEMS ON DELIVERY AND DONATIVE INTENT

1. Ambrose, a struggling young writer, wrote a long poem for which he was seeking a publisher. Between visits to various publishing houses, he wrote a letter which said: "Dear Beatrice, Thanks for your support. I know I promised to send my poem manuscript to you, but I'm still hawking it, though I still want you to have it. I wanted to confirm to you our understanding that you get 50% of the profits from my publishing my poem." Months later, Ambrose died without having executed any contract to publish his poem. Some months after that, his literary executor did execute such a contract, and the executor now has had a request from Beatrice for 50% of the royalties and profits from the publication.

There are at least two valid perspectives on the legal problem present here. The first involves a problem of identifying what was transferred. If it were the profits of publishing the poem, the problem is that no profits and no contract from which they could arise in the future were in existence at the time of the letter to Beatrice. No delivery could take place, the argument runs, because there was nothing to deliver. However, the writing may be a substitute for future profits (and is the subject of a symbolic delivery). It is a present gift of future profits and expresses a clear intent on the part of the donor to give future property. See *Rubenstein v. Rosenthal* (1988) (upholding gift of 10% of profits in land speculation); *Elyachar v. Gerel Corporation* (1984) (concerning gifts of stock income).

A second perspective involves evaluation of the letter as an assignment of a contract right. The assignment of a contract right was void at common law but valid as a gift in equity whether or not the contract right assigned is a present or future right. However, an instrument of gift is still necessary to evidence a clear intent to give a present interest.

Analogous, early common law cases provide precedent here and validated the transfer of an interest in the foal of a not-yet-pregnant mare.

2. Ambrose also wrote: "I know that I promised to send my poem's manuscript to you, but I'm still hawking it, though I still want you to have it." This second aspect of the confirmation letter involves a quite different problem. This gift of the actual manuscript fails for lack of delivery, although there is evidence of a present intent to give it away. What advice would you give Beatrice when she received this letter? Ambrose's retention of the manuscript for his own purposes is much like Mr. Cohn's reten-

tion of the stock for use in his business dealings. In this case, however, Ambrose's hawking it is not inconsistent with his making use of it for Beatrice's benefit when one considers the profit-sharing arrangement which his letter proposes. If Beatrice were to write back and say that "you keep my manuscript and get the best publishing deal you can for me," she would buttress an argument that Ambrose held the manuscript in trust for her. *Cochrane v. Moore* (1890). Here Beatrice has recognized that she has present rights in the manuscript and she (not the donor) has declared the trust.

3. What if Ambrose, after his rounds of the publishing houses and before he received Beatrice's suggested reply, stopped in a bar, then another, and finally went on a binge in about a dozen bars, losing the manuscript somewhere in mid-binge. Fortunately one of the publishers whom he had visited had photocopied the poem so that it was not lost, and when Ambrose next needed it he called the publisher just before leaving town on a speaking tour at colleges and universities around the country. When the publisher met him at the airport with the copy Ambrose said, while with his family and some friends, "Thanks. You've saved my career. I really need to publicize and read this poem during this trip. If you can find the manuscript, it is yours." The manuscript turned up a few days after Ambrose left town, and a few days after that an airplane on which Ambrose was riding crashed, killing all aboard.

Ambrose made a valid gift of the manuscript to the publisher. This gift revoked the prior, unexecuted gift to Beatrice, and because delivery was impossible at the time, his indication of a present intent to deliver the manuscript is as much as he could do. If this type of gift were found invalid, there would be no manner in which lost chattels could be transferred by gift. The manuscript was abandoned property. Such property is owned by him who next takes possession.

III.   GIFTS *CAUSA MORTIS*

A gift *causa mortis* is a gift of personal property made in contemplation of the donor's imminent death upon the condition that the donor die as he anticipates. The gift must also remain unrevoked before his death takes place. Delivery of the chattel is generally required along with proof of the donor's donative intent. Proof is often hard to adduce as the gifts are likely to be made in the course of hurried and private conversations. Moreover, the credibility of the proof is a matter left to the trial court which has the opportunity to assess the credibility of witnesses and the donee. Once found valid, such gifts are not likely to be invalidated on appeal for errors in interpreting the facts.

A gift *causa mortis* is a gift revocable at any time before the donor's death. His surviving the event from which he anticipated death also revokes the gift unless he subsequently regains full mental powers and reaffirms it, in which case the gift is validated as an *inter vivos* gift. A later will does not invalidate an otherwise valid gift *causa mortis*; the reason is that the will is not effective until the death of the donor, and the gift has previously taken the chattel out of the donor's power to place it under the control of his executor.

The death of the donor must not be a precondition to the validity of the gift. Instead, the gift becomes irrevocable upon the donor's death. The best evidence of the donor's intent comes from his own words, and some cases have made much of the donor's words of transfer. "If I die (from whatever death the donor is contemplating), this is yours," places a condition precedent to the gift, but "This is yours so long as I die" (from whatever) places a condition subsequent on the gift. The former phrasing invalidates the gift while the latter gift is valid. This distinction seems dry, especially so in the context of a gift which is only valid if made "in contemplation of death"—not of a lingering feeling of life's mortality but of a specific and reasonably immediate event. In such a context, it is too much to expect the donor to find the right phrase at a time when he is expected to be concerned with the innocence of his soul. Evidence of a donor's intent should not at such a time hinge on the words of transfer but should be ascertained more broadly.

The donor's surviving the event from which he anticipated death revokes the gift. It is not necessary that the donor state that he anticipates death from a certain event, nor is it necessary that the donor be *in extremis* when the gift is made. It is sufficient that the donor is apprehensive of death and be anticipating it.

This anticipation may be inferred from the context. Some cases present the situation in which the donor anticipates death on a hospital operating table, makes a gift, in fact recovers from the incision and the operation, but dies of the disease that the operation was intended to cure. Where there is no evidence that the donor revoked the gift between the time it was made and his later death, the gift will probably stand even though the lapse of time involved many months. If the sickness induced by disease is on-going, as with a progressive tumor, a cancer or a series of strokes or heart attacks, a context in which the donor might anticipate or contemplate death is established.

On the other hand, gifts by a soldier departing for combat in a war or by a person fearing an assassination which took place the next day, have been held insufficient contextual evidence of an anticipation of death. Neither is the putative donor's death by suicide a sufficient context, although some of these cases are influenced by a public policy against suicide and there is authority to the contrary. See *Scherer v. Hyland* (1976). In this case, a donor's leaving a negotiable check in an apartment shared by the donor with the donee, in a location where the donee would find it, is a constructive delivery by a donor. Moreover, a donor's delivery of the check in the manner just described, is made "in contemplation of death," when the donor then leaves the apartment bent on a suicide which occurred a few hours later. This context is sufficient to sustain a gift *causa mortis*. Indeed, an increasing recognition of the pervasive effects of mental illness may today put gifts preceding a donor's suicide on the same basis as gifts made in the course of many illnesses which ultimately prove fatal. Classifying gifts made in contemplation of death to be gifts *causa mortis* might also advance a policy against suicide because their revocable nature means that the donor may recover the chattel if the suicide is not completed. *In re Estate of Smith* (1997).

In many situations, however, the donor's suicide will be an insufficient context for a gift *causa mortis* because that context implicitly raises a question as to the donor's mental competency to form a donative intent. A better view is that, instead of invalidating such a gift for an insufficient context or "contemplation of death," a full examination of the circumstances of the gift, including the relationship between the donor and the donee, is warranted.

Analysis of whether the gift was made in anticipation of death often proceeds from the objective context to infer the state of mind of the donor. It does not (with some slight authority to the contrary) start and end with the subjective mind-set of the donor. In this sense, gifts *causa mortis* are not favored in the law, but that may be, in part, because they were a creation of equity. Their basis is a religious premise that when contemplating an imminent death, a donor will express his true feelings, will settle his debts and will altruistically disburse his property so as to ease his soul. For past generations, the flames of hell seemed more real than they perhaps do today and, in consequence, some of the religious basis for such gifts may be slipping away.

Other reasons for the law's dislike of them may be more practical. First, depending to any degree on the subjective state of mind of the donor will make the resulting legal rules difficult to apply. Second, because the donor is no longer around to testify, the donee may be unduly tempted to commit perjury and fraud. Third, unlike the gift *inter vivos*, any continued possession of the chattel by the donee does not indicate the donor's acquiescence in the transfer, and fourth, the validation of gifts *causa mortis* defeats the policy of the applicable Statute of Wills. In the face of the detailed and formal regulation of a testamentary disposition in such Statutes, the evidence for a gift *causa mortis* must be clear and convincing so that this line of cases can serve as a judicial corrective to such Statutes and the intestate laws of a state.

One state, New Hampshire, has drastically limited the common law pertaining to gifts *causa mortis* by requiring by statute that such a gift be the subject of an "actual delivery to the donee" proven in court, with a petition filed within 60 days of the donor's death and supported by "two indifferent witnesses." N.H.Rev.Stat.Ann. § 551:17 (2002). The elements of contemplation or expectation of death and donative intent are unaffected by this statute, but in requiring an actual delivery to the donee, the statute abolishes the rule that a gift *causa mortis* may be delivered somehow to a third party acting for the donee. Moreover, in raising the evidentiary standard for this type of gift well above the common law, the New Hampshire legislature seems to endorse the criticism some courts and legal writers have leveled at gifts *causa mortis*.

IV. ACCEPTANCE

Because the donee receives a benefit in having the gift bestowed on him, its acceptance is usually presumed. This presumption is a rebuttable one, and the acts of the donee can show rejection of the gift. What the donor intended as a gift of money can be accepted by the donee as a loan—the donee giving back a promissory note in recognition of this fact. Or, a donee can refuse the gift because he is in bankruptcy and to accept it would put the chattel in the hands of his creditors. Likewise, a donee might refuse for tax reasons.

A gift is normally a bilateral transaction, but where the donee does not know of the donor's donative intent (as with delivery to a third person, to a minor, or to an incompetent person), the law will presume acceptance, validating the gift until the donee has an opportunity to accept or reject it. The gift is presently effective, subject to a condition subsequent giving the donee the power to repudiate it. Thus the presumption of an acceptance functions to implement the intent of the donor.

Comparatively few cases discuss the element of acceptance in gifts. Where the donee does not know the precise intent of the donor in making the gift, but learns only that the gift was made (as where donor and donee are on different sides of a war zone and/or communication is impossible or sporadic), the donee may accept the gift in trust for the donor. Where this is done, the donee's knowledge of the gift must be incomplete in some respect, otherwise the ambiguous action might be construed as rejection of the gift. Similarly, accepting a bill of sale for a chattel but not claiming the goods within a reasonable time shows, not rejection, but that the donee has not made up his mind whether to accept the gift. While a donee should be free to reject a gift, its acceptance need not be contemporaneous with its delivery, particularly if after delivery the donor makes statements showing his intent as to the gift. On the other hand, the donee's filing suit to enforce the gift is sufficient to show acceptance and that he saw the gift as conferring some benefit on him.

V. CONCLUSION

Suppose A borrowed a thousand dollars from B and, when A was supposed to return the money, brought it to him in cash and put it on the table at which B sat. B said to A, "take it back—I don't want it." Without more being said, has B given A that money? There is no new consideration for the transaction, so B has made no contract that would permit A to have it, but has there been a delivery? Having studied the law of gifts, you can see how this gift might have been delivered, you recognize

B's expression of a donative intent, and you can easily imagine that A might freely accept the gift. Without knowing more about A and B—whether they are related, and how closely, or what their prior relationship has been—the transaction does not seem to be driven by a desire to maximize profit or economic growth, or preserve capital, so that the basis of the transaction is uncertain, unquantifiable, and little subject to proof; it also seems one-sided, in the sense that A gains and B loses; it further seems to be an act of willing self-denial on B's part. Does the law have to know more about them to uphold the gift? If so, how much more? Today the law of gifts recognizes that some transactions are beyond the calculus of contracts.

CHAPTER VIII

JOINT BANK ACCOUNTS

A specialized application of the law of gifts concerns multiple party or joint bank accounts, as well as other accounts and certificates of deposit held in the names of two or more parties. When establishing the account, the depositors may contribute unequal amounts to the funds on account. The issue immediately arising is whether one of parties intended to create a new ownership interest in the funds. Thus if A establishes an account in the names of A and B, B may thereafter think herself entitled to withdraw any or all of the funds. For a joint account to be created by gift, the gift must be proven in the same manner as any other *inter vivos* gift. *Beach v. Holland* (1943). There is, at the account's inception, no presumption of an irrevocable gift *inter vivos*, but a presumption does arise in more than half of the states that funds on account at A's death belong to B unless there is clear and convincing evidence otherwise or B exerted undue influence over A. *Estate of Maxfield* (1993) [citing two widely-adopted Uniform Probate Code (hereafter UPC) sections to this effect].

I. CONCURRENT INTERESTS IN PERSONAL PROPERTY

Personal property can be held concurrently by two or more persons using one of two common law estates—the joint tenancy and the tenancy in common. (A third concurrent estate, the tenancy by the entirety, is reserved for married persons, is used in only a minority of states, and is often inapplicable to personalty. See *infra*, Chapter XI.)

Joint tenancy is the concurrent ownership of a chattel by two or more persons who hold it as a unit. All have the right to reduce the whole of the chattel to possession. This is especially appropriate for many small objects of personal property because it provides the only manner in which they can be used. This unitary approach, however, also means that each joint tenant had to (1) take the same estate, (2) at the same time, and (3) from the same title, as well as (4) hold possession of the chattel together. These are the "four unities" of a joint tenancy—a unity of estate, time, title, and possession—and are today the four aspects necessary to establish this estate. Their presence means that each joint tenant is entitled to an undivided interest equal to every other tenant's. This joint possession of the whole leads to another more troublesome feature of a joint tenancy—the right of survivorship—by which the entire tenancy passes upon the death of any tenant to the surviving tenants until, at last, the sole surviving tenant takes the whole in absolute ownership.

If the right of survivorship was not express, the English common law had a presumption in favor of it. This presumption did not apply to a second type of concurrent interest—the tenancy in common, which is joint ownership lacking the right of survivorship.

The English presumption for the joint tenancy was rebuttable, and where an intent not to establish a joint tenancy was shown, a tenancy in common resulted.

The English preference for the joint tenancy was developed for real property and was fostered by a desire to avoid dividing the great landed estates among more than one heir. Where personal property is concerned, there is no comparable social policy to be served and, in any event, the English presumption had hardly gained a foothold in the United States before state legislatures in a few states abolished the joint tenancy entirely, or else abolished its right of survivorship or, as in the majority of states today, reversed the common law presumption in its favor. Thus the majority of American jurisdictions today require that there be an express manifestation of intent to create a joint tenancy before one is established; absent such an intent, a tenancy in common is presumed.

American common law as it developed in this area was applied to both real and personal property. But the affirmative manifestation of intent required in a majority of states to create a joint tenancy may, in the case of personal property, be oral and need not, as with real property, be in writing.

Furthermore, although a majority of states have a statutory presumption in favor of a tenancy in common the courts have not generally required that there be an express statement of an intent to form a joint tenancy in personal property. Likewise, statutes presuming that a deed to a chattel transferred to two or more persons is a tenancy in common, unless expressly declaring itself to be a joint tenancy, do not require that a right of survivorship be spelled out on the face of the document. Singling an item of personalty out of a decedent's estate does little harm to the decedent's heirs. Indeed, few reported cases in this country involve joint ownership of tangible personalty. Thus an intent to create a right of survivorship in personalty can be inferred from surrounding events and circumstances, except where each tenant has paid a portion of its purchase price or contributed ratably to funds on account; then a *pro rata* tenancy in common is established, with each tenant's share determined in proportion to his contribution.

II. JOINT BANK ACCOUNTS

A joint bank account is one established in the names of two or more persons. Although the rules of law applicable to bank accounts do not always square with those applying to joint tenancies and tenancies in common, the courts refer to such accounts as joint accounts. In particular, they do not require technical compliance with the four unities just because they call such an account a joint tenancy. Statutes of several types help courts achieve or provide for this result.

A.   STATUTORY TREATMENT
OF JOINT ACCOUNTS

One type of statute provides that a bank may pay any funds on account at the death of one account holder to the surviving holder(s) named in the account's documents and on signature cards. This type of statute is present in almost all states. Its purpose is to shield the bank from liability to other parties if the bank pays the surviving account holder in accordance with the terms of the account. Such statutes are not dispositive of ownership rights in the account, although more and more state courts use such statutes in resolving litigation between the surviving account holder and the heirs of the decedent, concluding that such a statute is at least presumptive evidence of a survivorship right. (The estate's money is typically available to pay for such litigation.) *Dyste v. Farmers and Mechanics Savings Bank of Minneapolis* (1930). Even in the absence of litigation, such statutes may not save the survivors from having to present evidence of a depositor's intent to create a survivorship right. To handle this possibility, some statutes provide that survivors may rely on the signature of a depositor as conclusive of his intent, absent other evidence of a fraud, misrepresentation, or undue influence in signing the card.

No such statute will shield a bank whose officials have knowledge of an actual dispute over ownership of the account. If it has actual notice of what they believe is a good faith dispute over the account, then at minimum it should be protected only when the parties to the dispute execute a release of the bank from liability for any withdrawal.

In twelve states and the District of Columbia, additional statutes provide that accounts established in two or more names become the property of all as joint tenants and that a right of survivorship attaches to the account when it is established. Such statutes sometimes preserve the common law's presumption of a joint tenancy for the special situation presented by bank accounts. This presumption may be rebutted by evidence to the contrary. *White v. White* (2001). Other states have gone further than this by judicial decision; here, as a matter of law, accounts established "in joint tenancy" create a joint tenancy with a right of survivorship, regardless of whether a contrary intent is evidenced, and indeed evidence of a contrary intent is inadmissible.

In nineteen other states, a uniform law has been enacted for joint accounts. It provides that the amounts on deposit belong "during the lifetime of all parties, to the parties in proportion to the net contribution by each to the sums on deposit, unless there is clear and convincing evidence of a different intent." UPC, § 6–103 (1989). It also provides that amounts "remaining on deposit at the death of a party to a joint account belong to the surviving party or parties as against the estate of the decedent unless there is clear and convincing evidence of a different intention at the time the account is created." UPC, § 6–104.

States adopting a variation of the UPC require that a statutory designation be used to reference the rights created by the Code. A failure to make such a designation runs the risk that the survivorship right in the account will fail, even though its creation was the intent of the account holders. Thus a few states require that survivorship be established by the documents and signature cards used to open the account. See Note, *The Creation of Joint Tenancy in Bank Accounts: The Old, the New, and the Uncertain*, 44 Ark.L.Rev. 199 (1991).

In successive waves of legislation then, these four types of state statutes become increasingly clear about the ownership rights created in joint accounts. Absent a statute, the law of gifts is applicable to the dispostion of joint accounts. Such statutes are not a complete answer to the problems that plague this area of the law. When the account documents and signature cards function as a substitute for the four unities requirement for creation of a joint account with a right of survivorship, the question of what those documents and cards need to say about the rights created sometimes arises. In addition, unlike tangible personal property held in joint names, a joint bank account has a fluctuating value as deposits and withdrawals are made. Common law rules in a jurisdiction may work a dissolution of the joint account's survivorship right at the time of a withdrawal of funds on account, thus severing the survivorship right from the bundle of rights otherwise held by the account holders. More on this problem later. Because of this, courts in many states have adopted more flexible rules for a joint bank account than would have been possible if it were just viewed as an application of a common-law joint tenancy. It has been called a gift, a trust, a contract, a testamentary disposition, as well as a joint tenancy.

B. ESTABLISHING A JOINT ACCOUNT

The establishment of a bank account in the names of two or more persons requires that the depositor or depositors and all other account holders sign signature cards at the bank. These cards generally define the type of account being established (e.g., joint tenancy or tenancy in common) by checking off the appropriate box. They also give each account holder the right to sign deposit and withdrawal slips for future transactions concerning the account. This is in effect the transfer of title to personal property to all the account-holders made by those who contribute money to the balance on account. As previously discussed, a transfer of title to two or more named persons will without more establish a tenancy in common in the funds on account, so it is at this point—the moment of creating the account—that the statutes previously discussed are first useful and must be consulted.

An optional type of signature card in use by many banks contains gift language to the effect that the signatory parties and the bank agree "that the funds placed in or added to this account by any one of the parties is and shall be conclusively intended to be a gift and delivery of such funds to the other signatory party or parties to the extent of their pro rata interest in the account." Several courts have held that this gift language is effective to overcome evidence that the account was a matter of convenience and worked no gift of the deposited funds. Such gift language on the signature card will not, however, prevent a court from looking for the elements necessary for a gift. Rather, the use of this card is evidence to be considered in the course of such an inquiry, but it is not by itself dispositive of the question of whether a gift was made.

Bank accounts are today widely used for holding money in joint ownership. Such accounts provide instances of the courts (1) formulating flexible rules pertaining to concurrent estates in this type of personal property, and (2) adapting the law of gifts to new uses. Legislatures have been reluctant to deal comprehensively with joint bank accounts because they are often used as a "poor man's will." They also facilitate inter-spousal transfers of family wealth.

The familial purpose of establishing a joint account is often tax-related—i.e., the avoidance of gift or estate taxes, or the transfer of the assets on account from one family member in a high income tax bracket to another in a lower bracket. Often too, such accounts function as a wallet shared by all account holders. The "wallet" and the "will" functions of such an account will now be separately examined.

C. THE "WALLET" FUNCTION:
THE *INTER VIVOS* RIGHT
TO WITHDRAW

In the situation where a bank account has been established in joint tenancy by two or more persons and one of these later withdraws his pro rata share or more of the account than he contributed to the balance on account, what is the effect of such a withdrawal? Many of the statutes previously discussed only deal with the intent of the contributor at the moment the account is established. Different evidence may be available as to his intent at the time of a withdrawal, and so courts may deviate from the rule provided in the statutes.

Most courts begin their search for a solution by reasoning from the attributes of a joint tenancy. For example, each joint tenant has the "right to possession" of all of the money on account, and from this some courts reason that each has the right to withdraw all the money on account without incurring any liability to the other account holders.

Other courts conclude that the agreement to hold the account in joint tenancy was only for the purpose of pooling the funds on deposit, but did not necessarily extend to an excessive withdrawal by any one of the tenants. Such courts look to see if the withdrawal was intended as a dissolution of the joint tenancy, either in whole or as to the withdrawn funds. If it is dissolved, a duty to account for any portion of the withdrawal in excess of his contribution to the account follows the withdrawing account holder and attaches to any property purchased with the withdrawn funds. A few states take the position that the withdrawal ends the right of survivorship that distinguishes a joint tenancy from a tenancy in common. The withdrawal severs or ends the joint tenancy and a tenancy in common replaces it. So the withdrawal of more than a *pro rata* share of the funds on account renders the withdrawing co-tenant liable to the other tenants for the excess.

A severance of a joint tenancy account might also occur when one co-tenant pledged the balance on account as security for a loan made to that co-tenant alone. Such a severance would occur when the other co-tenants know of and assent to the pledge. If they do not, some authority would still hold that a severance occurred when the pledge was made, whether or not the other co-tenants knew of it. Perhaps the better view is that no severance occurs when the loan was later repaid and the security was never needed—the non-participating co-tenants remaining ignorant of the loan all the while. A call on the security would, under any view, work a severance and change the joint tenancy into a tenancy in common thereafter. Finally, an even better view is that, even if there is a call on the security, or even if the account is called to satisfy a judgment of the depositing co-tenant, there is no severance of a joint tenancy when substantial funds remain on account. *Fleet Bank Connecticut v. Carillo* (1997).

Until 1990, California courts held that a joint tenancy in personal property, like a bank account, could not be severed unilaterally. Today unilateral severance is possible and an account holder can defeat the right of survivorship by withdrawing funds on account. *Estate of Propst* (1990). While there is nothing inherently wrong with a unilateral severance, courts typically permit it only when the non-severing tenants have been given notice of it.

In a tenancy in common, the presumption is that the co-tenants contributed equally to the funds on account. This presumption is, however, often a rebuttable one. Whether the bank account is held in either joint tenancy or tenancy in common, some courts have a presumption that where the contributing and noncontributing account holders are husband and wife, the contributing tenant intended to make a gift of one half of the funds on deposit to the other tenant. This last presumption is used to promote the stability of spousal relations as a matter of public policy and is virtually irrebuttable whether or not a withdrawal turns a joint tenancy into a tenancy in common. In such jurisdictions, neither the fact that the withdrawing tenant had been the sole owner of the funds prior to deposit nor the fact that he removed the balance in the account and used it for his own purposes is sufficient, singly or in combination, to rebut it. Whether the withdrawn funds are still in existence or not, the gift to the spouse was complete upon deposit.

One more distinction worth noting in this area is attributable to different patterns of usage of savings as opposed to checking accounts. The tracking of a contribution through a bank account is often more easily accomplished with a savings account where deposits and withdrawals are less frequent and in larger amounts than would be the case with a checking account. Checking deposits and withdrawals will be more frequent, smaller, and much more difficult to track. From this difficulty an inference might be drawn that a gift of deposited funds was intended to any checking account holder making a withdrawal in any amount, even one in excess of his contribution. At least one court has refused to impose a liability on a checking account holder for amounts withdrawn in excess of contribution although, if the funds can be tracked through an account, there is no need to make this distinction between savings and checking accounts dispositive of any case. Indeed, modern banking practices and mutual fund money market accounts tend to blur the once clear distinction between these two types of accounts. The pattern of use is one fact from which intent might be determined, but not the only one.

Indeed, it is difficult these days for many to figure out who is a banker. Although this section deals with bank accounts, much said here can also be applied to mutual fund, money market, and stock brokerage accounts in joint names with a check cashing feature. See *First Wisconsin Trust Company v. United States* (1982). In the future, the rules used for bank account cases are likely to be used to decide similar controversies involving accounts held by companies functioning like bankers, though not regulated as such. Also seldom subject to statutory regulation are survivorship disputes involving personal property in jointly held safety deposit boxes; in the absence of statutes, the common law of gifts applies to such disputes.

D. THE "WILL" FUNCTION: GIFTS TO SURVIVING ACCOUNT HOLDERS

Absent a statute to the contrary, a gift of the balance on account to a surviving account holder is invalid unless the signature cards establish an express or implied right of survivorship. The earliest reported cases on survivorship rights were decided under the law of gifts. Where a depositor opened an account in joint names but thereafter retained some control over the passbook, checks, or account records, the question arose as to whether there was a delivery. However, because the retention could also be construed as a completed gift with a survivorship right, courts often look to the execution of the signature cards as a deed of gift that substituted for an actual, manual delivery. In other early cases, courts regarded the signature cards as a depositor/bank contract for the benefit of the other account holders as third-party beneficiaries of the contract. So gift and contract theories often exist side by side in a jurisdiction's case law to give surviving account holder's rights in the funds on account.

In some states the signature card which opens an account in joint names creates a presumption that a survivorship right attached to the account. This presumption is rebuttable, but only by clear and convincing evidence. Rebutting evidence generally goes to show that the account was opened for the convenience of the depositor and created an agency relationship between the depositor and the other account holders. In such a case, no survivorship rights will be found where the depositor (1) could withdraw all the funds on account in his sole discretion and (2) was ill and the account was needed to order his financial affairs through an agent. An aged depositor whose illness might require all funds on account, but who opened an account with a nurse who never withdrew funds for personal use, could argue successfully that his intent was to retain control of the funds during his life. Here, if any right in the account for the nurse is intended at all, it will arise only at the death of the depositor. At this time the agent's authority to use the account is terminated by his principal's death, but the survivorship right may have been given as payment for the agent's services. This arrangement is in effect a joint account in which one account holder, if he has any rights at all, has only survivorship rights. Such a result is less plausible where a depositor is in the same aged and ill condition but is nursed by a spouse to whom many courts would accord more discretion in withdrawing funds on account. However, if the nursing spouse withdrew all the funds a day before his spouse's death, he might still be held to have severed a joint tenancy and would lose half of it to his spouse's estate. If, on the other hand, he had waited a day he would have received the whole account as a surviving account holder. Compare *Estate of Gray* (1965) with *Zander v. Holly* (1957).

Courts may ignore a regulatory statute's literal wording, even with regard to a statute purporting to establish a joint tenancy as a matter of law, and permit the parties to a dispute to litigate the issue of ownership of the funds on account. When the deceased has deposited all or most of his funds in such an account or the survivor has not contributed his share of the funds on account at the time of the death, the courts look beyond the statutes to review the alleged transfer of the funds to the survivor(s). Even in these situations, the statutes still count for something: they extend the possibility of survivorship rights in account holders who have not contributed to the funds on account, although the funds are all or most of the corpus of the deceased depositor's estate. These cases are fact-sensitive. In them, courts sustain survivorship rights (if they do) on one of three theories. The first involves contract law, another trust law, and yet a third involves viewing the deposit as a gift to the survivor.

(1) If the deposit of the money with the bank creates a contract between the depositor and the bank, the surviving account holder who has not contributed money to the bank balance might be viewed as a donee, third-party beneficiary to that contract. It is a transaction between the actual depositor of the money and the bank for the benefit

of another account holder. Then a third party need not sign the agreements establishing the account. *Malek v. Patten* (1984) (noting that stringent application of the law of gifts would require the beneficiary's signature, but that "[m]odern commercial practice relies heavily upon contractual theory rather than gift theory."). If the supposed beneficiary has in addition signed a signature card, then the contract is a three-party one. This contract is also enforceable without regard to the law of gifts.

(2) Alternately, the depositor who places his money in a joint tenancy account might be regarded as the settlor of a revocable trust. It is revocable in the sense that the depositor retains access to the balance up until the time of his death. Such a view of the joint tenancy bank account is in conflict with the normal requirement that the settlor of a trust relinquish all title and control over the corpus of the account. A combination of factors may, however, persuade a court to overlook this rule: the convenience of the account, a decline in the adherence to the policy underlying the Statute of Wills, the difficulties of probate, and the bank's account-opening formalities, impressing upon the depositor the fact that he is giving up total control over the account.

Of course, a deposit may be expressly made "by S in trust for B." These words would constitute a formal declaration of a trust, and when accompanied by other evidence of the settlors' intent to create a trust, such as giving some checks or the passbook to the beneficiary, such trust is valid. In this case, the courts of some jurisdictions assume the trust is irrevocable but that the settlor has retained a management power over the balance in the account. Such a trust may, however, still be found in violation of the Statute of Wills, and cases in some jurisdictions have so found.

(3) A third view of the joint tenancy bank account involves the law of gifts. The courts of many states have litigated the question of delivery for these accounts. Delivery and donative intent are required. Arguably, the delivery of the funds to the bank is a delivery to a trustee for the co-depositor donee, especially when the donee acquires a present right to make withdrawals from the account. As to the donor's intention to make a gift, the courts have split in finding such an intent in a situation where typically the donor has given access to the funds to the donee but can himself withdraw them, and so has not relinquished total control over the balance in the account. If access through checks or the passbook is provided the donee, many courts have sustained the gift even though the donor has only shared control over the account. So, in situations where both the donor and donee have access to the account, the holdings of these cases are an exception to the general rule that the donor must relinquish all control over the subject of the gift. Either that relinquishment is inferred from the donor's acquiescence in the donee's access, or else the donor is estopped to deny that the access created a survivorship right in the donee, and thus it is the donee's access to the account that proves dispositive in these cases. It is irrelevant whether or not the right

to withdraw was ever used or that the donee only actually used the funds in the account for emergency purposes. Acquisition of access and a potential right to control the account is sufficient.

A gift of the balance to the survivor in a joint bank account is not testamentary in nature. As a gift, it operates at the time the account is established, that is, during the donor's lifetime. Some courts have presumed the validity of the survivorship gift without looking more deeply into the matter. Other courts, however, have found that the gift is void for noncompliance with the Statute of Wills applicable in the jurisdiction. Courts have hesitated to make this finding, however, since a good faith codepositor will then be held to account for any withdrawals he made. Only where such withdrawals are made with notice of a rival claim on the funds, such as might be made by the estate of the nonsurviving depositor, will courts impose this liability. Otherwise, the donor's providing access to the funds is evidence of acquiescence by the donor to the gift.

Once the donor is dead, courts show an increasing reluctance to disturb the joint bank account arrangement. A survivorship right in a bank account may not be revoked by will. *Estate of Steed* (1994). Even when the will is express on the matter, the attempt at revocation is only effective after the survivorship right had taken effect. Other courts use the donor's intent as their guide. The notion of when both the will and the right is effective is too formal when contrary to the donor's intent. Because an earlier will can be revoked by a later one, these courts reason, a joint bank account's survivorship right should be revoked by a later will as well. A contract or a trust, for that matter, might be similarly revoked. In any event, a will substitute, functioning in the meanwhile like a wallet, should be treated no differently than an earlier will would have been. It can be, if courts distinguish clearly between the two very different functions served by joint accounts.

This area of the law is by no means crisp. The confusion of theories results in opposing and contrary holdings. Recent cases in Ohio and Rhode Island, reviewing the three theories, have rejected the cases using the depositor's intent as their principal guide, and concluded that, absent fraud, the manner in which an account is opened—that is, including an express right of survivorship or not—"shall be conclusive evidence" of the depositor's intent with regard to the disposition of funds on account at depositor's death to either the depositor's estate or to the surviving account holder. *Robinson v. Delfino* (1998). The drum beat of litigation, however, continues to be steady because joint tenancy bank accounts are in wide use and function as an everyman's will.

No matter what legal theory is used, the alleged transfer will be held void upon proof of fraud, duress, misrepresentation, mutual mistake, or incapacity. Such has been the traditional rule in matters of gifts, so when a domineering person escorts a transferor into the presence of a third party like a bank officer, it would be inequitable to hold that the same grounds for invalidating the transfer are not available just because the theory supporting the transfer has changed and is now contractual or trust-oriented. No matter what the theory, proof of one of these grounds for invalidation shows that the transfer does not reflect the intent of the parties. *Lowry v. Lowry* (1976); *Estate of Bowlin v. Ables* (1988).

1. The Totten Trust

The idea that a joint bank account can serve as a will substitute without first being a wallet is, when viewed through the lens of the trust theory, akin to a revocable trust—traditionally almost a contradiction in terms. Nonetheless, a depositor's placing his own funds in a savings account "in trust for" or "as trustee for" another is generally held to establish a revocable or tentative trust during the lifetime of the depositor. Restatement (Second) of Trusts, § 58 (1959). It is revocable at will because the depositor retains access to the funds and because of a judicial policy against self-declared trusts. Title to the funds stays with the depositor and so the beneficiaries named in the account have a mere expectancy, not a vested right to them. This trust may be completed by delivery of the passbook to the beneficiary or by any other unequivocal act of the depositor. If not revoked during the life of the depositor, a presumption arises that an irrevocable trust is created at his death. In some states, the title to the funds passes by operation of law to the persons named; this means that no evidence to the contrary is admissible because there is no presumption on which the contrary facts might work. The corpus of this trust consists of whatever funds are on deposit at death.

This tentative trust is called a Totten Trust, so-called after the case of *In re Totten* (1904). Totten trust funds are generally considered to pass outside the estate of the depositor, now decedent. See Kara Marcus, *Totten Trusts: Pragmatic Pre–Death Planning or Post–Mortem Plunder?*, 69 Temp. L. Rev. 861, 865 (1996). They can be subjected to claims made on him or his estate by his creditors. *Farrell v. Coulter* (1995) (depositor's continuing authority over the deposit during his life justifies creditor's ability to reach it to satisfy judgment). However, they are not everywhere subjected to a spousal right to elect against the will of the decedent. Compare *Dalia v. Lawrence* (1993) (no spousal right to elect) with *Estate of Amundson* (2001) (conferring such right). An agreement not to create a Totten Trust to defeat spousal rights will be enforced. *Blackmon v. Estate of Battcock* (1991). As to creditors, the logic is that if the depositor could have used the funds to pay creditors, the latter should be able to reach the funds by judicial process.

A formal revocation of the tentative trust by the depositor is not necessary. Any action, disavowal, or declaration will do. Any withdrawal of funds by the depositor will revoke the tentative trust as to the funds withdrawn but *not* as to the funds remaining. So will any withdrawal by a person with the depositor's general power of attorney. If the passbook is used as collateral or security for a loan to the depositor, the trust is revoked to the extent of the debt of the depositor on the loan because he has shown an intention to use the funds in a manner inconsistent with the terms of the trust. This is so because the alternative of holding that a trustee of only a tentative trust has violated his fiduciary duty seems harsh. Upon revocation by withdrawal, the beneficiary may not trace the funds (that is, show their final use) or hold the depositor liable for them.

If the beneficiary predeceases the depositor, a Totten Trust is terminated. If the payment of the trust funds to the beneficiary is not to be made at the depositor's death, and instead a successor trustee is appointed, or the payment is conditioned on some event after the depositor's death, such as the beneficiary's reaching a certain age, the trust is not a Totten Trust and the traditional rules of the law of trusts are applied. *Estate of Bischof* (1989).

A residuary clause in a will, stating that "all the rest and residue of my property" go to a person other than the beneficiary of a Totten Trust, will not by itself revoke the trust. However, evidence that a testator intended to revoke it with his will is admissible. *Estate of Bol* (1988).

At the depositor's death, the money is normally paid out to the beneficiary, although the issue of whether it should be paid out involves an interpretation of the terms of the trust. Since the first judicial recognition in New York in 1904, Totten Trusts have been adopted in eighteen other jurisdictions, including good opinions from Florida and

Illinois. *Estate of Morton* (1987). In addition, statutes permitting banks to pay out funds on account to surviving depositors, often provide an argument for courts that there is no policy objection to the recognition of Totten Trusts. *In re Estate of Adams* (1990); *In re Estate of Stokes* (1987). Other states' community property statutes may protect the depositor's spouse and limit the usefulness of such trusts because community funds may not be unilaterally placed in this type or any type of trust; there only half of the depositor's account passes to the Totten Trust's beneficiary. *In re Estate of Wilson* (1986).

CHAPTER IX

ADVERSE POSSESSION OF PERSONAL PROPERTY

Adverse possession is the use of a chattel in a way inconsistent with the right of the true owner of the title to it. The title to a chattel can be transferred by adverse possession. Using this method of transfer, even a convertor who holds a chattel for the requisite, statutory period of time, using it in an exclusive, open and notorious, continuous, hostile—and so generally adverse—manner receives title to it. The passage of time involved in the period of adverse possession bars the true owner's or prior possessor's cause of action in either replevin or trover. *Henderson v. First National Bank of Dewitt* (1973).

Each of the previously stated elements of adverse possession raises issues of fact. Was the convertor in *exclusive* physical possession of the chattel? Did he hold it for all his neighbors and the world to see—that is, *openly and notoriously*? For a *continuous* or uninterrupted period of time? In such a *hostile* manner as to put the world, including the true owner or prior possessor, on notice that he was holding it so as to bar any other rights in it?

338

All the elements of adverse possession typically examine the behavior of the adverse possessor. However, there are two deviations from this tradition in the law of adverse possession for personalty. One involves the so-called "demand and refusal" element in an action for replevin or trover. New York's case law has examined this. The other is the use of the so-called discovery rule in interpreting the statute of limitations for chattels. New Jersey has used this.

The *open and notorious* element of adverse possession will often provide the adverse user of chattels with the greatest difficulties of proof. After all, many chattels are just not big enough to make their possession notoriously apparent to all. Their open use may nonetheless be inconspicuous. Thus it is not surprising that many adverse possession cases are difficult to decide because they involve two innocent parties and revolve around the issue of when the statutory period starts—rather than when it ends. *State of New York v. The Seventh Regiment Fund, Inc.* (2002). On this issue, state statutes of limitation for replevin, trover and conversion, and conversion alone, are seldom helpful.

The typical period for bringing such actions is either three or six years in over one half of the states—and four or five years in most of the rest. A majority of United States jurisdictions have a two to four year statute of limitations. See Jodi Patt, *The Need to Revamp Current Domestic Protection for Cultural Property*, 96 Nw. U. L. Rev. 1207, 1215, n. 67 (2002); Patti Gerstenblith, *The Adverse Posses-*

sion of Personal Property, 37 Buff. L.Rev. 119 (1988).

Adverse possession was originally a real property doctrine that was in the 19th century applied to personalty. It has several purposes. First, like any statute of limitations, it bars the litigation of stale claims because of the evidentiary problems that would otherwise result. Second, it aids in the quieting of title to chattels, settling expectations and giving commercial security and reliability to later sales and other transfers. Third, it often protects good faith purchasers of chattels. Finally, it punishes the true owner who is not diligent in pursuing his rights. This final purpose is more important with chattels than it is in the comparable case law involving realty.

I. ADVERSE POSSESSION AND STATUTES OF LIMITATION

Where do the elements of adverse possession come from? The required exclusivity, openness, continuousness, hostility and adversity are a gloss on statute of limitations provisions found in all state codes. They are judge-made law. Such statutes typically provide:

No person shall commence an action for the recovery of a chattel or land, or make any entry on land, unless within ... years after the right to bring such action or make such entry first accrued, or within ... years after he or those by or under whom he claims, have been seized or possessed of the chattel or premises.

The period of time required to lapse under such provisions is 10 to 20 years for real property, but often only two to six years for personal property. In one leading case, two counters were installed in a shop. The shop's premises were later mortgaged and the mortgage included all fixtures within it (including the counters). Can the vendor of the counters reclaim them after the statute of limitations for personalty has run but before the real property limitation period has run? This was the issue in *Chapin v. Freeland* (1886).

Holmes, J., held that he could not, but gave an answer that made it necessary to determine the type of property involved. The cause of action brought by the plaintiff, who purchased the premises at the sale foreclosing the mortgage, was replevin which lies for the recovery of personal property. The defendant had installed the counters in 1867 and had repossessed them in 1881. Once repossessed and in his hands, what had once been a real property fixture reverted to being personal property; the court held that the shorter statute of limitations for personal property applied and had already run at the time of the repossession.

The dissent in *Chapin* takes issue with Holmes' application of the statute of limitations for personalty. It thought that the defendant was entitled to have the benefit of the longer limitations period in the real property statute which had not been tolled at the time of the defendant's seizure of the counters. Since the chattels became fixtures and so part of the real property when installed *by the plaintiff,* the defendant should have the benefit of the limitations period chosen by his opponent.

The counter-argument to this is a practical one to the effect that persons like the plaintiff should be encouraged to modernize and improve their property with personal property permanently affixed to their real estate. To permit the defendant to have the benefit of the longer limitations period for real property would be to weaken the plaintiff's ability to realize the profits of the modernization by subjecting the title to the fixtures to uncertainty for a longer period.

Another advantage of Holmes' position is that it discourages self-help and the violence that might attend it. The vendor of a chattel that becomes a fixture on realty must assert his right (if any) to self-help within the period of limitations for personalty or be barred. This, too, will tend to give the improver of realty an incentive to modernize by confirming his title to the fixtures all the sooner.

Further, Holmes argues that no repossession or self-help was possible because the statute of limitation was intended to bar the right to the chattel as well as the remedy for infringement of that right.

It is this last proposition to which the dissent in *Chapin* takes exception. Barring the right along with the judicial remedy is the traditional view of the effect of an adverse possession statute concerning real property. The dissent, however, thought that in Massachusetts the remedy was barred, but not the right. In a sense, the vendor still had a right or a title that the courts would not reduce to possession. If the underlying right or title of the vendor survives, then self-help is available to him to enforce his right to the counters.

However, the Massachusetts statute bars "the action for replevin and all other actions for the taking, detaining, or injuring of goods or chattels." This inclusiveness suggests that the actions of trespass, detinue, and trover, as well as the action of replevin, are barred under this statute. With both damage actions as well as those for specific recovery barred, then the personal property statute bars both the tort and property causes of action involved in adverse possession and operates as a complete bar to recovery of the chattel.

Holmes also has the better of the argument over whether there should be a right without a remedy. His underlying premise is that the courts should not permit a right, even if derived logically, for which there is no practical remedy and for which there is no judicial review to prevent its abuse. Self-help might be permitted, he might say, but not to this extent.

A. THE U.C.C. AND *CHAPIN*

Today, in about one half of the states, the holder of a mortgage or other security interest in fixtures who files his interest on the public record obtains a priority of lien over pre-existing recorded mortgages on the underlying real property under the Uniform Commercial Code, § 9–313(4)(a), 1972 version. This priority is an exception to the usual rule of the recording statutes for real property whose rule is usually "first to record, first in right." For fixture filings, the rule is "last to record, first in right." Such a drastic exception is permitted only because of a strong policy to encourage the modernization and improvement of real property.

The exception to the normal priority is itself subject to an exception, but it is one that reenforces the underlying rationale; that is, the fixturizer's priority of lien is itself subject to a lien for a construction loan on the same property. Because the construction lender energizes improvement of the whole property, a fixturizer, as one who improves only a part of it, takes second place to him. UCC § 9–313(6) (1972).

II. ADVERSE POSSESSION AS A GLOSS ON STATUTES OF LIMITATIONS

Chapin shows that the elements of adverse possession are a judge-made gloss on statutes of limitations and an extension of rules originally applied to real property. It is the rare case, however, that allows a judge to delve into the causes of action underlying these statutes, for in many jurisdictions the law of adverse possession will have hidden its statutory roots in a maze of cases. These cases will outline the facts necessary to make out the elements of adverse user for both real and personal property.

These statutes of limitations provide that no person shall commence an action for the recovery of chattels unless they do so within up to six years running from the time his right or title to the chattel first accrued, or within six years from the time the plaintiff last possessed the chattel or had the right to possess it. Several of the phrases in this paraphrase are indicative of the present-day elements of adverse possession. First, the idea that the plaintiff must assert his "right or title" suggests that his interest in the chattel must be recognized— i.e., *open* and *notorious*. Second, that his "possession or right to possess" the chattel is at issue suggests that his interest in the chattel must be *continuous*. Third, that a "right to possess" may be considered as well as possession itself, suggests that the interest will usually be an *exclusive* one, but may on occasion be constructive or at least as exclusive as custom and usage permit.

Six years was the period of limitations in England for trespass, detinue, trover and replevin actions. A similar period has been adopted in many states in this country. Its passage bars both the title and the right to possession of the true owner or prior possessor when he was out of possession for that period, and meanwhile the adverse possessor satisfies all of the elements of adverse use. The good or bad faith of the adverse possessor makes no difference— the statute of limitations runs in either case.

Many adverse possession cases involving real property revolve around the claim of title of the adverse possessor: is there evidence of legal ownership? With regard to real property, this evidence is known as color of title. Often (probably more often than will be the case with real property) the holder of a chattel will not have a bill of sale, deed of gift, or other evidence of a claim of title. So color of title is not required to acquire adverse possession of a chattel. This being the case, some courts have heard with sympathy the claim that when a stolen chattel leaves the jurisdiction or when it is hidden, the statute stops running and starts to run again when the thief holds it openly within the jurisdiction. If he leaves once more, the statute stops running and does not begin running again until his return—and so on, until the statutory period is tolled in fits and starts. Often this result is accomplished by statute, but one court put the rule this way:

> The statute of limitations on an action to recover stolen personal property in the hands of one who in good faith purchased the personalty for value, begins to run from the time the latter acquired the possession and not from the time the owner first had knowledge of the whereabouts of the property, provided there was no fraud or attempt at concealment. . . . However, the action is barred only when the property is held openly and notoriously for two years, so that the owner may have a reasonable opportunity of knowing its whereabouts and of asserting his title. . . .

Riesinger's Jewelers, Inc. v. Roberson (1978). This quotation makes two points about the law of adverse possession. First, the function of its five elements is to provide the true owner or prior possessor of the chattel with notice that non-assertion of his rights will bar his claim after the statutory period runs. Second, the elements are a judicial gloss on a statute of limitations and as such are intended to mollify the harsh effects of the statute alone; they are meant, in other words, to do justice between the parties to a dispute over a chattel.

Some cases hold that the doctrine of tacking (or substitution) between adverse users applies to personal property that is adversely possessed, just as it applies to realty. However, there are some cases to the contrary, holding that a new cause of action begins to run against each successive adverse possessor of a chattel. See, e.g., *O'Keeffe v. Snyder* (1980). Although the purposes and the policy of the statute of limitations remain the same for both realty and personalty, each successive transfer of the chattel is also a new basis for an allegation of conversion. So the adverse use of a chattel must be open and notorious enough to provide notice to its owners and prior possessors that its present holder is seeking to receive title in himself. Successive transfers are likely to be the most public acts available as proof that the open and notorious elements of adverse possession have been fulfilled. Tacking therefore seems justified, otherwise most adverse users would not be able to prove this element of their cases. On the other hand, if each successive transfer gives rise to a new cause of action in conversion, then tacking is not justified. The rule closest to the procedural origins of adverse possession law is that tacking is not permitted for personalty. This rule also best protects chattels' true owners.

Once an adverse possessor acquires his title, he is entitled also to all of the rents, income and profits derived from a chattel for the period of time during which he has been running the statute. These are known as mesne or interim profits. In the same manner, one acquires the rights in any off-spring born to adversely-possessed animals, crops grown on land adversely possessed, and any other chattels affixed to land adversely possessed. In these situations, the title of the adverse possessor, once acquired, is said to relate back to the date on which he began to run the statute in his favor.

A. "OPEN AND CONTINUOUS" ADVERSE POSSESSION

Unlike land, a chattel cannot easily be held for all the world to see. Even if it is not secreted away or hidden, it is likely to be in the user's home and unlikely to be on public display. Its adverse user will thus be subject to the argument that he has not openly used the chattel and so cannot prove all the elements of adverse possession.

A leading case illustrates this point. In 1946, the artist, Georgia O'Keeffe, had three of her paintings stolen from a New York City art gallery. From then until 1975 the paintings were lost, and O'Keeffe, thinking them lost forever, did not report the theft until 1972 when, for the first time, it was possible to report stolen works of art and have them put on an international registry. In 1975, the painting turned up in the Princeton, N.J., gallery of a purchaser who did not verify the title of the person who sold him the paintings. O'Keeffe made a demand upon the gallery owner to return the works. He refused and she sued him in replevin. *O'Keeffe v. Snyder* (1980).

Since this suit was brought more than 20 years after the supposed theft of the paintings and the applicable statute of limitation was six years, the first issue in the case is whether the statute of limitations has run on this cause of action. What then is it, precisely, that starts a statute of limitations running? The answer is a general one—the accrual of the cause of action. When does a cause of action first accrue? One answer might be that it accrues when the last element of the cause of action falls into place. In the case of replevin, the plaintiff must allege: first, some right to the chattel in the plaintiff; second, the loss of the chattel by conversion—some wrongful taking or detention of it; and third, the defendant's retention of it at the time of the suit, after a demand by the plaintiff and a refusal to return it by the defendant, by which, fourth, the plaintiff suffers damages.

The third element of the cause of action—the retention at the time of the suit—is generally proven by a demand and refusal. The plaintiff demands the chattel back and the defendant's refusal shows that he retains it in the face of his knowledge of the plaintiff's claim to it. A demand and refusal cannot be made until the defendant is located. In practical terms, this is good for the plaintiff in replevin because he then argues that until the defendant is known to him, his cause of action is not complete and the statute of limitations cannot run against it. At least one state (New York) has cases which accept this point of view. *Menzel v. List* (1967). There the demand puts the innocent possessor on notice of the plaintiff's claim. Thereafter, his possession of the disputed chattel is a knowing interference with the plaintiff's rights. The knowing retention of the chattel completes the conversion underlying the cause of action; indeed, it constitutes an entirely new act of conversion and in some states may start the statute running anew.

However, this view of replevin has limitations. The demand is not, of course, the first time that a bad faith possessor is put on notice of another's rights. He is, presumably, already adversely possessing the chattel and his possession is a continuous conversion of the plaintiff's chattel.

Making a demand and refusal a necessity for replevin will prejudice innocent purchasers more than ones with bad faith. In any event, few defendants will be prejudiced by the absence of a demand; indeed, the plaintiff's bringing suit against them will itself provide notice of the claim. The good faith or bad faith of an adverse possessor is

not and should not be dispositive of adverse possession questions; rather, the type of user is.

A more general weakness of the argument that a
demand and refusal is a substantive element of
replevin is that, whether the defendant is known to
the plaintiff or not, the defendant typically has
retained the chattel for the statutory period. So the
better view is that the demand and refusal is not a
substantive element of replevin; it is merely one
method of proof of the third element in this cause of
action. In some jurisdictions, it may even be *the*
traditional method of proof. But only that. As evidence rather than a substantive requirement of
replevin, a demand and refusal is not necessary to
the bringing of the cause of action, and the statute
runs regardless of whether or not it is made.

In states which reject demand and refusal as a
substantive element of replevin, the courts remain
concerned that the adverse possessor of a chattel
not hide it for the statutory period and prevent the
true owner from finding it until it is too late. So
normally the concealment of a chattel stops the
running of the statute. Where the defense to the
replevin action is a title in the defendant by adverse
possession, the defendant will have the burden of
proof to show each of the elements necessary for
such possession. In the instance of a concealment,
he will fail to show "open and notorious" possession. The focus of the court's inquiry will be on the
defendant's actions, rather than the need for a
secure title in a later possessor and equitable defenses such as laches. To decide whether the statute

ever began to run, therefore, some courts examine the plaintiff's actions including, but not limited to, whether he made a demand for the chattel's return.

The *O'Keeffe* court said that the difficulties of applying the law of adverse possession to chattels dictate that the statute not start to run until the discovery of the chattel in the defendant's possession if, in the meantime, the plaintiff has been diligent in seeking to discover its whereabouts. The burden of showing this diligence is on the plaintiff. Running the statute of limitations is deferred only so long as this diligence lasts, and thereafter, it runs and the defendant must show that he satisfied the elements of adverse possession.

Subsequent uses of the *O'Keeffe* case as precedent make plain that, in many instances, the true owner of the chattel as a plaintiff is the one to benefit from the use of the discovery rule, in that it extends the time during which an action is available to him. See e.g., *Mucha v. King* (1986) (involving artwork sought by the artist's heir); *DeHart v. First Fidelity Bank, N.A./South Jersey* (1986) (involving conversion of negotiable instruments owned by a bank).

Use of the discovery rule in *O'Keeffe* downplays the fact that the defendant was not a bad fellow; indeed, he has some of the traits of a good faith purchaser. It was the difficulty of establishing what constitutes open and notorious possession of the paintings that persuaded the court that the burden of first establishing those elements of adverse possession should not be imposed on the defendant.

Rather, the true owner has the burden of showing diligence, although why that diligence is less difficult to show is unclear. Meanwhile—that is, while the true owner is being diligent (if he is)—how is the possessor supposed to learn of this diligence and thus learn of the (in)security of his right to continued possession of the chattel? The answer is that he cannot know, and so can't be secure in his claim. This is particularly true of the good faith possessor. The *O'Keeffe* court solves one problem by creating another.

This "discovery rule" has been used in other areas of the law (e.g., torts) to protect causes of action which would otherwise not be brought due to ignorance. It is particularly apt when the plaintiff is injured—or when there is an injury to property not immediately evident—and the defendant is a bad fellow. (Notice, however, this was not the situation in *O'Keeffe*.)

The use of the discovery rule permits a court to balance the injustice to the defendant (whether through the difficulties of defending a stale suit, his innocence, or the injury which he will suffer) against the benefit to a plaintiff in allowing the replevin action. The rule is an invention of equity and permits the plaintiff to bring replevin when he can show due diligence under the circumstances of the case. Moreover, it considers degrees of due diligence—whether the defendant was blind to facts he should have seen, was intentionally idle, made some efforts, or was faced with an impossible task. It renders the title of a remote possessor that much more uncertain but gives force to the rule that, with stolen chattels, the thief acquires no title and cannot transfer good title to others regardless of their good faith or ignorance of the theft.

Today reliable, computerized, and well publicized registries for reports of art theft are operated by various law enforcement agencies. Once these registries are widely available and customarily used, true owners who promptly report thefts to the police and such registries can expect, in discovery rule states, to satisfy the due diligence elements of *O'Keeffe's* discovery rule.[1]

The *O'Keeffe* case was not the start of a trend in the courts or legislatures. *Mucha v. King* (1986). California amended its statute of limitation to reflect it. Cal. Civ. Proc. Code. § 338 (c) (1993). However, the New York Court of Appeals rejected the case. *Solomon R. Guggenheim Fdn. v. Lubell* (1990). While stating that, after discovery of the stolen chattel, the true owner was subject to the equitable doctrine of laches and so cannot unreasonably delay the demand upon the possessor for its return, this court thought that imposing on the true owner the burden of proving due diligence was a retreat from the traditional protection afforded owners. Moreover, the court said, all true owners should not be expected to behave alike, so that

1. A similar rule is used in Western states for rustled cattle: the true owner of livestock bearing a registered brand is not held to have an action in trover or replevin until he knows of their whereabouts, as brands were commonly recorded and branding thus became a sign of diligence in sorting out ownership. See, e.g., Utah Code Ann. 78–12–26(2) (2001).

crafting a rule of due diligence would become very difficult. Some will not want the notoriety of advertising the theft. Some will think their chance of recovery greater if they don't advertise it. In addition, were the rule otherwise, the court said, the possessor able to hold onto the chattel for three years (the applicable limitations period) would be able to retain possession unless the true owner is able to show due diligence. (That is, the court fears that a procedural rule would quickly turn into a substantive one.) Due diligence, while not irrelevant to this court, is thought best considered by way of an estoppel or laches defense. Thus the Court of Appeals protects the true owner when he is the victim of an art theft by placing the burden of tracing the title of the art object—or provenance, in the parlance of the art trade—on its purchaser.

The statute of limitations rules in the holdings in *O'Keeffe* and *Lubell* has no effect on the moral rights of artists. Although little accepted in this country, the doctrine of moral right holds that an artist has, even after selling his work, the right to preserve its integrity, to prevent its being exhibited up-side down, or copied in a way that distorts its meaning. This doctrine has been codified in seven states. See e.g., McKinney's—N.Y. Arts & Cult. Aff.L. § 14.03 (2002). The artist's cause of action under this type of statute arises when the integrity of the work is threatened.

When a museum is the purchaser or donee of a work of art or other chattels, the law of adverse possession is often used as a title-quieting device.

Thus, after the delivery as a gift of a collection of historical documents to a museum holding them for the statutory period, the transferor of a heretofore unqualified delivery cannot seek to reacquire them on the ground that the documents were the subject of a bailment or loan. *Wilcox v. St. Mary's University of San Antonio, Inc.* (1973). This decision is based on the rule (discussed in Chapter VII) that a delivery unqualified on its face cannot be cut back by a condition unstated at the time of delivery or not appearing in the deed of delivery.

This title-quieting function is often seen today in international law to protect the repose of artifacts that are on permanent exhibition in or are owned in one country, but which another country claims as its cultural property. In this context, some present possessors are likely to have to return artifacts; so a dealer or museum should know enough to investigate their title and the export papers. *Autocephalous Greek–Orthodox Church of Cyprus v. Goldberg & Feldman Fine Arts* (1989). A similar fate awaits the heirs of any WWII soldier possessing art objects acquired in wartime and hidden in his basement during his lifetime. While United States courts assess the clarity and due process accorded in foreign laws asserted in derogation of the rights of United States citizens, nothing prevents the courts from enforcing those cultural property United States v. McClain *(1979)*.

Several difficult disputes between true owners and good faith purchasers involve the wartime loss of personalty. A further difficulty was involved in the case of Hebraic manuscripts about to be destroyed, but smuggled out of Nazi Germany by giving them to a scholar with an exit visa and headed for the United States. See J.D. Bleich, *The Controversy Concerning the Sotheby Sale*, 8 Cardozo L.Rev. 91 (1986) (discussing the Talmudic law of gifts and the case of *Abrams v. Sotheby–Parke–Bernet*]. The Talmudic rule is that the possessor of stolen chattel may convey valid title, provided that the victim of the theft has despaired of recovering the chattel—a rule akin to that of *O'Keeffe*, applied even when the possessor does not actually know of the victim's despair. At common law, the smuggling scholar's use of the texts is consistent with a bailment for the period of time the texts were in danger of destruction. Whether the scholar should benefit from Talmudic law raises anew issues of custom explored earlier, in discussing *Ghen v. Rich* in Chapter I.

III. CONCLUSION

New York's general rule is the so-called demand and refusal rule: a true owner's cause of action in replevin against even a good faith purchaser does not arise until the owner makes a demand that the purchaser return the chattel and the purchaser refuses. This rule does not apply to a thief; no demand need be made of a thief, and the cause of action against a thief is available upon discovery of the chattel. Some lower appellate courts in New York have also indicated that the date on which the owner has the right to make the demand, even if she does not actually make it, is the date on which the action accrues.

By contrast, in New Jersey's so-called discovery rule, the cause of action runs from the date on which a diligent owner actually discovered or should reasonably have discovered the chattel, but thereafter balances the evidentiary problems created by the passage of time against the hardship on the owner and considers the equitable claims of all parties.

The discovery rule is little more than a fact sensitive, ad hoc, facts and circumstances inquiry. It illustrates the difficult balance courts seek in adjusting the law of adverse possession to cases involving two such innocent parties as true owners and good faith purchasers.

CHAPTER X

ACCESSION AND CONFUSION

I. ACCESSION

In earlier chapters, we saw that the true owner of a chattel could reach down the chain of possession and bring an action in replevin against subsequent possessors of the chattel, so long as the subsequent possessor chosen as a defendant did not assert the rights as good faith purchaser or there was no entrustment of the chattel. There are some other limits to his reach, and we will now discuss one of them—the doctrine of accession.

Accession is the addition of labor to the chattel of another that, without the latter's consent, so changes the chattel that the title to it is transferred to the laborer. Thus one defense that may be offered in an action of replevin is that the physical identity of the chattel is so changed that it is no longer the same piece of property, and the cause of action should not lie when the identity of the goods was so altered. *Wetherbee v. Green* (1871). This is so because the title to the chattel has, by the addition of labor, been transferred to the laborer. The title to the affected chattel should lie with the claimant who contributes the most value to the final product.

In *Wetherbee,* the defendant cut timber worth $25. He mistakenly thought that the timber was his to take and, after doing so, made it into barrel hoops worth $700—28 times the original value. The true owner of the timber sued to replevy the wood. Judge Cooley concluded that a judicial inquiry based solely on the physical identity of the chattel was difficult to apply. He cited the instance of grain becoming malt, coins melted down into a cup, and timber made into a house—all instances of altered identity—and compared them with cloth made into garments, leather into shoes, or trees sawn into timber, all instances in which the alteration was insufficient for the title to be transferred to the laborer. He then decided that title should go to the person contributing the most value. Assuming that an appraisal of the components of value is not too difficult, this rule has ease of application to commend it.

This does not necessarily mean that the party who is allocated more than 50% of the appraised new chattel's improved value wins. The labor added in *Wetherbee* made the chattel 2700% more valuable—meaning that a lesser increase might yield the same result. Later cases have not resulted in a fixed and certain percentage or number, so in some measure this rule of relative value is subject to the same charge which Cooley laid at the door of the physical identity rule. It, too, is hard to apply and uncertain of application.

One limitation on a transfer of title to a laborer often applied is that the labor must be added innocently and in good faith or, in other words, under a belief that the chattel is rightfully his. This limitation arises from the facts and the holding of *Wetherbee* and has been followed in other cases, though not uniformly; there are cases in which a knowing appropriator received title.

In an industrial age, when the addition of labor comes through expensive manufacturing processes, requiring organization and capital on an unprecedented scale, the relative value rule might be expected to have great appeal in many jurisdictions. Such was the case, and after *Wetherbee*, the relative value rule quickly became the majority rule in this country.

This majority rule came into the law from *Wetherbee* in at least two forms: first, the physical identity rule continues to be the law unless the laborer can show that the work added substantially to the value of the improved chattel. Or else, second, the relative value rule supplants the physical identity rule. The latter possibility is more straightforward as well as the easiest to apply. If Cooley meant otherwise, he would not have criticized the old rule as he did.

What if, then, the property falls back into the hands of the prior possessor in its improved, value-added state? Can the innocent laborer recover for the value of his work? The traditional answer is no. If the law were otherwise, a possessor of property could be forced to become the debtor of another acting without his consent. A debtor-creditor relationship should be established only by mutual consent. *Isle Royale Mining Co. v. Hertin* (1877). Today when an owner or prior possessor of personality does not know of or otherwise encourage repairs innocently provided, the laborer has no claim against that owner or possessor and the latter may recover the chattel as accessorized. *Tom Growney Equipment, Inc. v. Ansley* (1994) (concerning an automobile). Thus a laborer repairing at the request of a thief or any person unauthorized by the owner, has no such claim.

A. CONVERSION AND DAMAGES

When the true owner's writ of replevin is denied, he is still permitted to recover damages measured by the value of the chattel in its unimproved state. *McKee v. Gratz* (1922). This damage action is for the conversion of the chattel. It is not a trover action since that would require the successful original possessor to give over title in a forced sale, and this after the accession he cannot do.

Measuring the prior possessor's recovery by the unimproved value is the usual rule, but it works best when the laborer has done no more than innocently converted the possessor's chattel. The possessor is compensated for his loss, and the laborer is not penalized for an innocent action. However, if the laborer's conversion, trespass, or other type of appropriation is willful, some authority exists for measuring the possessor's damages by the value of the chattel in its improved state, as if the possessor has been denied the opportunity to improve it himself and is being compensated for the lost opportunity. In natural resource cases, because an action for conversion only lies for damage to personal property, it is additionally reasoned that giving damages based on (say) the trees or other natural resources rather than the timber or other product made from them is to give damages for real rather than personal property. This reasoning requires a measure of damages based on the improved value of the chattel, whether the laborer was innocent or willful.

If the improved chattel has been sold by the laborer to a third party, the measure of damages applied when the prior possessor sues the purchaser depends on whether the purchaser acted in good faith and without notice of the prior conversion. If the purchaser acted in good faith, the unimproved value alone will be recovered; if he knew of the conversion, then the improved value is the measure of damages.

B. INCORPORATION OF CHATTEL INTO ANOTHER'S PROPERTY

Traditionally if one person's chattel is incorporated into another's and if the attachments can be removed without damage to what is remaining, the doctrine of accession is not applicable. The two chattels have not changed into one; rather, one chattel has been attached to another. However, with the advent of the relative value rule, the scope of the law of accession was broadened.

Its new scope can be seen in cases dealing with automobiles. If new tires are purchased for a car owned free-and-clear, they are not permanently attached to the car, but their removal will occasion a loss of value for the car as a whole. It will not run without them, the value of a running car being out of all proportion greater than the value of the tires alone, and so title to the tires is transferred to the possessor of the car. The same might be said of a new clutch, transmission, or engine, but the rule of relative value has its limits. As the value of the accessory rises, the likelihood of its being accessed falls: for example, the value of a car's engine is sometimes so great a portion of the car's overall value, that the relative value rule appears inapplicable and results in a contradiction: the greater the utility of the part, the less likely it is to be subject to accession under this rule. As we shall see, however, automobile mechanics and repair shop operators fight against the uncertainties of the rule by using conditional sales agreements for car parts and accessories installed while a car is in the shop.

The limits of the relative value rule can be seen readily when a thief steals three automobiles of the same make and model, using the body of one, the chassis of another, and the engine of a third, in order to construct what then becomes a fourth car. The rule stands helpless in the resolution of such a case. In this event, it is better for each true owner to retain title and follow his part into the newly constructed car. *Atlas Assurance Co. v. Gibbs* (1936) (using this hypothetical).

When, however, there is a chattel mortgage on the car (bought on the installment plan), the preexisting mortgage holder can obtain, by the same law of accession, title to any accessories added after the mortgage was executed. Typically the same result is achieved in the chattel mortgage by the insertion there of an "after acquired" accessory clause, subjecting later installed parts to the prior lien of the mortgage. The title to such accessories passes to the possessor of the car, and when the possessor has "his" car repossessed by the holder of the mortgage, his title is taken away as well, and since that title includes the added accessories, title to them passes to the mortgage holder. The latter presumably bargained for a working car and so accessories were presumably intended to become permanent additions to the car. Their removal lessens the utility of the car as a working vehicle and certainly lessens its collateral value as security for the automobile loan. So the lender repossessing the car gets title to its accessories and the former owner loses the right to remove them.

If the accessories are themselves sold under a conditional sales contract, and the title to them does not pass to the possessor of the car, the Uniform Commercial Code § 9–314 provides that a security interest in goods which attaches before installation takes priority over the prior lien on the car, except as to certain types of creditors or purchasers of the whole who take without knowledge of pre-existing liens on the whole. The purpose of such a provision is to encourage maintenance and repair of a mortgaged car, on the assumption that a running vehicle is good for both its possessor and the holder of a prior chattel mortgage on it. The holder of a security interest successfully asserting its priority must, however, compensate the car possessor for any severance damages incurred in removal of the accessory. Instead of occasioning a dispute about title to the accessory, then, the UCC here gives the conditional vendor of the accessories installed or affixed a security interest or lien to perfect.

The retention of title to the part installed by the mechanic under a conditional sales agreement provides its vendor with more than a lien remedy. Relying on the common law in this area, some courts have held that detachable parts to an automobile do not become accessions and so are not subject to the lien of the prior chattel mortgage if the vendor of the part retains the title under the agreement. The logic of this position runs as follows: because the owner mortgagor of the auto does not have title to what was installed, the lien of the prior chattel mortgage cannot attach to it and any after-acquired accessory clause has nothing on which to work. Thus in disputes between conditional sale vendors of parts and prior chattel mortgagees, the vendor has an action for the value of the parts. *Bank of America v. J. & S. Auto Repairs*

(1985) (an excellent opinion collecting recent authorities on such disputes).

For purposes of such disputes between two out of possession parties, the definition of what is a "detachable" part is broad indeed. *Clark v. Wells* (1872) (a leading case finding the running parts of a wagon not subject to accession). The relative value rule discussed previously is little used in this line of cases. Even the engine is not subject to an accession.

One must, however, be sensitive to the action brought to resolve such disputes. If the vendor's action is trover and conversion, what is detachable and so subject to trover can be defined broadly because the plaintiff does not want to take the engine out and the question is academic. If the action is replevin, however, one would expect close analysis of whether the part can in fact be removed without injury to the whole. That—"removal without injury"—is what is typically meant by detachable. Conversely, when the vendor has repossessed the part, replevin by the mortgagee will include what remains, but not include the repossessed part because the action affects only the property to which the lien of the mortgage attached. If the mortgagee drafts its complaint for conversion, however, the timing of the vendor's repossession may matter: the vendor will have to act after the owner's default under the conditional sales contract, but before any demand for repossession by the mortgagee in order to avoid conversion liability.

C. ACCESSION TO REAL PROPERTY

A chattel can occasionally become an accession to real property. For example, suppose a laborer contracts to build a house on one parcel of land and instead builds it by mistake on another. Because the value of the house will be many times more than the value of the unimproved parcel of land, the doctrine of accession implemented by a rule of relative value, if permitted to have its customary effect, would transfer the title to the land to the laborer. However, the law does not work that way. It regards the personal property—the house—as becoming affixed to and part of the real property—the land—with the result that the title to the chattel passes to the rightful possessor of the land. *Sponseller v. Meltebeke* (1977).

Thus at law the title holder to the real property can refuse to pay for the unexpected windfall of the house unless equity intervenes to soften this harsh result. The hardship on the builder itself may justify equitable relief, but other factors enter into such cases as well: the negligence of the builder in not checking the title to the ground on which he labored may be a basis for denying relief, or the landowner's conduct leading the builder into the subsequent error may be a basis for granting it. The tendency of recent cases has been to protect the innocent improver or laborer. If the value of the real property is substantially increased by the accession of the added improvement, the hardship created by the doctrine of accession is sufficient for a court to find that the laborer has stated a cause of action in equity. And there is some authority for an equity court to grant relief because of the hardship on the builder, as well as the windfall unearned by the possessor of the land. If the latter attempts to bring an equity action to quiet title to the improvement, he can be made to pay first for the improvement on the theory that he who seeks equity must simultaneously do equity.

II. CONFUSION

Confusion is the intermingling of two or more pieces of personal property so that the property rights in each can no longer be distinguished. Thereafter, no specific identification or separation of the formerly separate chattel is possible. Such an intermingling occurs with fungible goods like gas, oil, grain, mineral ore, or unmarked timber.

Where confusion of chattel of the same type and quality occurs, each prior possessor receives a *pro rata* share of the whole. Each proves what he put in and receives a like amount back again. If no *pro rata* division is possible, then each receives an equal share of the whole which is thereafter owned by all as tenants in common, each holding undivided fractional shares in the tenancy. Where, however, one of the possessors negligently or intentionally confuses chattels, that confuser either loses his share or has the burden of proof to show what his share was. If he fails to carry this burden, he also loses his share.

III. FIXTURES

A fixture is personal property that has been attached to real property. It is an accession[1] to realty; this implies that it is personalty having a possible existence apart from realty, but which may be assimilated into it and become part and parcel of it. It is traditionally defined using a three element test. *Teaff v. Hewitt* (1853). That is, property is a fixture which has been (1) *annexed* to the realty, either actually or constructively, (2) *adapted* or applied to the use or purpose to which that part of the realty to which it is connected is appropriated, and (3) *intended* to become a permanent accession to the realty. *Wyoming State Farm Loan Board v. FCSCC* (1988); *Kent Storage Co. v. Grand Rapids Lumber Co.* (1927). Thus inventories of goods are not fixtures. Whether a chattel is a fixture or not is a question of fact. *Stone v. Livingston* (1915).

Annexation refers to the act of attaching personal property to realty. Traditionally personalty will not acquire the status of a fixture unless it is in some manner or means, however slight, attached to the realty. The attachment may be either actual or constructive. That is, if the object is not attached to the land or to some structure or appliance which is attached to it, it will retain its character as personalty, even though intended for permanent use on the premises. For example, a mobile home may

1. Accession, here as elsewhere in this Chapter, implies a transfer of ownership and control over property inferred by operation of law from a change in its character.

become a fixture when it is put on a foundation, hooked up to utility lines, or even heavily landscaped. *W.H.V., Inc. v. Associates Housing Finance, LLC* (2001) (a dispute between two lenders, one lending on the security of the land and another on a mobile home).

If an object is not physically affixed to the realty, it may acquire the status of a fixture by constructive annexation. Personalty that are constructively annexed to the realty are those whose weight and heft forbids removal or whose removal from it impairs both their value and the value of the realty. For example, cable television equipment may be removable, but would not be re-used. Context matters too. In an office building, spare parts for repair of the heating and cooling systems, replacement windows and doors, or wall partitions are all necessary for making the office space rentable. They may be fixtures, but office furniture will not be. Similarly, in a steel mill, molten steel solutions might be constructively annexed to a furnace: they are useless without it, are used only in connection with the furnace, are not stock in trade, merchandise, or inventory, and are analogous to the detached special parts or special tools for a machine. *Los Angeles v. Times–Mirror Co.* (1933). When the principal part of the machine is a fixture due to actual annexation to the realty, its components, even though not actually annexed, are also fixtures because they would, if removed, leave the machine unfit for use, and because in themselves they are incapable of general use elsewhere. So constructive annexation occurs when personalty that are not themselves actually or directly annexed to realty, but are part of, or accessory to, personalty so annexed.

Adaptation to the use of the realty is the second element. It is the relationship between the chattel and the use made by the annexor of the underlying realty. Coolers in a retail grocery are an example. They are introduced onto the realty and become a fixture when necessary or convenient or at least a useful adjunct to the realty, considering the purposes to which the latter is devoted.

An *intention* to make a permanent accession to the realty is the third element defining a fixture. In English law, annexation was the most litigated of the three elements; in American jurisdictions, it is the annexor's intention. To determine it, only objective visible facts are examined. *State Highway & Transportation Comm'r v. Edwards Co, Inc.* (1979). The objective intention is that of an ordinary, reasonable person and is based on the surrounding circumstances in the record. The intention must be to make the article a permanent accession to the realty. The surrounding circumstances determine the intent of the annexor, not the annexor's secret or subjective intent. The law of fixtures is very clear on this last point: objective, not subjective intent, is the guide. This is so because annexation is dependent on the actions of one person, and if his subjective intent were dispositive of litigation, there would be no point to the lawsuit; instead of litigating, we could just ask him what his intent was. Ronald Polston, *The Fixtures Doctrine: Was It Ever*

Really The Law?, 16 Whittier L. Rev. 455 (1995). Intent, then, must be inferred from the nature of the article affixed, the purpose for which it was affixed, the relation and situation of the annexor and the policy of the law thereto, and the structure and mode of the annexation. So the chattel's nature, the way it was affixed, the purpose it serves on the realty, and the annexor's relationship to it and the realty matter.

The law of fixtures is generally applied to three sets of facts: (1) when a vendor removes an item from realty after agreeing to sell it to a purchaser who expects it to be there when he takes possession [*Everitt v. Higgins* (1992) (holding a wood stove for cooking not a fixture)]; (2) when a mortgage lender forecloses on realty, and expects to sell or take possession of realty that may then be sold to recoup his loan [*City of Hydaburg v. Hydaburg Cooperative Ass'n* (1993)]; (3) when a landlord claims an item at the termination of a lease. Fixtures law prevents vendors from stripping realty after sale, borrowers from denying lenders security for a loan, and lessees stopping landlords from quickly re-renting premises. It serves to keep realty useful and personalty mobile. Because the finding of the facts of the case is so important to a determination of what becomes a fixture, judges who are competent triers of fact are unlikely to be reversed on appeal.

CHAPTER XI

COMMON LAW ESTATES IN PERSONALTY

The applicability to personal property of some of the rules and doctrines comprising our system of common law estates is generally assumed, but there are exceptions. Just to show that personal property *may* require different treatment than does real property, consider the case of *Scott v. Shuffler* (1973) where the court stated that "an item of personal property could not be held in fee simple." Why so? The court was thinking that *seisin* is inherent in the fee simple absolute in realty, but does not apply to personalty. If this is so, then no interest to which *seisin* attached at common law— no freehold interest—could be created in personal property. This would mean no life estate, fee simple determinable, fee simple subject to a condition subsequent, or future interest could be established in personalty.

Not so. The *Scott* court is only technically correct. It is preferable to speak of true or absolute ownership of a chattel, rather than of a fee simple absolute in it—and if ownership is not absolute, then it is proper to say that such ownership is qualified. However, the notion of *seisin* is now lost in the mists of *stare decisis* and cannot affect many applications to personalty of the common law's system of estates. As noted in this Chapter, however, the lack of *seisin* for personalty serves on occasion to limit the application of the estate system to personalty.

I. PRESENT ESTATES AND REMAINDERS

It is therefore harmless error to say, along with many courts, that personal property may be held in fee simple absolute, fee simple determinable, or fee simple conditional (or subject to a condition subsequent). Likewise, there is nothing that would prevent personalty from being held in a life estate followed by a vested or contingent remainder. *Innes v. Potter* (1915) (containing a good, short historical discussion of these matters). However, there is less authority on the use of a contingent remainder and generally there may be some question of the prudence of tying tangible personalty up in this manner; income-producing, intangible personal property may be a more likely subject for such an arrangement.

If the remainder is a contingent one, it could at common law be destroyed by natural termination, merger, or forfeiture; this common law doctrine of the destructibility of contingent remainders has generally been held inapplicable to personalty. This is so because the doctrine evolved out of the requirement of the common law that *seisin* never be in abeyance after the date of the conveyance or the date on which the devise is effective. Because *seisin* is irrelevant to questions involving personal property, the doctrine of destructibility is irrelevant as well.

A. THE RULE IN SHELLEY'S CASE

Where real property is conveyed "to X for life, remainder to X and his heirs," X took a fee simple absolute in the realty transferred. This result was called the Rule in Shelley's Case and is, as a rule of law, inapplicable to personal property. *Society National Bank v. Jacobson* (1990) (calling this the "prevailing view" but relying on an Ohio case to the contrary). It may, however, still be applicable to a devise or inter vivos transfer of personalty as a rule of construction. *Id.* (collecting the cases). The Rule is abolished by statute in most states, and where such statutes apply only to realty, this abolition may leave it applicable to personalty. *Ray v. Ray* (1967). Where the Rule still applies, as to a will effective before an abolition statute is enacted, it may be applied to a devise of realty subsequently converted to personalty (money). *City Bank and Tr. Co in Dixon. v. Morrissey* (1983).

B. FEE TAILS

Suppose there was a transfer of personal property "to X and the heirs of his body" or "to X and his issue." Whether or not any issue or heirs were alive at the time, this would be an attempt to create a fee tail in personalty. This is impossible because the validity of the fee tail depended on English land law and the English Statute DeDonis. This statute, by its terms, applied only to estates in realty invested with *seisin*. Even before this early statute, "heirs" meant only persons who acquired land by intestate succession. *Society National Bank v. Jacobson* (1990). Whether X takes absolute ownership immediately, or absolute ownership subject to a condition subsequent that X have no descendants, or a life interest followed by absolute ownership in X's heirs, would likely depend on an interpretation and application of a state statute, available in all but a few states, abolishing the fee tail.

C.　THE RULE IN WILD'S CASE

If the language in a transfer of personal property were to read "to X and his children," such language would raise the applicability of the Rule in Wild's Case. With regard to realty transferred in this way, X has a fee tail at common law if X has no children on the date of the devise, but if X has children, X and his children take concurrently. Such rules apply only to real property; they are inapplicable to personalty, whether the transfer is made by devise or *inter vivos* transfer. If X has no children alive at the time of the transfer of personalty, X has absolute ownership of the chattel. He is the primary and earliest beneficiary of the transfer, and the mention of children may reasonably be regarded as an expectancy or contingency. If there are children alive, some courts have concluded that X and his children hold concurrently.

D.   THE DOCTRINE OF
WORTHIER TITLE

This doctrine is fully applicable to personal property in both its testamentary and inter vivos branches. That is, if personal property is the subject of a devise and the devisee is under the law of descent given a same estate as he would take under the will, he is deemed to take by descent and not by devise. If the personal property is subject to an *inter vivos* conveyance and is thereby conveyed to the transferor's heirs, the estate given to the heirs is void. The testamentary branch of the doctrine makes a difference in estate planning in a few specialized areas, but many authorities think it obsolete. Not so for the *inter vivos* branch: where O conveys personalty to X for life, remainder to the heirs of the transferor (O), the heirs take nothing. From the date of the conveyance, X's life estate is followed by O's reversion, not by the heirs' remainder which is void under the doctrine. A transferor wishing to avoid the doctrine should specify his heirs by name in his will or conveyance.

II.   FUTURE INTERESTS

All five types of future interests—reversion, remainders, executory interests, possibilities of reverter, and rights of reentry—may, according to the weight of authority and the Restatement of Property, be created in personal property. However, a future interest cannot be created in consumable personal property. A transfer of such an interest is

usually taken to have transferred absolute ownership in the transferee. A consumable is an article of
personalty that is worn out or destroyed by normal
use: crops, farm implements, and hogs ready for the
butcher are examples. Dairy cattle, furniture, and a
grist mill are non-consumables. The line between
consumables and non-consumables is not firm, nor
should it be. Nor is the rationale for this exception
to the rule that a future interest may be created in
personalty firmly established. If use of a chattel
results in its consumption, then that consumption
is integral to the thing itself, and ownership must
be absolute—in other words, possession is tantamount to ownership in this case, and a future
interest in it would be a legal superfluity.

A. THE RULE AGAINST PERPETUITIES

The Rule Against Perpetuities applies equally to
real and personal property. As such, it serves to
limit the vesting of future interests in personalty to
a period of time extending over lives in being at the
time of the transfer plus a period of twenty-one
years.

III. CONCURRENT ESTATES

Both the **tenancy in common** and the **joint tenancy** with its attendant right of survivorship, may
exist in personal property, although the former is
seldom seen. The latter is often used for checking,
savings, and stock brokerage accounts. However,
there is a split of authority as to whether the

tenancy by the entireties, limited to property held by legally-married husbands and wives, can exist in personal property. At common law, because the husband became the owner of the wife's personalty, it did not exist for personalty. After the Married Women's Property Acts were enacted in all states, a split in the case law developed. Some states held that the Acts made this estate available to husbands and wives. Others held that the Acts did not change the gender-neutral rule that spouses as such could hold personalty only in one of two concurrent forms—the joint tenancy or the tenancy in common.

INDEX

References are to Pages

ACCESSION
Chattel mortgage and, 366
Conversion and, 362
Damages for, 362–63
Definition, 359
Good faith, 359, 363
Incorporation of chattel, 363–67
Lien, 366
Physical identity rule, 360–61
Attachment, real property, 368–69
Relative value rule, 360–61
Replevin, relation to, 359
Security interest, 365–66
    Conditional sales agreement, 364–366
    Chattel mortgage, 364–66
Transfer, title, 360
Value, 360–61

ACTIONS
Bailment, 193–94
Conversion, see Conversion
Election of, 102–03, 105–08
Replevin, see Replevin
Trespass, see Trespass
Trespass on the Case, see Trespass on the Case
Trover, see Trover and Conversion

ADVERSE POSSESSION
    See also Open and Continuous
Concealment, 351
Discovery rule, 352–54
Demand and refusal rule, 357
Elements, 338
Fixture, 341–44
Function of, 355–56
Interim profits, 348
Self-help, 342–43
Statutes of limitation, 339, 344–48
    Real property, 341–42
Stolen chattel, 346
Tacking, 347–48
Title quieting function, 355–56

AGENCY
Apparent agency, 253
Donor's agent, 288–89
Transfer agent, corporate, 292

ATTORNEY
Agent, donor, 288–89

AUTOMOBILE
Insurable interest, 248–50

BAILMENT
Automobile, 196–98, 202–03
        Bailee
    see Negligence, this topic
    Due care, 193, 209
    Duty to deliver, 193, 216–17
    Injuries, 192–94
    Liability over, 192
    Standard of care, 208–09
Bailee for hire, 201–02
Benefit of, 208–9
    Bailee, 208–09
    Bailor, 208–09
    Finder, 208
Burden of proof, 211–13
Car, 196–200
Closed receptacle, 183–85
Common carrier, 220
Constructive bailment, 184

BAILMENT—Cont'd
Definition, 182–83
Distinguished from
    Lease, 195, 200
    License, 197, 200
    Sale, 203–04
Finders, 185–190
Fungible goods, 207
Implied contract for, 188
Innkeeper, 233–35
Involuntary bailee, 185
Knowledge of bailee, 185–86
Measure of damages, 214–16
    Actual value, 215–16
    Sentimental value, 215
Misdelivery, 205, 216–17
Mutual benefit, 209
Negligence, 210, 211
    Presumption of, 211–14
        In contract, 211
        In tort, 211
Negligent entrustment, 202–03, 257
Possession "for approval", 203
Postal service, 116
Reasonable person, 210
Safe deposit box, 195–96
Sole benefit, 208–09
Strict Liability, 193
Transfer by bailee, 244
Warehouseman, 218–19

BURDEN OF PROOF
Clear and convincing evidence, 293, 305
Confusion, 369
Negligence, bailee, 211–14

CADAVER
Burial, 91
Quasi-property in, 91
Right to possession, 91
Trade in, 98

CHATTEL
    See also Automobile; Crops; Domestic Animals; Human Cells;
      Wild Animals

CHATTEL—Cont'd
Bulky, 156
Cadaver as, 91
Concealment, 351
Definition, 1–2
Dividend checks, 178
Embedded, 154–56
Engagement ring, 298
Fungible, 207–08
Horse, 275
Insurable interest, 248–50
Logs, 131–36
Manure, 68–69
Manuscript, 356–57
Mare, 274
Meteorite, 84–91
Paintings, 348–49, 355
Prior possessor, 104–05, 114–15, 118
Small, 156
Stolen, 129
Supermarket carts, 175–76
True owner,
Unclaimed, 177–81

COMMON CARRIER
Bill of lading, 220
Standard of care, 218, 220

COMMON LAW ESTATES
See also Concurrent Interests; Future Interests
Doctrine of Worthier Title, 378
Fee simple, condition subsequent, 374
Fee simple, determinable, 374
Fee tail, 376–77
Life estate, 374
Personal Property, 374–80
Remainders, 375
Destruction, 375
Rule against perpetuities, 379
Rule in Shelly's case, 376
Rule in Wild's case, 377

CONCURRENT INTERESTS
Joint tenancy, see Joint Tenancy
Tenancy by the entireties, see Tenancy by the Entireties
Tenancy in common, see Tenancy in Common

CONFUSION
Definition, 369
Division, 369
Negligence, 369

CONTRACT
Assignment, 304
Third-party beneficiary, 292, 329–30

CONVERSION
Accession and, 362–63
Adverse possession, 350
Allegations in, 94
Cadaver, 91
Demand, 258
Demand and refusal, 75, 349–51
Exercise of dominion, 73
    Seriousness of diversion, 76–77
Forced sale, 76
Intent, 77–78
Logs, 131–36
Measure of damages, 77
Theory, 76
    Compared with trespass, 72–73
Trover and, 110–113

CORPORATE STOCK
Certificate, 290
Delivery, 290
Gift, 290–93
Registration, 292
Transfer Agent, 292

CROPS
Agricultural crops, 79
Bailment, 206
Emblements, 70
Marijuana, 71
Pecans, 70
Seed, 206–07
Severance, 71

DEED
Bill of Sale, 236
Gift, 277–79
    Under seal, 277
Uniform Commercial Code, 254

DOMESTIC ANIMALS
See also Estrays
Bailment of, 208
Definition, 17–18
Pets, 24–25
Dog Bite Statutes, 25
Trespass by, 26

EQUITY
Estoppel, 266, 273
Equity of recission, 246
Trust, 289–90, 316

ESCHEAT
Generally, 176–77
Abandoned Property, 178–81
Dividend Checks, 178
Unclaimed Property Acts, 177–81

ESTRAYS
Damage by, 24
Statutes on, 24
Auction of, 24
Liens, 24
Title to, 24

FAULT
In broken engagements, 298–300

FINDER
Abandoned chattel, 143,151, 163
Abandoned Shipwreck Act, 161–62
Adverse possession of, 146
At sea, 163
Bailee as, 144, 186–90
Currency, 144–45
Definition, 143
Employment, 157
Escheat, 176–77
Independent contractors, 157
Landowner's rights against, 149–57
Lost chattel, 150–51
Luck of, 158–59
Marine antiquities, 159–60
Mislaid chattel, 151
Place of find, 149–50
Public place, 149

FINDER—Cont'd
Place of find—Cont'd
    Private place, 150
Possession, 146–49
Reward, 171
    Contract to pay, 174
    Lien for, 171
    Statute, 175
Search for true owner, 153–54
Small chattel, 156
Statutory duty, 169–71
Successive finders, 131, 145
Treasure trove, 152, 159–61
Wreck of the sea, 161

FISH
    Capture of, 11–13

FIXTURES
Generally, 370–73
Accession, 370
Adaptation, 372
Annexation, 370–71
Definition, 370
Intent, 372–73
Under Uniform Commercial Code, 270

FUTURE INTERESTS
    Generally, 374, 378–79
Consumables, 378–79
Executory interest, 378
Intent to create, 279, 294
Possibility of reverter, 378
Remainder, 378
Reversion, 378
Rule against perpetuities, 379

GIFT
Acceptance, 311–12
Bank account balance, 327, 331–32
Causa mortis, 273, 306–11
    Contemplation of death, 306–09
    Revocation, 306
    Suicide, 308–09
Condition, 297
Courtship gift, 298

GIFT—Cont'd
Deed of, 273, 277–79
Delivery, 273, 240, 273, 274–77, 281–90, 293
    Affected by statute, 279
    Constructive, 284
    Symbolic, 283–285
    To third party, 287–89
Donative intent, 279–80, 290–96, 302–03
Engagement gift, 297–301
    Affected by heartbalm legislation, 300
Hebraic manuscript, 357
Horse, 275
Inter vivos, 273
Parol, 276
Revocation, 287

GOOD FAITH PURCHASER
Accessed chattel, 363
Codification of rights, 252–57
Definition, 237–38, 255
Entrustment, 257–63
Honestly held belief, 247
Insurable interest, 248–50
    Settlement claim, 248–50
    Subrogation, 248–49
True owner legislation, 251
Uniform Sales Act, 252
Void title rule, 240–41, 251
    Legislative reversal, 251

HEBRAIC MANUSCRIPT
Gift, 357
Talmudic rule, 357

HUMAN CELLS
    Generally, 91
Consent to research with, 93
Conversion, 93–96, 98–99
    Strict liability for, 94
Fetal Tissue, 100–01
Fiduciary duty, 94
Leukemia, 92
Patent on, 93
Possession, 88–89
Replevin of, 99
Spleen, 92–93

INNKEEPER
Negligence, 235
Statutory duty, 233–34
Strict liability of, 234

JOINT BANK ACCOUNT
See also Gift
Actual notice, 319
Balance,
    Gift, 327
    Pledge, 324
    Survivorship right in, 315–20, 327–28
Definition, 317
Functions, 322–23
    As gift, 323–27
    As will, 327–30
Good faith dispute, 319
Joint tenant, 319
Presumption, 319
Signature cards, 318, 320–22
Spousal transfer, 325, 328–29
Surviving account holder, 315–20
Survivorship right, 315–21

JOINT TENANCY
Bank account, 319
    Definition, 315,
Intent, 316
Severance, 324
Survivorship, 315–20
Unities, 315, 318

JUS TERTII
Defense of, 28, 119–22, 125

LARCENY
Effect on good faith purchaser, 253
Fish, 13
Human tissue, 92

LIENS
Chattel mortgage, 268, 365–66
Codification in Uniform Commercial Code, 269–71
Common law, 267–69
Conditional sales contract, 268, 364–66
Estrays, 24
Finder's, 174

LIENS—Cont'd
Pledge, 267–68

NEGLIGENT ENTRUSTMENT
Generally, 202–03
Scienter, 203
Negligence, 203

OPEN AND CONTINUOUS
Accrual, 349
Adverse possession, 339, 350–52, 355
Concealment of chattel, 351
Conversion, 350
Demand and refusal, 350–51
Discovery, 352
Due diligence, 352–55
Good faith, 350
Open and notorious, 351
Replevin, 349–51
Talmudic law of gifts, 357

PAWNBROKER
Protected purchaser, 262

POSSESSION
Cadaver, 91
Capture, 7, 52–53
Constructive possession, 28
Custom, 13–16
First possession, 1
Intent to possess, 7
Interference with, 3, 11–12, 28–29
Landowner's right to, 26–27
Presumption of title, 133
Prior possession, recovery of, 113–15
Ratione soli, 26–27, 33

PRESUMPTION
Acceptance, gift, 311–12
Donative intent, 301–03
Equal contribution, bank account, 325
Negligence, bailment, 221
Survivorship, 316–17, 318–19, 328

PURCHASER
See also Good Faith Purchaser
Identity, 264–67

RELATIVITY OF TITLE
Generally, 113, 117, 133–34
Good faith purchaser, 253
Larceny and, 13

REPLEVIN
Generally, 79–82
Accrual, 349
Demand, 349–52
Abolition of, 82
Accession, 359
Adverse Possession, 83, 349–52
Allegations, 78–79
Bailor and, 191
Bond, 81
Constitutionality, 81
Damages, 82
Demand, 83, 349–51
Distraint of landlord, 79
Preliminary hearing, 81
Relation to detinue, 80
Relation to trover, 83, 191, 193
Specific recovery, 80
Theory of, 80–81
Prior Possession, 117

RESTATEMENT OF PROPERTY
Future interests, 378

RESTATEMENT OF TRUSTS
Totten trust, 345

SALVAGE
Finder, 164–66
Logs, 141
Nature of right, 46, 165–66

SEISIN
Common law estates, 374–75

RESTATEMENT OF TRUSTS
Totten trust, 334

TENANCY BY THE ENTIRETIES
Applicability to personal property, 380

TENANCY IN COMMON
Definition, 316, 379

TENANCY IN COMMON—Cont'd
Definition—Cont'd
   Statutory presumption for, 317

TITLE
Accession, 359–61
Deed, gift, 273–79
Equity of recission, 246
Markets overt, 240
Transfer, 243
   Fraud, 244
   Misrepresentation, 244
   Mutual Mistake, 244
Transfer to joint bank account, 321
Void, 240
Void title rule, 240–41
   Codification in Uniform Commercial Code, 252, 265
Voidable, 243–46, 253, 265

TRANSFER
Corporate Stock, 290–292
Fraud, 333
Good Faith Purchaser and, 254–55

TREASURE TROVE
   Generally, 46, 159–60
Abandonment, 162–63
Concealment, 160
Salvage, 159–61
Wreck of the Sea, 161

TREATISES
   See also Restatement of Property
Bracton, 5
Fleta, 5
Justinian, 5

TRESPASS
Definition, 2, 12, 72–73
Domestic animals, 17
Interference with possession, 72
On posted land, 34–35
Poaching, 34

TRESPASS ON THE CASE
Definition, 2–3
Firing a gun, 11

TRESPASS ON THE CASE—Cont'd
Procedure, 5–6

TROVER AND CONVERSION
See also Conversion
Damages, 139–41
Definition, 76
Double liability, 125, 137–38
Jus Tertii, 134–41
Measure of damages, 139
Relation to replevin, 83
Subrogation, 125
Theory of, 76

TRUST
Acceptance of gift in, 311–12
Constructive, 275
Judicial recognition, 336–37
Revocation, 330–31
Totten trust, 334–37
    Bank account, 334
    Revocable trust, 334
Trustee for donee, 287–90
Declared by donor, 288–89

UNCLAIMED PROPERTY
Definition, 179
Escheat, 176–77
Purpose, 181
Uniform Unclaimed Property Acts, 177–81
    Litigation concerning, 181
    Report, 179

UNIFORM COMMERCIAL CODE
See also Common Carrier; Fixtures; Warehouseman
Burden, 211–13, 221–27
    Of persuasion, 212–13,
    Of proof, 211, 223
Buyer in the ordinary course of business, 258, 260
Collateral, 269
Commercial practice, 255
Entrustment, 257–63
Good faith, 253–55
Good faith purchaser, 247–48, 250–55
Presumption, negligence, 221
Purchase from inventory, 262, 263

UNIFORM COMMERCIAL CODE—Cont'd
Secured party, 269, 271
Security agreement, 269
Security interest, 269–71
Transaction of purchase, 253, 257
Transfer, 253–54
Vendor in possession, 263

WAREHOUSEMAN
Bailment, 218
Definition, 218
Effect of Uniform Commercial Code on, 219, 221, 225
Limitations, liability, 230–32
Misdelivery, 229
Standard of care, 219
Theft, 227–28
WHALING
Custom, 13–16
Harpoon, 14

WILD ANIMALS
Bees, 21–22, 31–33
Capture of, 7–8
Common property, 1
Control, 7, 9–13
Escape, 9
Foxes, 2–8
Governmental ownership, 1, 37–41
    Purpose, 39
    Theories of, 37–38, 40–41
Habitat, 20
Hunting of, 2–8
    Custom, 13–16
    Regulations, 41–44
    Posting of Private Land, 35–37
Intent to return, 20–21
Landowner's right to pursue, 26–30
Mortal wounding, 10–11
Natural Liberty, 10
Oysters, 22–23
Pursuit of, 6–7, 9–10
Trespass, 2, 26
Trespass on the case, 2, 11–12

†